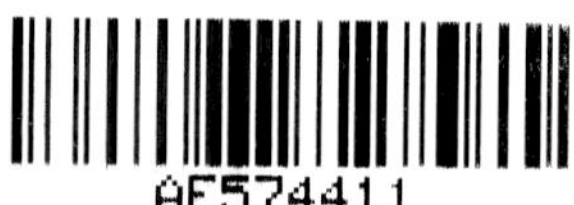

IMAGES
of America

PENDLETON

On the Cover: Native Americans and Pendleton residents pose together for this publicity shot for the Pendleton Woolen Mills. The native peoples, the mills, the Round-Up, and Hamley & Company always had a symbiotic relationship. (Pendleton Woolen Mills.)

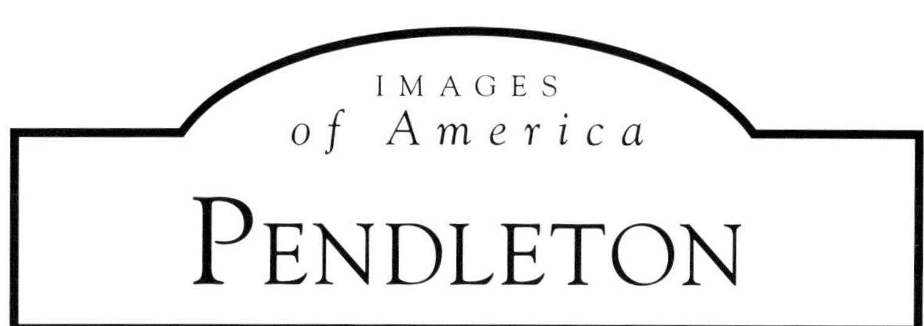

Elizabeth Gibson

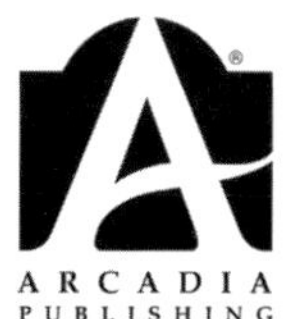

ISBN 978-1-4671-3000-4

Published by Arcadia Publishing
Charleston, South Carolina

Printed in the United States of America

Library of Congress Control Number: 2012955162

For all general information, please contact Arcadia Publishing:
Telephone 843-853-2070
Fax 843-853-0044
E-mail sales@arcadiapublishing.com
For customer service and orders:
Toll-Free 1-888-313-2665

Visit us on the Internet at www.arcadiapublishing.com

Contents

ACKNOWLEDGMENTS

I would like to thank everyone who helped in putting this book together, from providing images and reliving family histories to having faith in me to paint a portrait of Pendleton's robust history. Specifically, I would like to thank Lee Moorhouse and the Tamástslikt Cultural Institute. Without your help, a gigantic piece of Pendleton's history would have been lost to the winds of time.

I would also like to thank my family for their continuing support and for putting up with me on this crazy journey!

Introduction

Pendleton is one of the oldest cities in Oregon. It 1862, Abram Miller filed a claim on a 160-acre homestead on the north side of the Umatilla River in northeastern Oregon. He built a home on a small lot on the south side of the river. Several years later, Moses Goodwin traded Miller a team of horses for the property. Goodwin then set up Goodwin's Crossing a block south of the river. In 1865, he built a bridge across the river where the Main Street Bridge stands today. He also built Goodwin's Hotel nearby. Lot Livermore, who would later become the first mayor, built a store next to the hotel. It was not long before other businesses sprang up around this central point.

The first industry was wool. Jacob Frazier brought the first sheep about 1865. Several large herders came to the area, but the biggest was probably Charles Cunningham, who came in 1871. He crossbred prime Merinos with the local breeds for top-quality wool. He became a major supplier to the woolen mills that began in the 1880s. At first, the mills produced Indian blankets, but they later supplied other types of clothing as well. By the early 1900s, sheep in the area numbered in the hundreds of thousands.

Pendleton became the seat of Umatilla County before it was even an incorporated city. Initially, Umatilla City was the county seat, since it had a larger population. However, Pendleton was more centrally located, so, in 1868, the county seat was moved. The home of Judge G.W. Bailey was home to the city offices and the jail.

The first major event to affect the area was the Bannock War of 1878. The native tribes of southern Idaho, the Bannocks and the Paiutes, had been harassed by miners and ranchers. They tried to get the Umatillas, Cayuse, and Walla Wallas to join them in fighting the white man. They killed many settlers in outlying areas before reaching the Umatilla Reservation, which had been formed in 1855. The war ended when Umatilla chief Umapine killed and beheaded Bannock chief Egan. Full-scale war was averted.

After that, things settled down a bit, and Pendleton was incorporated on October 25, 1880. The county commissioners named their city for George Hunt Pendleton of Ohio, a Democratic candidate for vice president in 1864.

Gold was discovered in the John Day area of the Blue Mountains, and railroads were built from Celilo, on the Columbia River, to Pendleton. Both developments brought Chinese immigrants to the area. They used tunnels that were originally built by city planners for the easy transportation of gold, money, alcohol, and other goods for laundries, restaurants, and opium dens.

Another early industry was wheat and flour production. William S. Byers built the first flour mill in 1875 on Fifth Street. Other mills were built in 1887 and 1920. To support the agricultural base of the city, two canneries opened, one in 1937 and one in 1945. Both have since closed their doors.

In 1881, William Roesch owned the first brewery in Pendleton. During the peak of pre-mechanical agriculture, when many cowboys and sheepherders were in town, they enjoyed their liquor. Prohibition only sent the businesses underground, not out of business. There were also many gambling halls and card rooms.

Pendleton has long been known for the Pendleton Round-Up, a weeklong affair of rodeo events. The event began in 1909 as a fair with bronco riding, war dances, sack races, and other activities. There was such a positive response that the next year, the nonprofit Northwest Frontier Exhibition Association was created. The association held the first Round-Up, which has grown ever since. The profits from the first year were used to build a grandstand for the following year. The association also procured 15 acres of property, where the Round-Up is still being held today. In 1916, the Happy Canyon Pageant was added. The program portrays the lives of the Indians, the coming of pioneers, and the eventual settlement of the West.

The face of the city changed when farms became more and more mechanized. Fewer cowboys and sheepherders were needed, and many businesses that catered to horsepower, such as saddle makers and blacksmiths, began to disappear. The farms themselves became larger in order to use the mechanical equipment, and smaller farmers went out of business.

The city experienced another boom for a short time after the Army airbase was built in 1939. The James B. Doolittle raiders trained at the base. In an interesting twist, the bordellos, long an eyesore in the community, stayed open to serve military personnel. Upstanding citizens worried that their young women would be prey to the Army men, and so they lobbied for the bordellos to remain open. The last one finally closed in 1953.

Agriculture still forms the base of the city's economy, and the Round-Up is still its number-one claim to fame. However, there are also several businesses, such as the Pendleton Woolen Mills and Hamley & Company, that have been in business for over 100 years. The town still celebrates its connection with the Wild West days with the annual Cattle Barons Weekend, the Old Iron Show, and the Wildhorse Pow Wow.

One

NATIVE AMERICANS

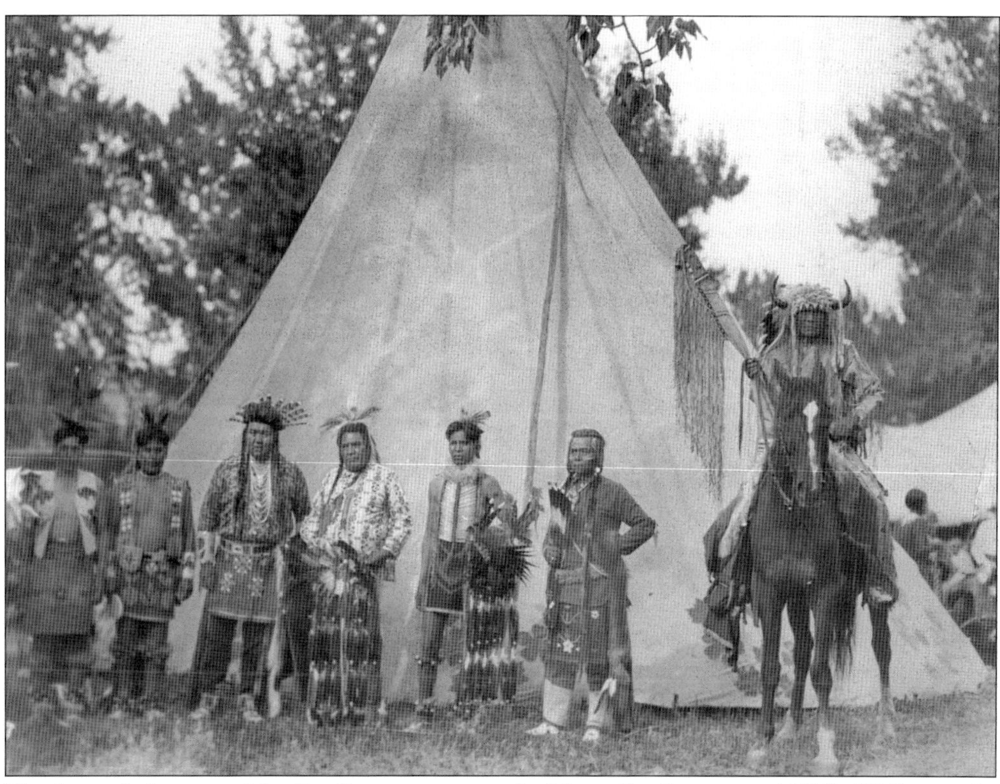

The first inhabitants of the Pendleton area were the Umatilla, Cayuse, and Walla Walla people. They were generally peaceful toward white men who traveled through to the West Coast and to the nearby gold mines. They refused to participate in the Bannock War, which threatened to overflow into their area in 1878. Seen here from left to right are Cane Shippentowner, Francis Shillal, Clarence Burke, unidentified, McKinley Williams, Johnson Chapman, and James "Poker Jim" Burke. (Tamástslikt Cultural Institute.)

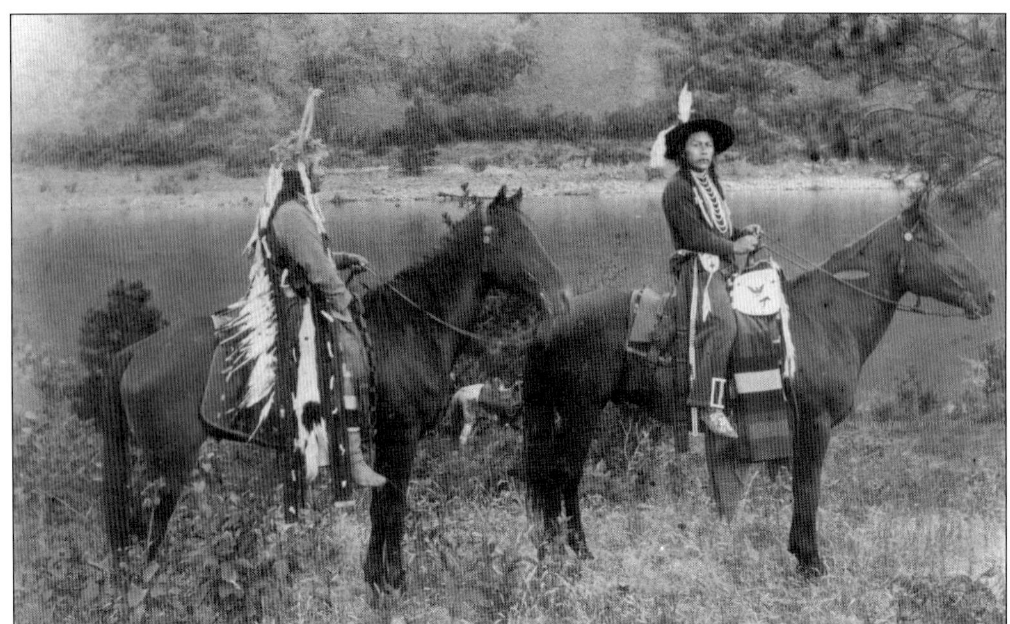

Seen here are Too-kay-am-lik (left) and Jesse Spotted Eagle, likely of the Nez Perce people. The Nez Perce, Umatilla, Cayuse, and Walla Walla spoke Shahaptian languages, though the Nez Perce language was used as a common language among all the eastern Oregon and Washington tribes. (Tamástslikt Cultural Institute.)

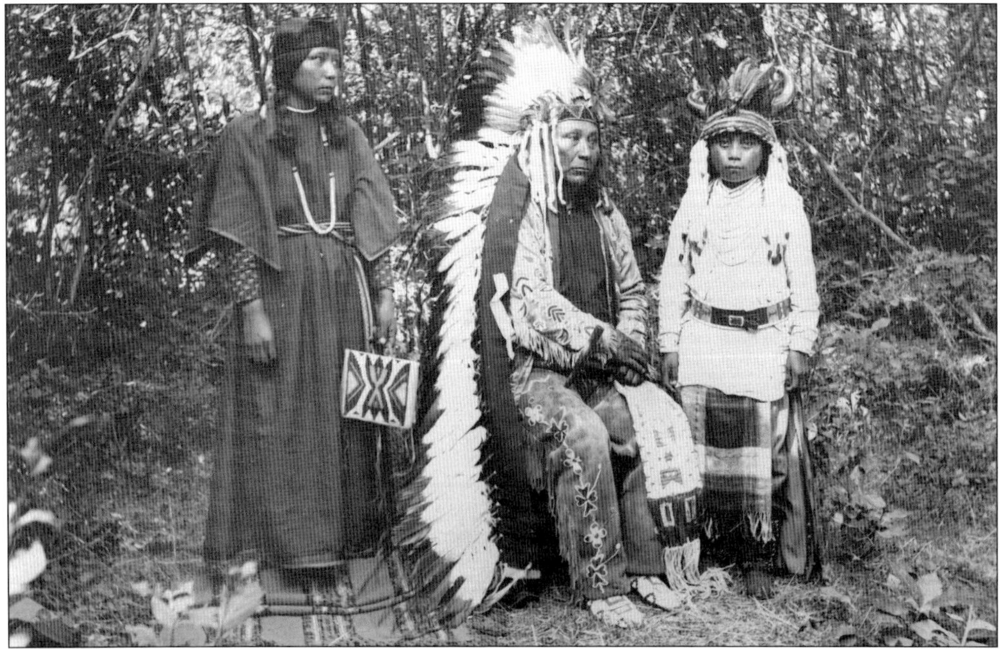

Chief Peo was a chief of the Umatilla tribe. Later, when Presbyterians were building a church on the reservation property, Chief Peo was one of several leaders who donated property for the church grounds. His daughter Jennie trained at an Indian training school and became an interpreter. Peo attended services when he was in good health. He died in approximately 1909. (National Museum of the American Indian, Smithsonian Institution [P27431]; photograph by Lee Moorhouse.)

Paul Show-a-way became the chief of a band of Cayuse about 1880. He succeeded a man named Howlish Wampo, who died about that time. Chief Show-a-way was an educated man and spoke good English. He often represented his people at delegations on the East Coast. (National Museum of the American Indian, Smithsonian Institution [P27417]; photograph by Lee Moorhouse.)

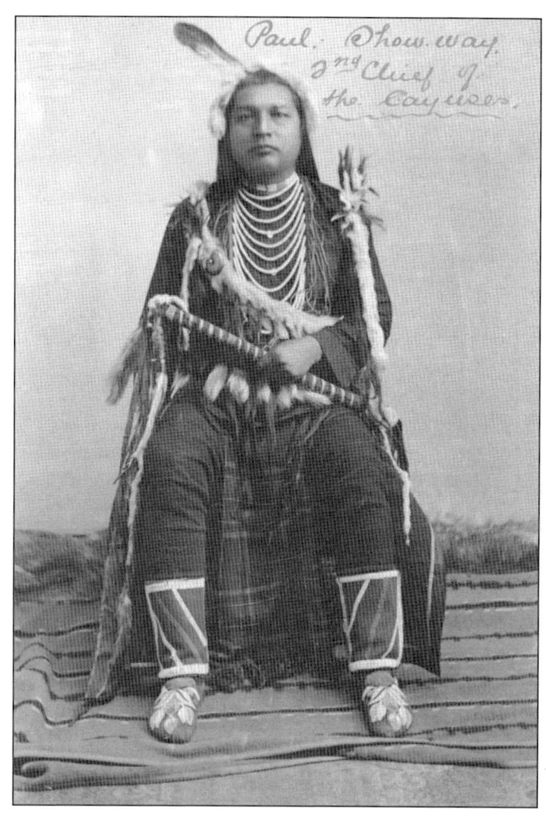

The Cayuse Indian below was known as Pai Shamkain, Charley Shaplish, and, most commonly among whites, Dr. Whirlwind. He carried dispatches for Col. George Wright and Col. Edward Steptoe during the wars of 1855 and 1856. A medicine man, he was known for performing medicine dances while holding live rattlesnakes. He died when he was bit by a rattlesnake during one such dance in the early 1900s. (Tamástslikt Cultural Institute.)

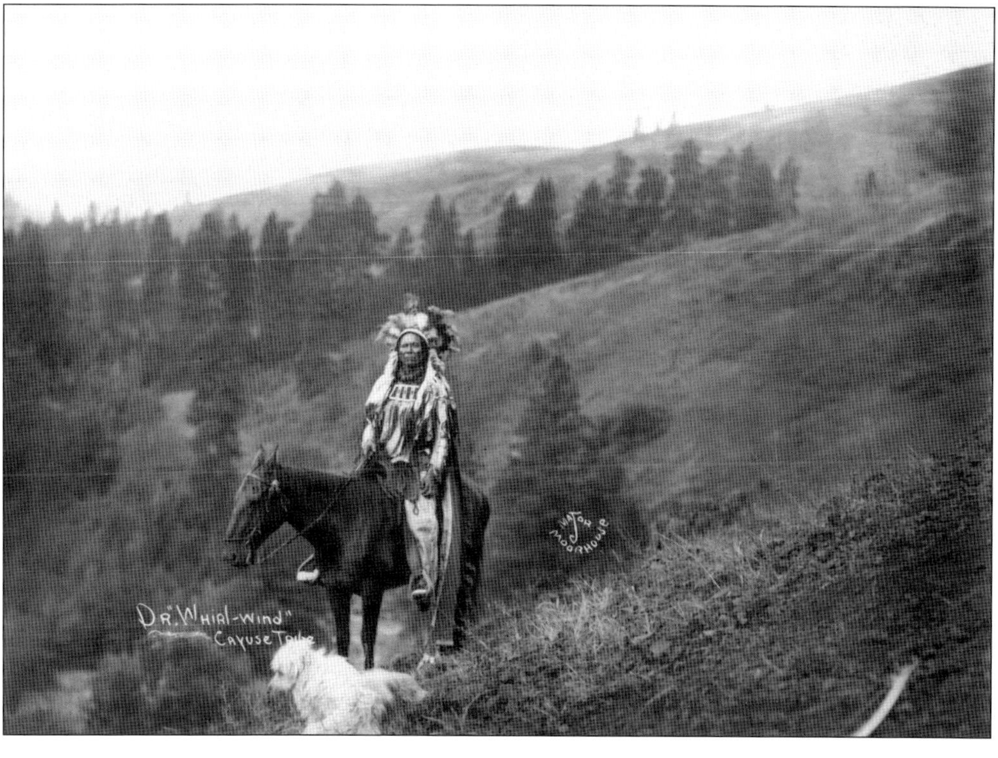

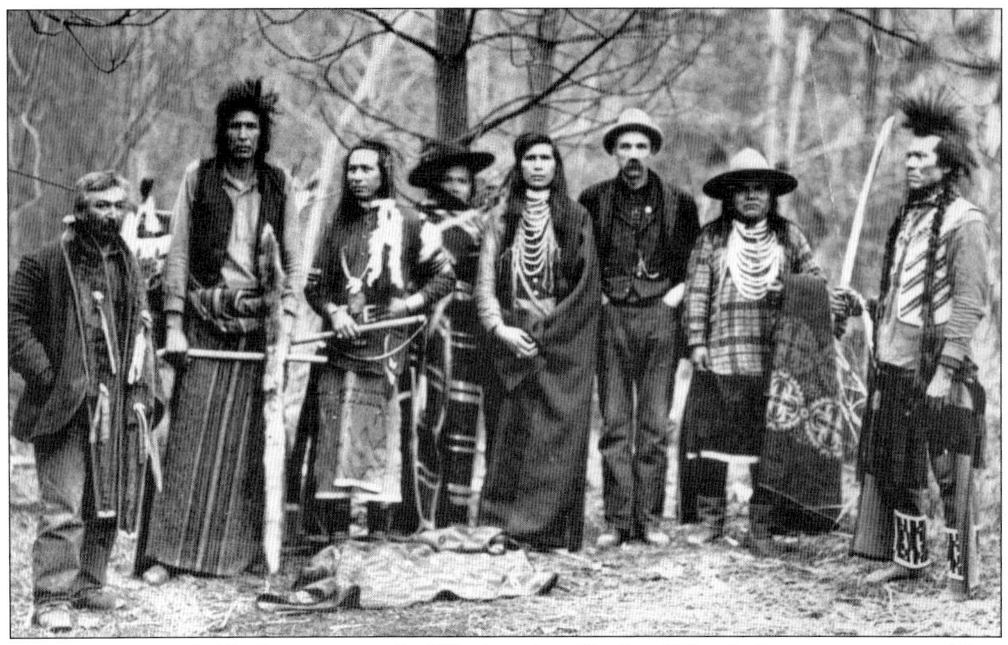

These men are probably Cayuse, since Dr. Whirlwind and Isadore Whitebull are among them. They are, from left to right, unidentified, Charles Whirlwind Jr., Towatoy, unidentified, Paka Whirlwind, unidentified, Isadore Whitebull, and Dr. Whirlwind. (Tamástslikt Cultural Institute.)

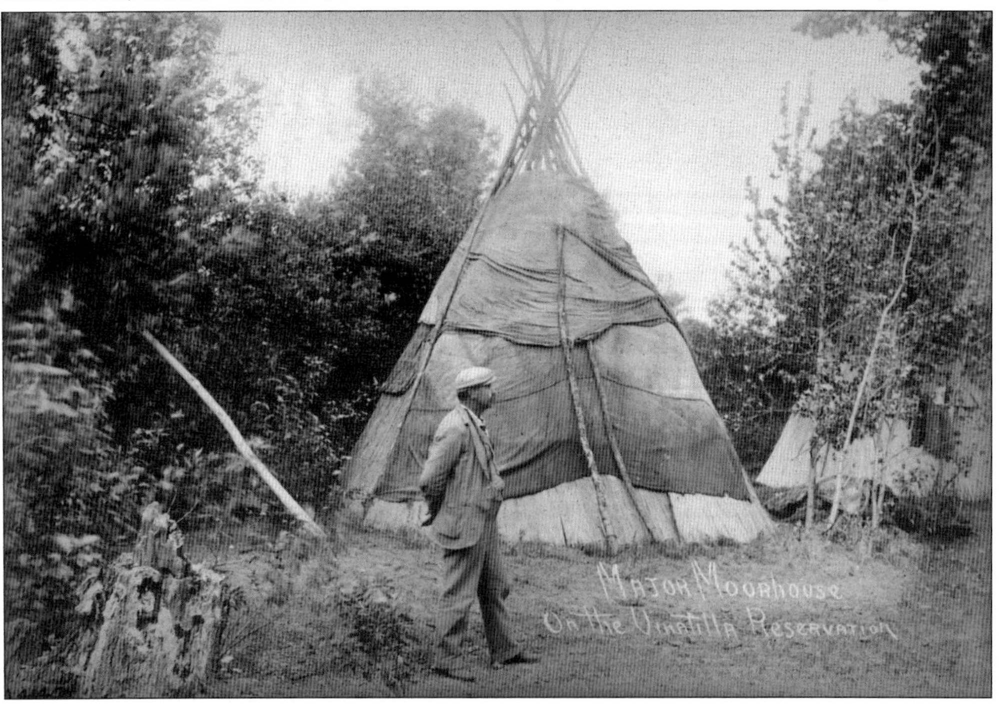

Lee Moorhouse served in the state militia and reached the rank of major. He then served as the county surveyor and as a field secretary to Gov. Stephen Chadwick during the Bannock War of 1878. He was a Pendleton businessman and property owner in the 1880s. In 1889, he was appointed as an agent of the Umatilla Indian Reservation. (Tamástslikt Cultural Institute.)

Moorhouse published a book of Indian photographs, many of which are seen in this book. Seen here is Anna Kash Kash, a Cayuse princess. She was the model for two of Moorhouse's photographs. One picture was entitled *Princess We-a-lote, Cayuse Maiden*, and the other was entitled *Wal-lu-lah*. She was educated at the Carlisle Indian School in Pennsylvania. She later taught there, as well as in Oklahoma. She also lived on the Umatilla Indian Reservation. (National Museum of the American Indian, Smithsonian Institution [P07697]; photograph by Lee Moorhouse.)

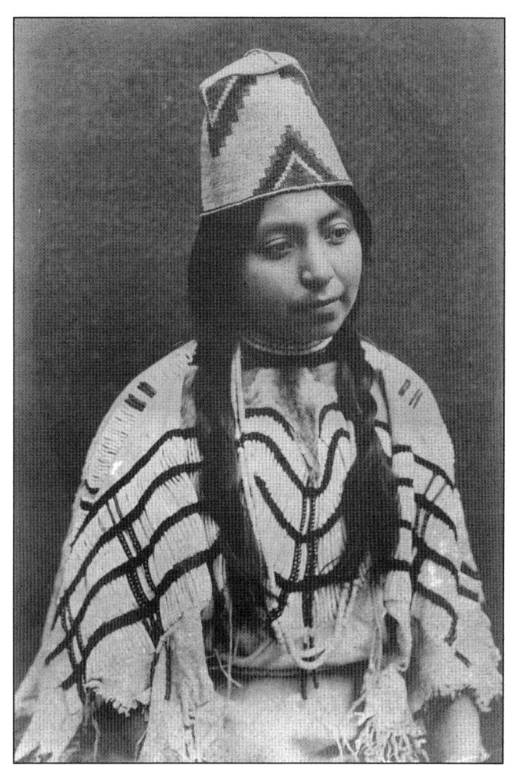

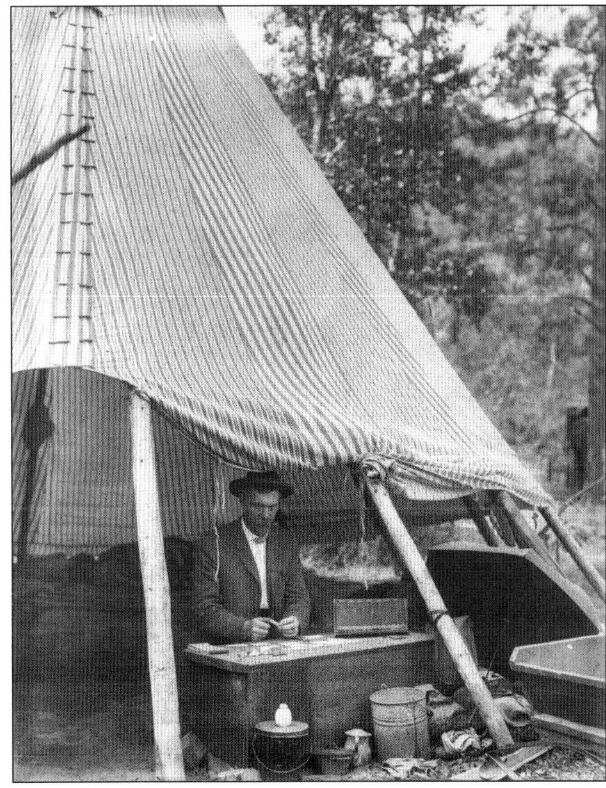

As an Indian agent, Lee Moorhouse was well respected by the tribes he served. They often entrusted him to dispatch letters, and they gave him gifts. He was also responsible for establishing an educational system on the reservation and was an advocate for Indian rights. For example, if trains killed livestock or started fires that destroyed property, he went to the railroad to ask for compensation. (Tamástslikt Cultural Institute.)

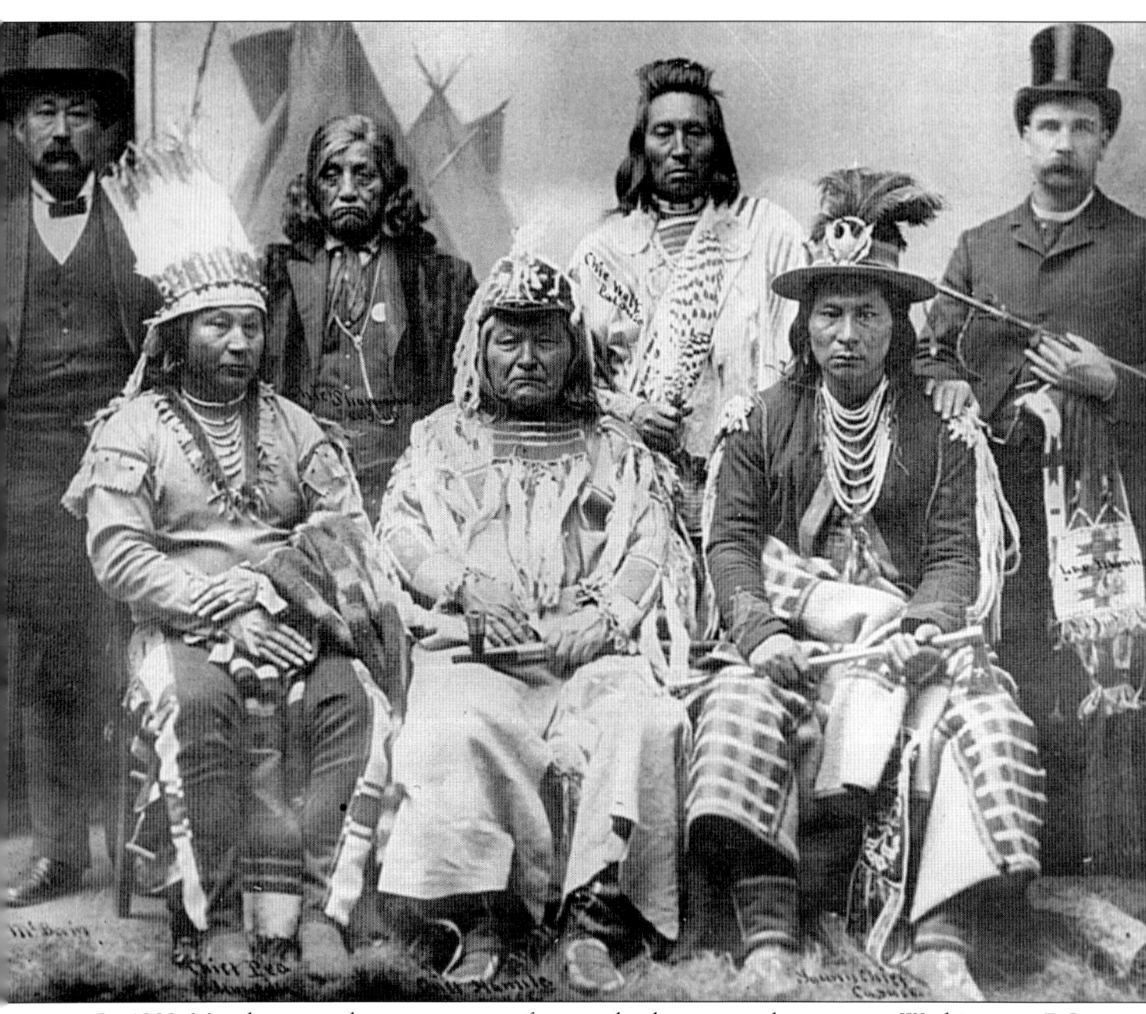

In 1889, Moorhouse took a contingent of native leaders on a pilgrimage to Washington, DC. Seen here from left to right are (seated) Chief Peo of the Umatillas; Chief Homli of the Walla Wallas; and a young chief of the Cayuse; (standing) John McBain, an interpreter; Chief Showaway of the Cayuse; Chief Wolf of the Palouse; and Moorhouse. They met with Thomas J. Morgan, the commissioner of Indian affairs. Though not a resident of the reservation, Chief Wolf was allowed to speak on behalf of his people. The group also met with Sen. Joseph Dolph, Sen. John F. Mitchell, and Rep. Binger Herman to discuss reparations still due the tribes after the 1878 Bannock War. (Yakima Valley Museum.)

This photograph of a pair of Cayuse twins is one of Lee Moorhouse's most famous. He got the mother's permission to take the babies' pictures. They started crying afterward, which he also recorded on film. The image, taken in 1898, sold 150,000 copies. The twins were named Al-om-pum and Tox-e-lox. (National Museum of the American Indian, Smithsonian Institution [P22465]; photograph by Lee Moorhouse.)

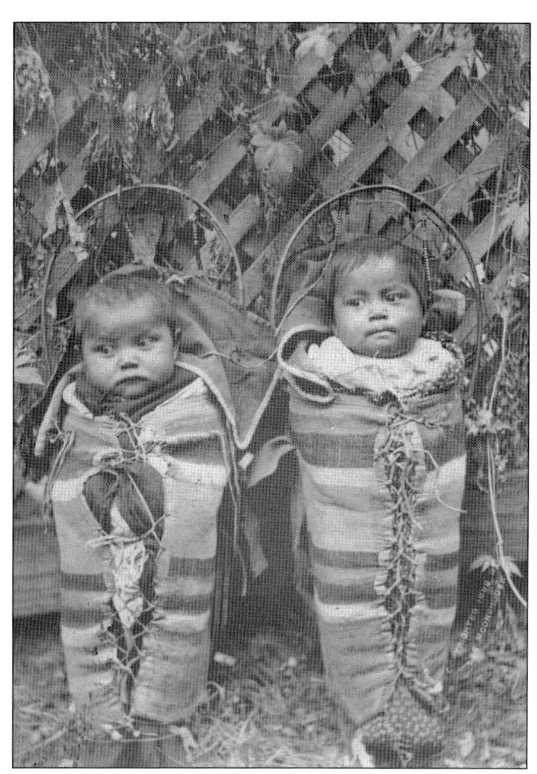

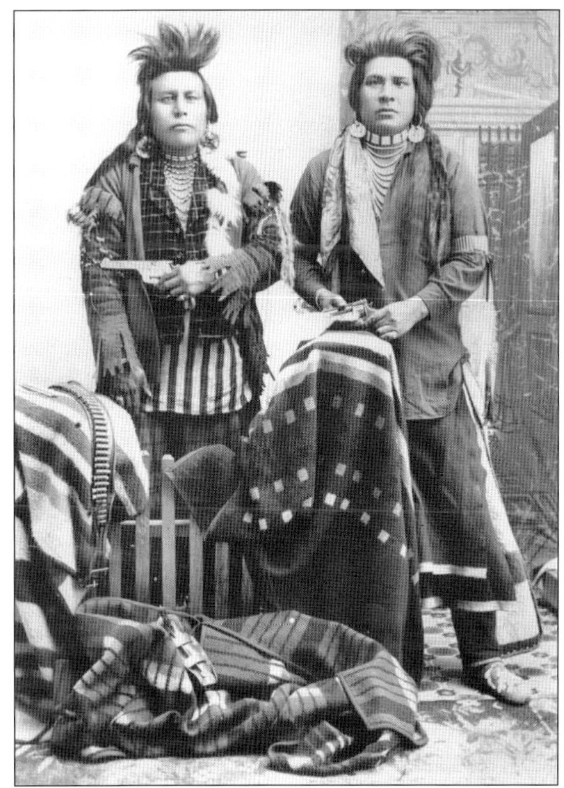

The two men in this classic Lee Moorhouse photograph are identified as George Howlish and James Badroads. Moorhouse took many photographs in his personal studio, and the poses were often stiff and formal. The subjects were given props from Moorhouse's personal collection that were not always authentic to the subjects. He used a fabric-covered backdrop outside his back door, which provided good natural light for his photographs. (Tamástslikt Cultural Institute.)

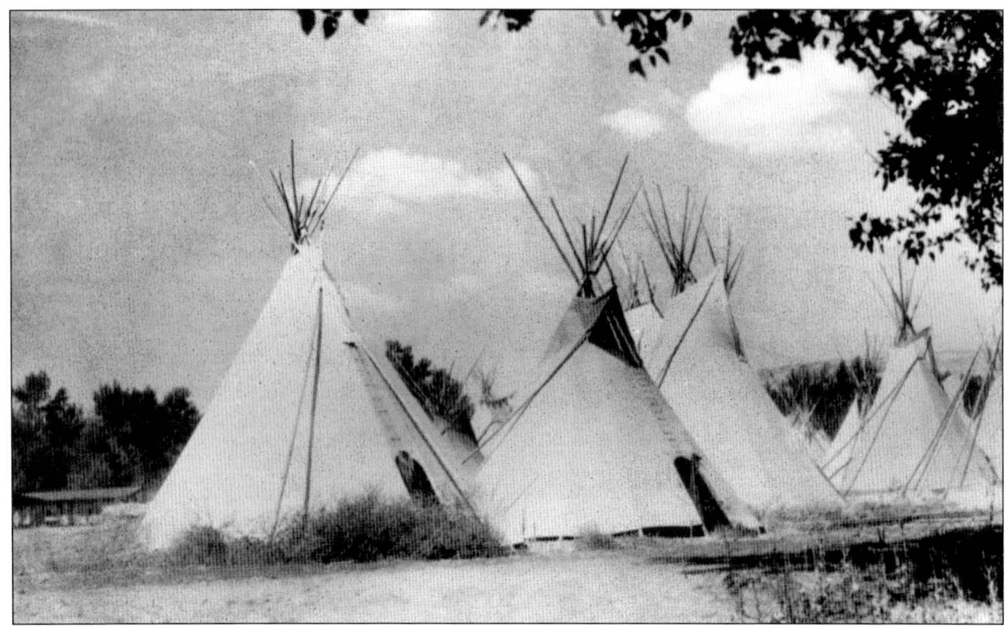

These tepees are typical of Cayuse and other Plateau tribes. Unlike Plains tribes who made dwellings from hides, these are made from tule mats. Tules grow along rivers and in other moist areas. The tules are lightweight and can be transported easily. They also act as a good insulator during the wintertime to keep in the heat. They were also used for flooring inside the tepees. (Tamástslikt Cultural Institute.)

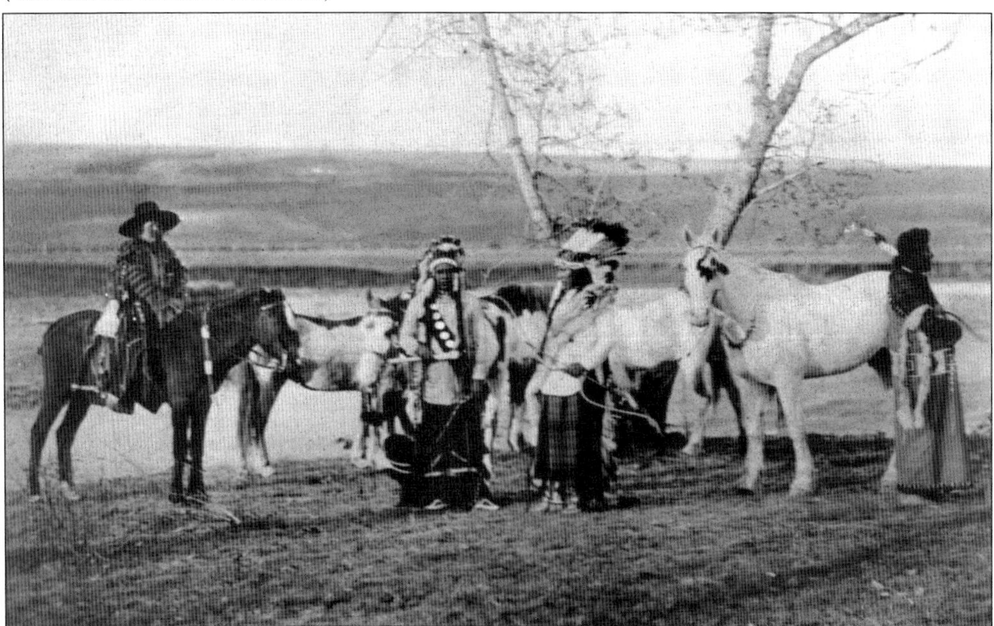

These men are probably from the Umatilla tribe. Their exact identity and the date of this photograph are unknown. It was likely taken on the banks of the nearby Columbia River, where natives went to fish. At one time, these tribes owned large herds of horses. The Cayuse horses were stout, strong animals that could move easily through the nearby mountain ranges. (Tamástslikt Cultural Institute.)

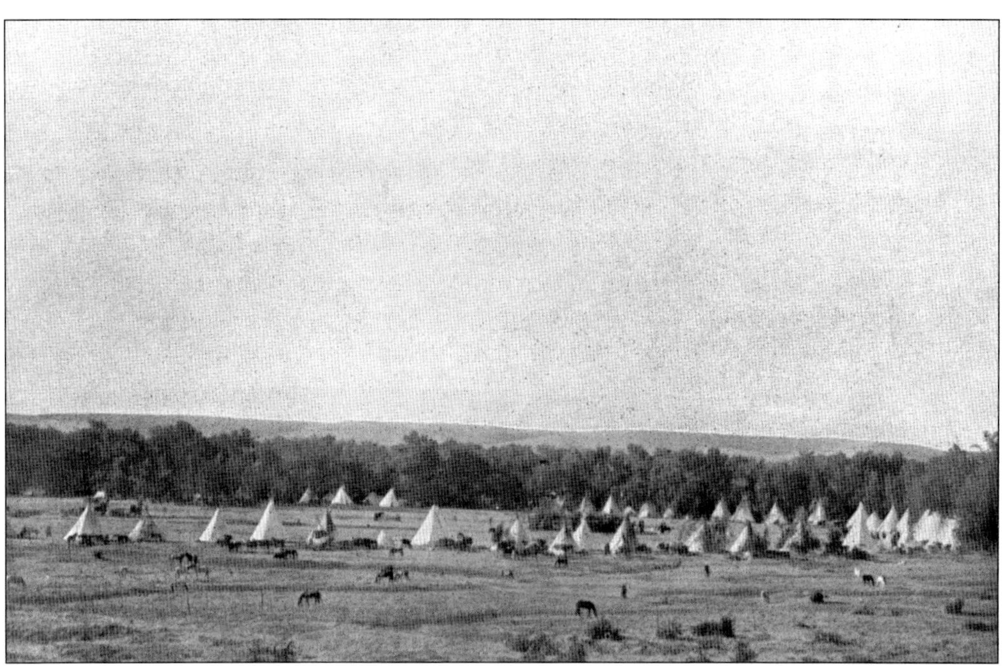

The Indian campground above was located on the Umatilla Reservation. This photograph, taken in approximately 1906, shows a typical village encampment with horses grazing. At this time, some tribal members were living in wooden houses, but many were still living in a traditional manner. (National Museum of the American Indian, Smithsonian Institution [P27462]; photograph by Lee Moorhouse.)

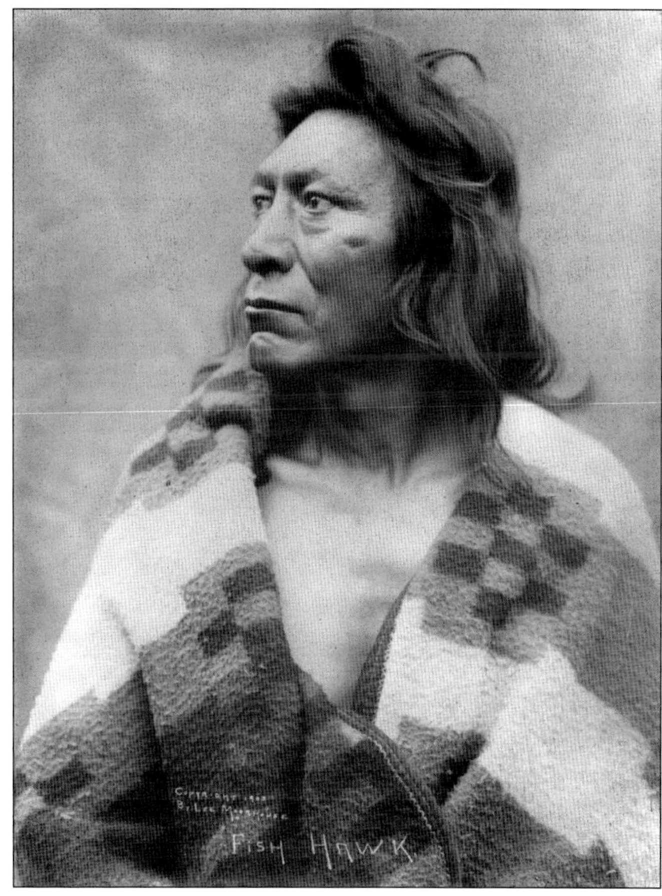

This photograph was taken in approximately 1903. Fish Hawk was the head Cayuse war chief. He was also the son of a Cayuse chief. In 1901, he converted to Christianity at the Presbyterian church located on the reservation. Rev. Enoch Pond and Philip and Robinson Minthorn officiated the ceremony. (Tamástslikt Cultural Institute.)

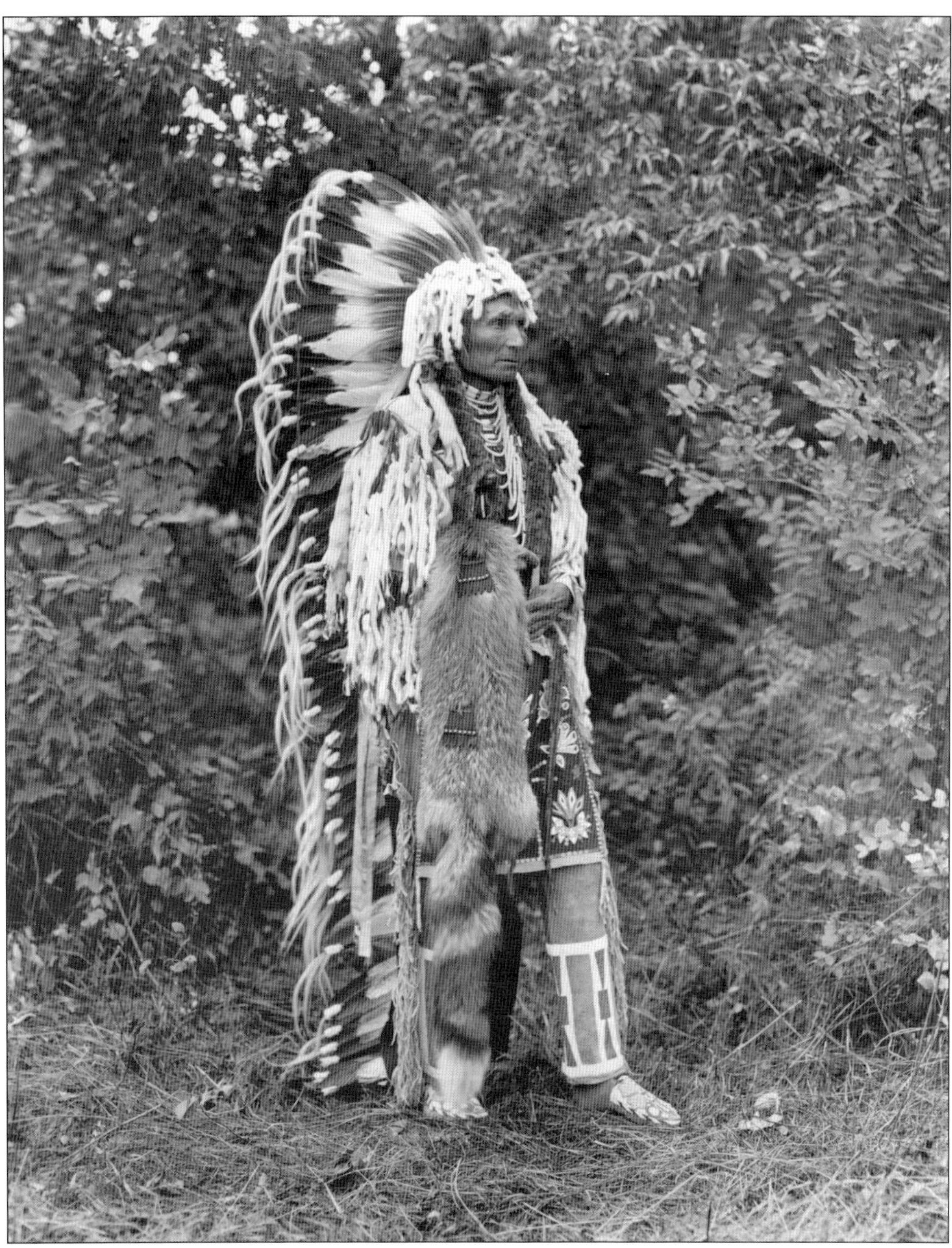

This photograph of Chief Umapine was taken by Dr. Joseph K. Dixon during what was known as the Wanamaker Expedition. Rodman Wanamaker sponsored three trips between 1908 and 1913 to record the tribes of the northern plains. Umapine was a Cayuse chief known to them as Wa Kon We La Son Mi. He was known for killing Chief Egan of the Bannock tribe, who had been harassing white settlers during the Bannock War of 1878. His death was thought to have saved Pendleton area residents from attack. In 1914, a small town in Umatilla County was named after him. (Library of Congress.)

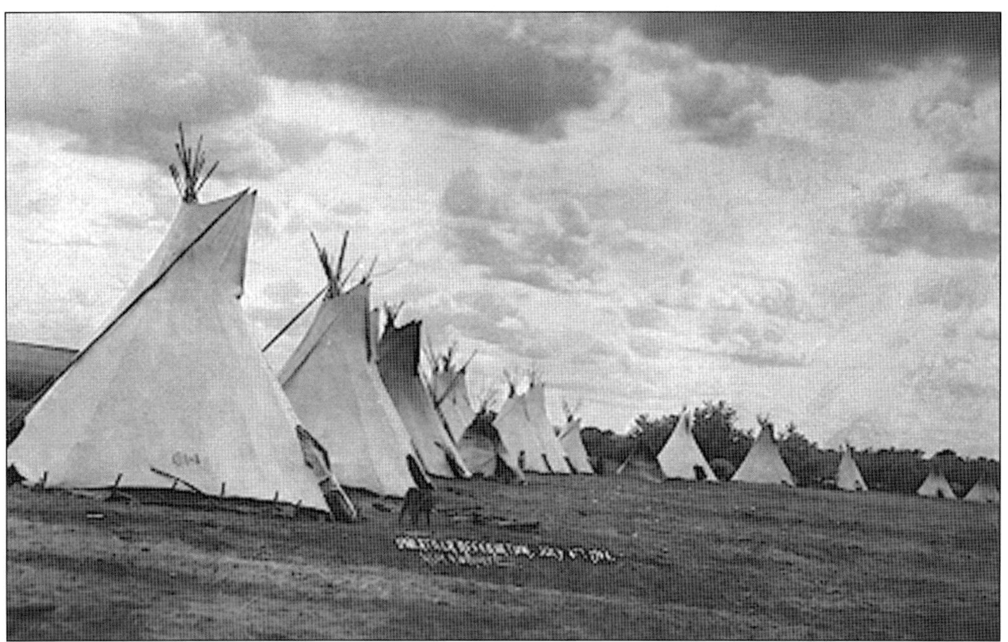

This photograph is dated July 4, 1914, and likely shows an annual celebration of local settlers or a typical native camp of the time period. (Fort Walla Walla Museum.)

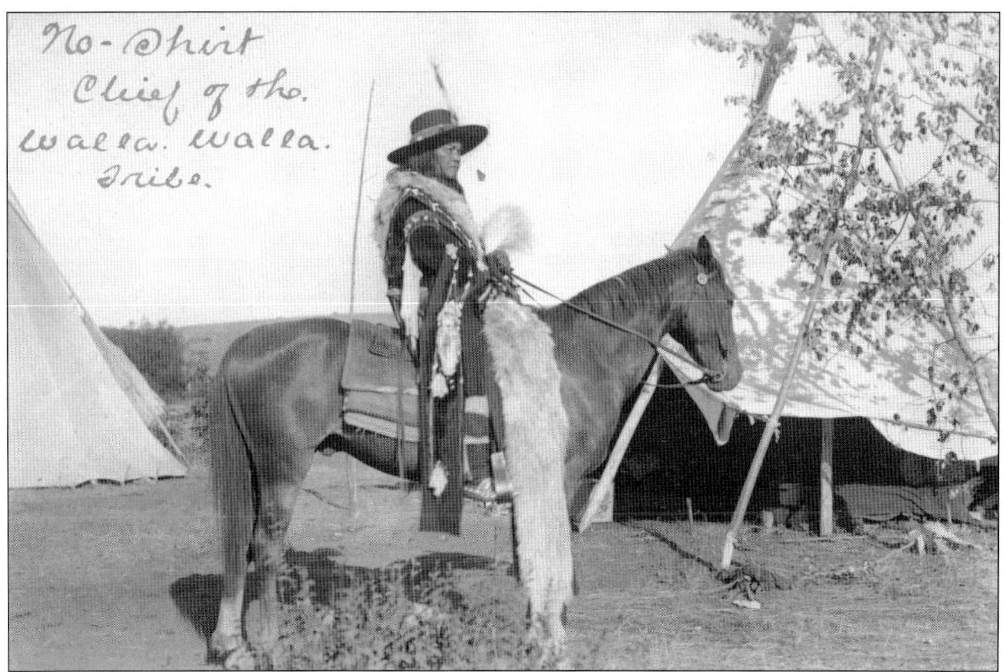

Chief No Shirt of the Walla Walla tribe was born in 1845. He was one of the first chiefs to bring his people to the Round-Up grounds. He passed away in 1917 at age 72. He was inducted into the Pendleton Round-Up Hall of Fame in 2012. (National Museum of the American Indian, Smithsonian Institution [P27435]; photograph by Lee Moorhouse.)

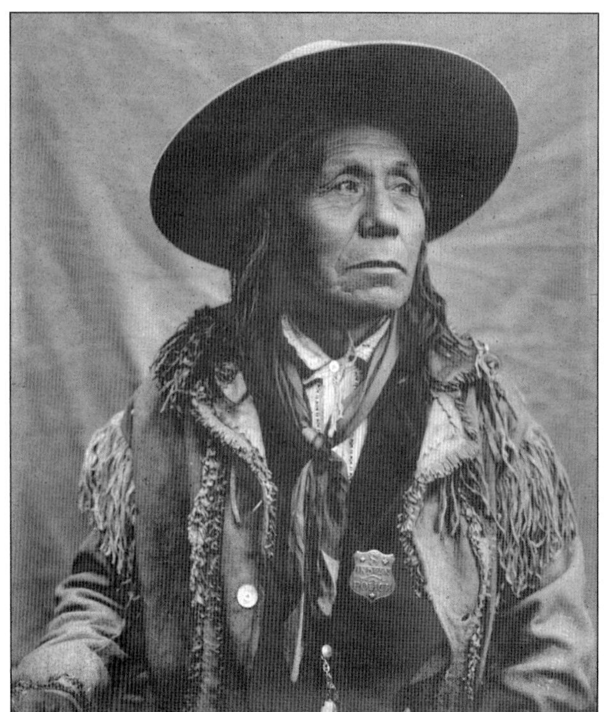

Sergeant Tiloukaikt was a Cayuse warrior who served as a scout for Lt. W.C. Brown, US Cavalry, after the Bannock War of 1878. He was one of about 20 young men recruited to track down renegades who had fled to Idaho. He was later known as Captain Som-Kin, or Sumpkin, because he served on the Umatilla Reservation police force. (National Museum of the American Indian, Smithsonian Institution [P26752]; photograph by Lee Moorhouse.)

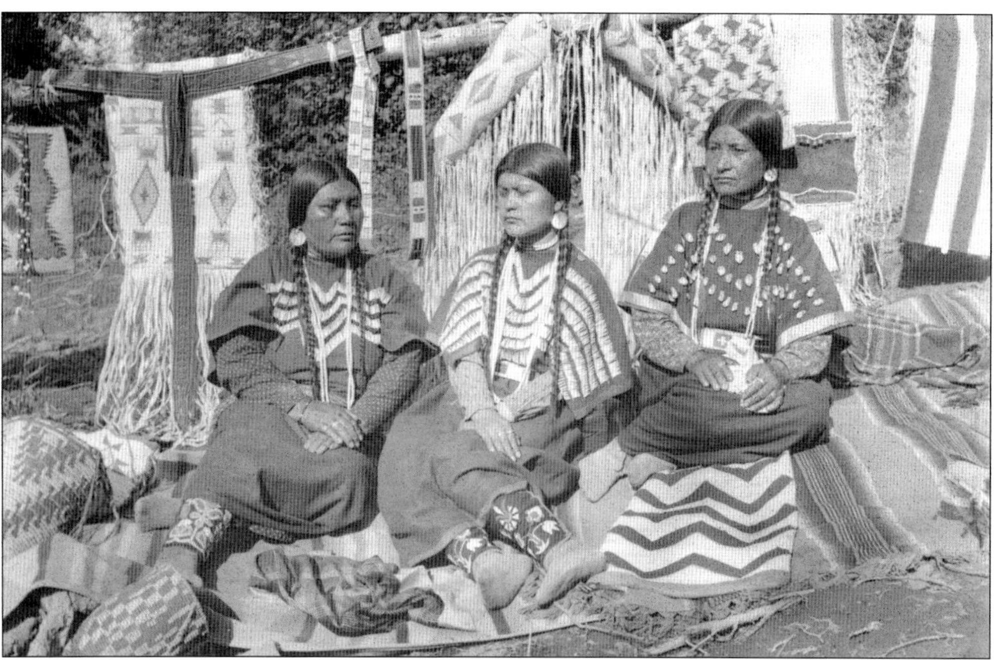

These women may be Walla Walla or Cayuse. They are shown with typical native basketry, beadwork, and clothing. Baskets, hats, and bags usually depicted icons that told a story important to history. They did use cotton and wool, which were introduced by white men, but they decorated them in a traditional way, with cowrie, dentalium, shells, and elk teeth around the yoke. They wove blankets with bright geometric and plaid designs. (National Museum of the American Indian, Smithsonian Institution [P27429]; photograph by Lee Moorhouse.)

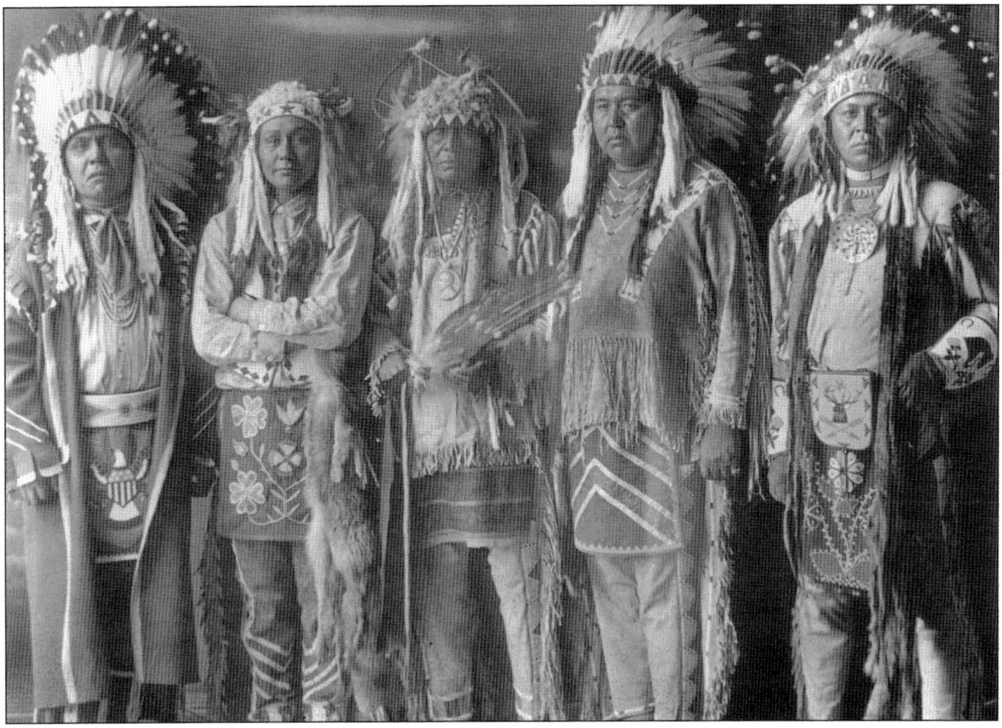

Seen here from left to right are Lucian Williams, Richard Burke Sr., James "Poker Jim" Burke, Clarence Burke, and Charley Johnson. The Burkes are members of the Umatilla tribe and have long been involved in leading Indian participation in the Pendleton Round-Up. (Tamástslikt Cultural Institute.)

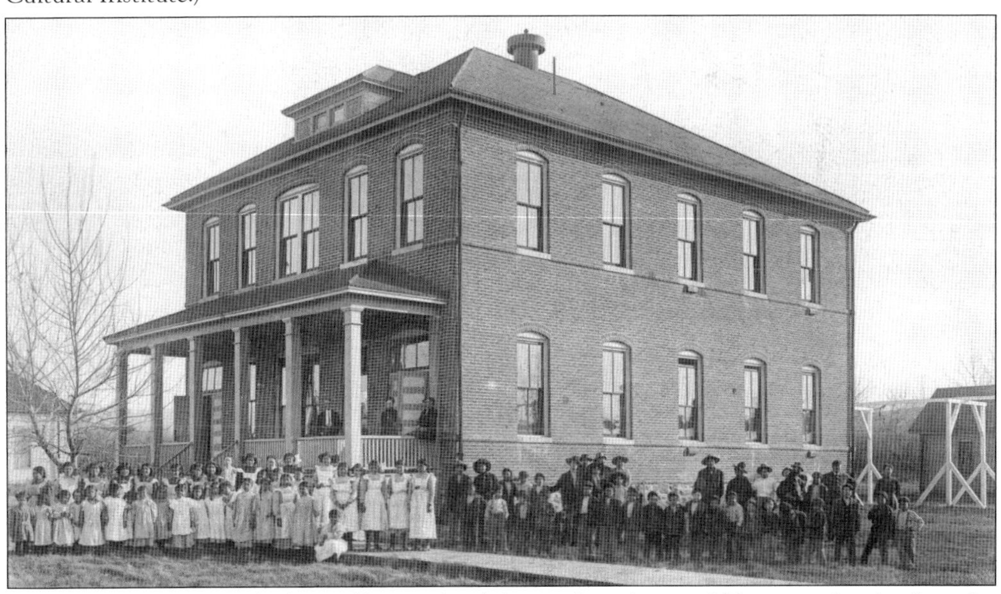

It is unknown exactly which Pendleton school this is, though it could be an early school on the Umatilla Reservation. It does appear that both white and Indian children were in attendance. Multiple age groups stand out front, so this building likely housed all grades from first through 12th. (Tamástslikt Cultural Institute.)

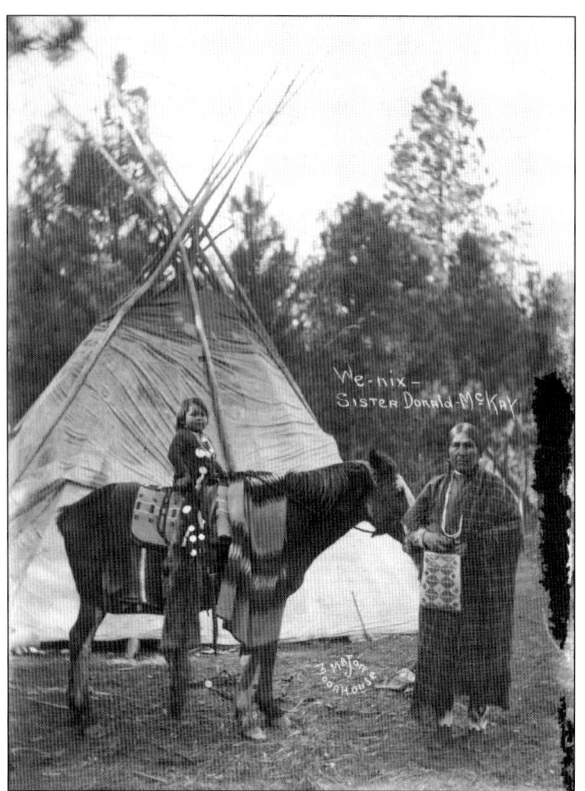

Seen here is We-nix McKay, the sister of Indian Agency interpreter Donald McKay. Their parents were Thomas McKay and a Cayuse Indian woman. They also had a half-brother, William Cameron McKay, whose mother was a Chinook Indian woman. William McKay served as the agency doctor for many years. The child on horseback is unidentified. (Tamástslikt Cultural Institute.)

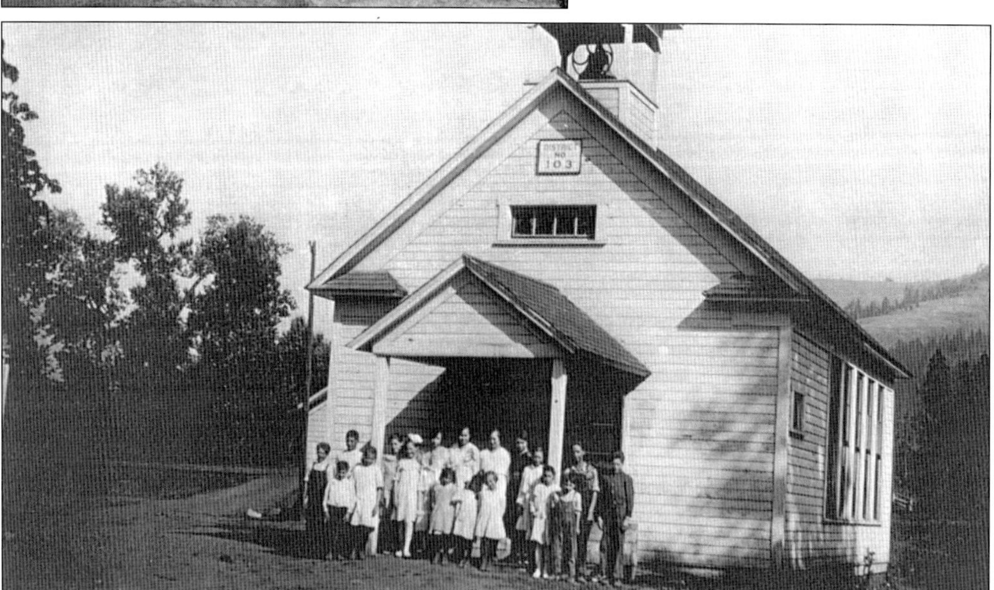

Gibbon was a railroad station named for Maj. Gen. John Gibbon, the commander of the Department of the Columbia from 1885 to 1886. The name of the station was later changed to Bingham Springs, but the name of the post office remained Gibbon from 1892 until 1966. The Gibbon school served both Indian and white children through at least 1940. The unincorporated town still exists along the Umatilla River on Umatilla Indian Reservation property. (Tamástslikt Cultural Institute.)

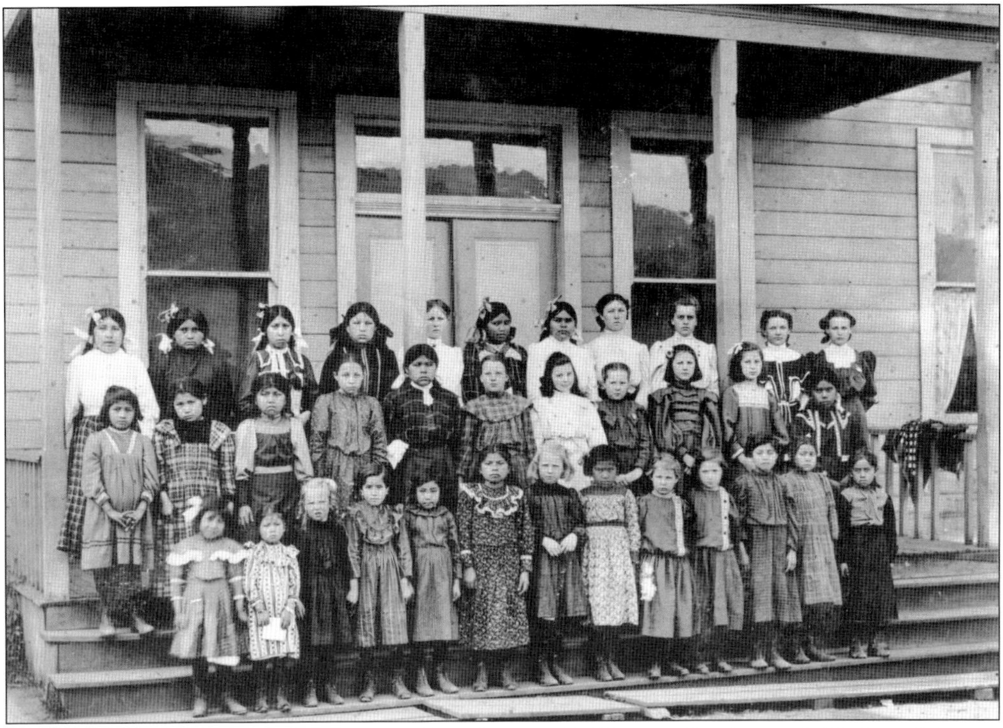

Originally called St. Ann's Mission and then St. Joseph's Mission, St. Andrew's Catholic Mission was established four miles southeast of the agency headquarters of the Umatilla Indian Reservation. The mission, established in 1883, was named for Monsignor J. Andrew Stephan, the director of the Bureau of Catholic Indian Missions. The associated boarding school, called the Kate Drexel Institute, opened in 1890 with four resident nuns and 13 students. (Tamástslikt Cultural Institute.)

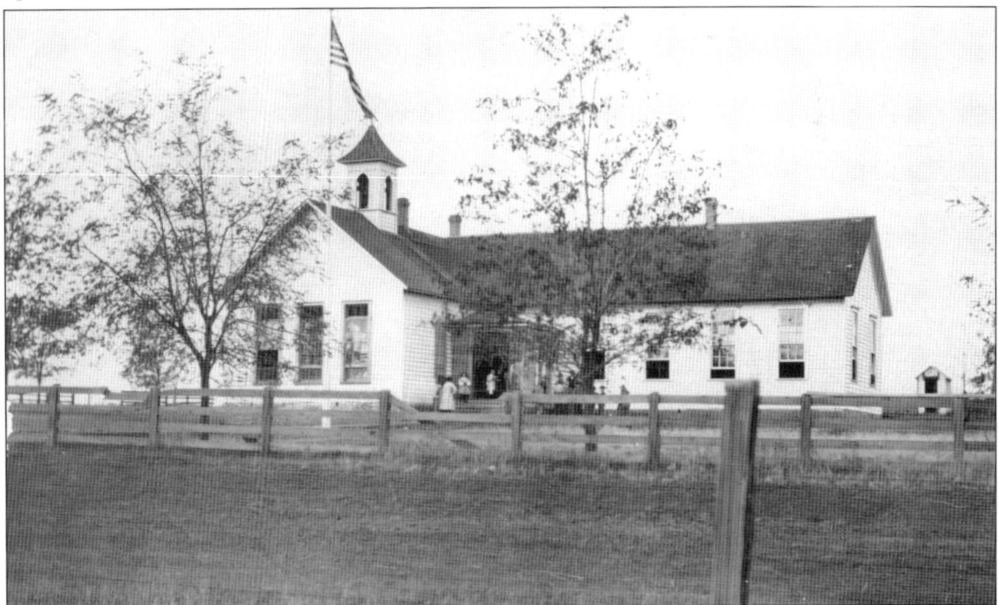

It is not known exactly which school this is, although it could be the St. Andrew's school, which has had various buildings over the years. (Tamástslikt Cultural Institute.)

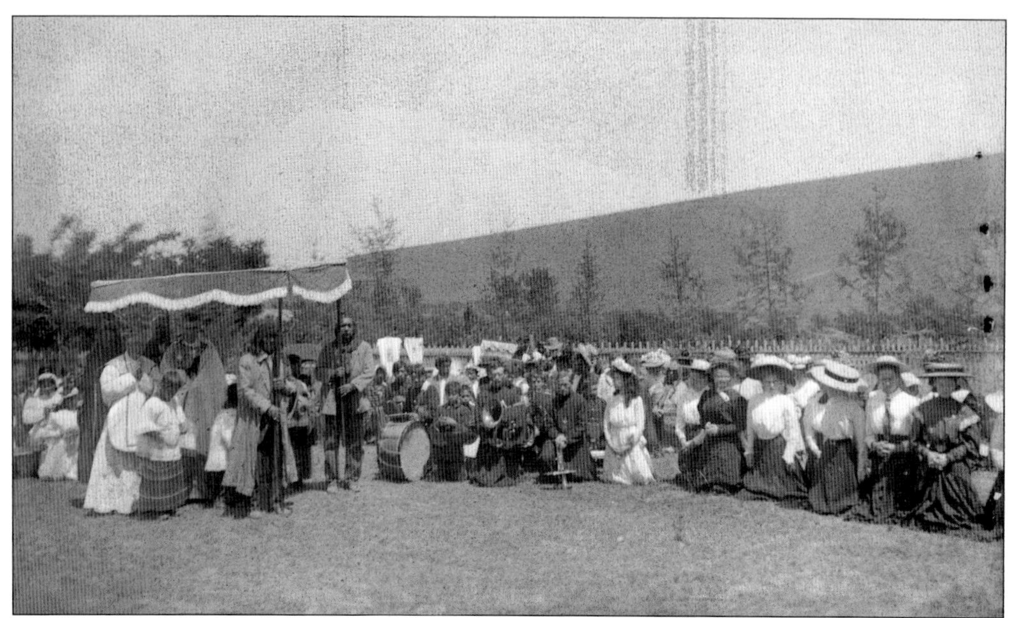

During the era of the Catholic missions, various Catholic dignitaries visited from time to time. Bishop Charles J. O'Reilly of the Baker City diocese is seen here visiting the Umatilla Reservation. This photograph is believed to be of a 1909 visit to the Umatilla Reservation. Fr. Joseph Cataldo, a longtime resident priest in the area, acted as interpreter. (Lee Moorhouse Collection [PH036 1374], Special Collections and University Archives, University of Oregon.)

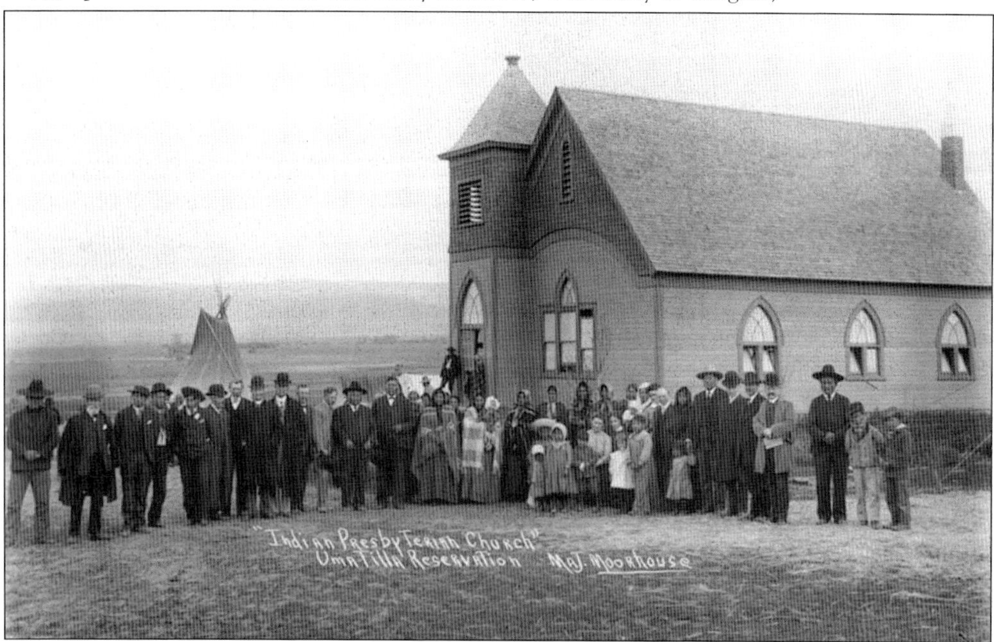

Tutuilla Presbyterian Church, on Tutuilla Mission Road on the Umatilla Reservation, still looks very much as it did when it was established in 1882. It was organized by Rev. Robert Williams, Reverend Deffenbaugh, and Rev. William Wheeler. For the first 15 years, Nez Perce members served as ministers. Rev. James M. Cornelison arrived in 1899 and served there for 40 years. Tutuilla Creek runs from southeast to northwest near the church. (Tamástslikt Cultural Institute.)

When Rev. James M. Cornelison came to the reservation, he lived in a lodge, similar to how the Indians lived. With the help of Fr. Joseph Cataldo, he developed a written Nez Perce language. He then provided services in that language. He also worked hard to desegregate the schools, succeeding when Esther Motanic became the first Indian girl accepted into Pendleton High School. (Lee Moorhouse Collection [PH036 2493], Special Collections and University Archives, University of Oregon.)

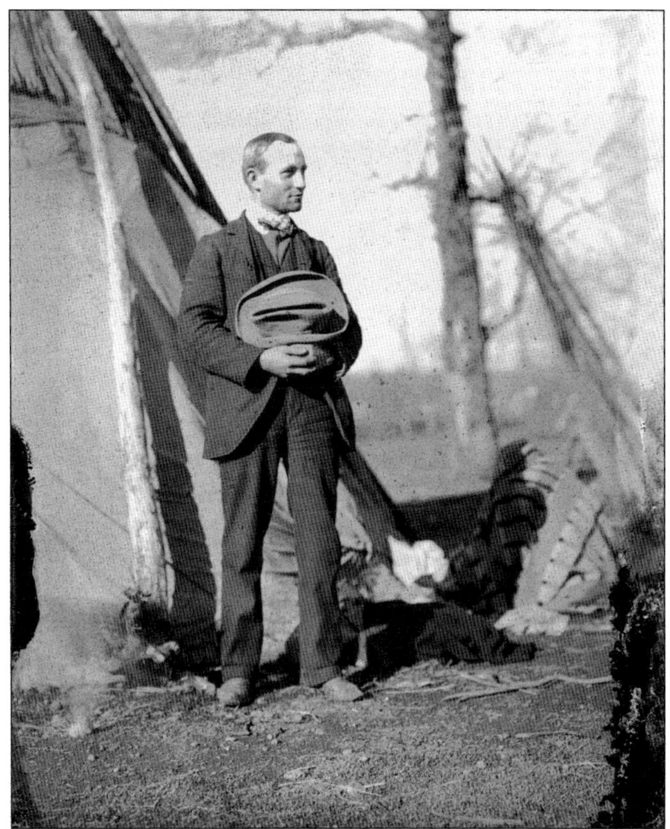

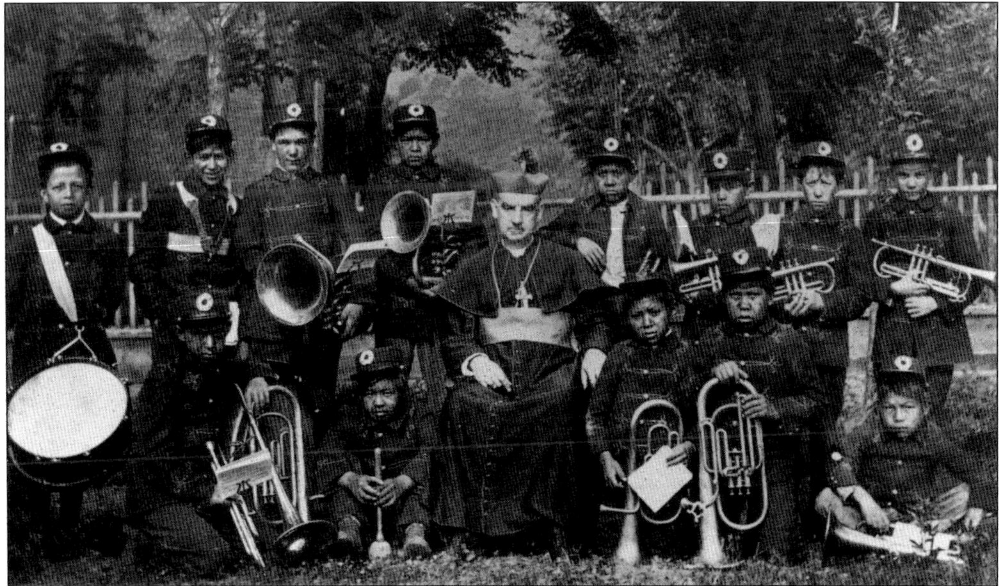

The Catholic Boys brigade at the St. Andrew's school is seen here. During the early days of the agency school, there was a boys' dormitory and a girls' dormitory. The school had a large orchard with nearly 200 trees. There was also a 10-acre garden and 40 acres of wheat. Boys at the school were charged with maintaining the gardens and orchards. (Tamástslikt Cultural Institute.)

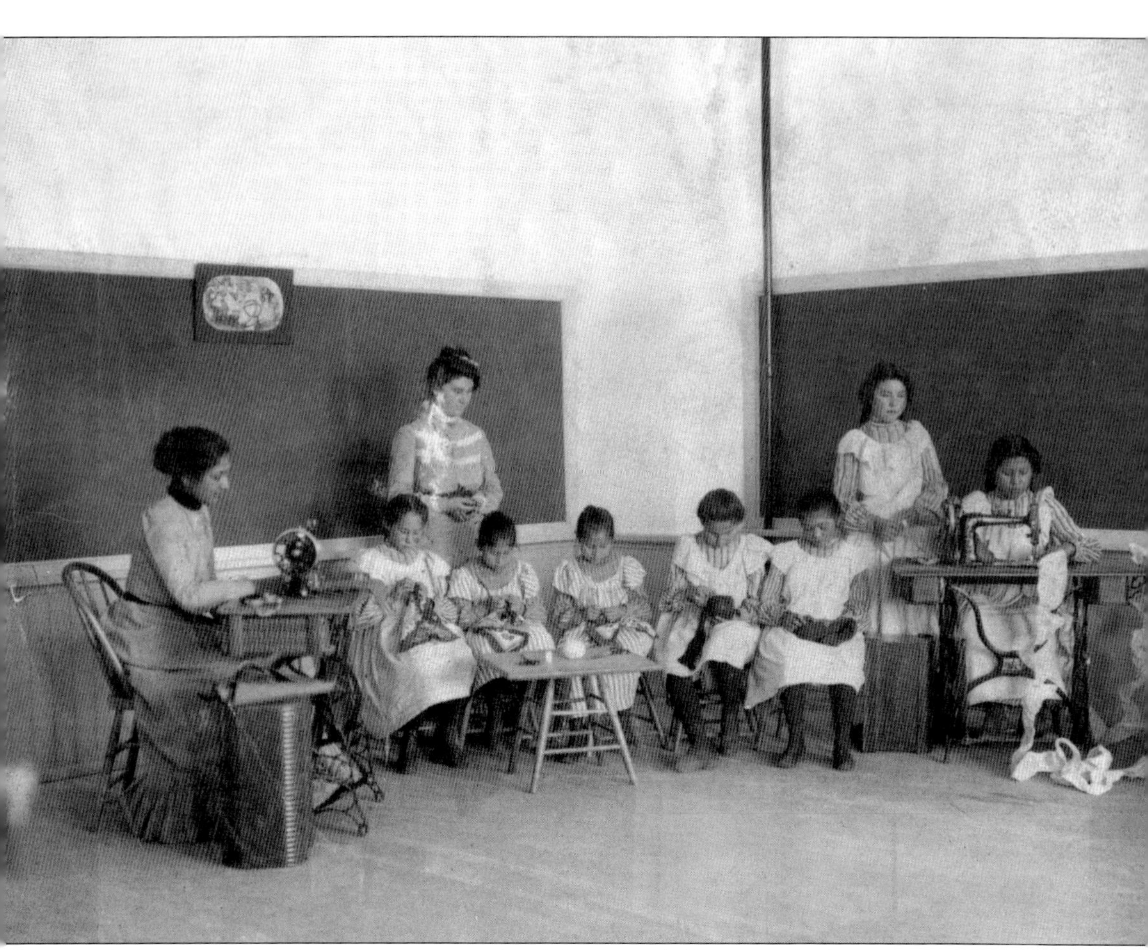

Girls were expected to learn vocational and domestic skills just as the boys were. Girls were also taught housekeeping skills and nursing. They learned to work in the dairy, the kitchen, the garden, and the laundry. The girls in this photograph, taken about 1906, are learning to sew. Mary Johnly Hines is third from the right. (Tamástslikt Cultural Institute.)

Two

EARLY DAYS

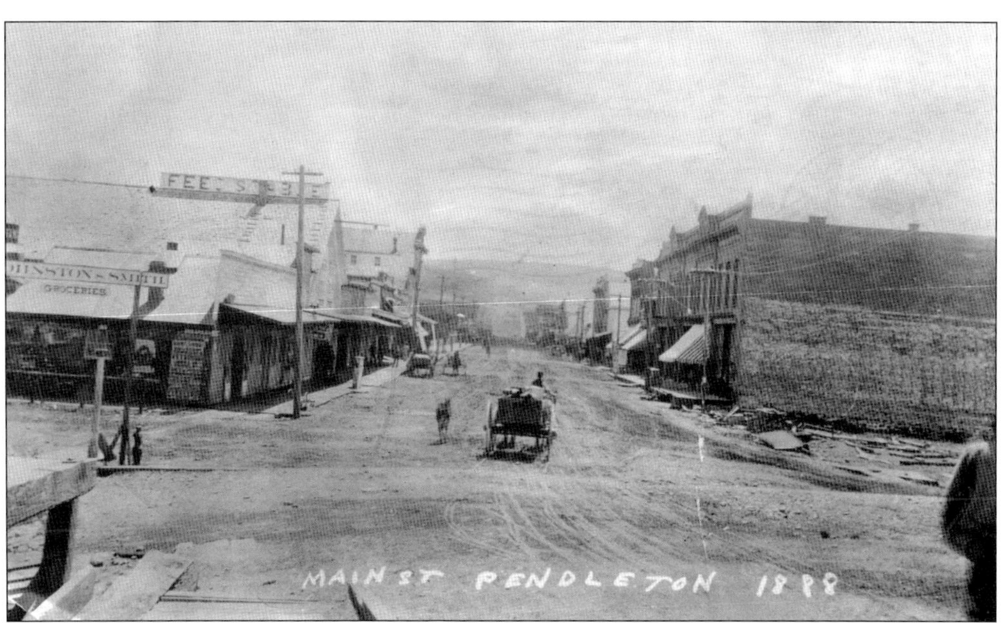

As is the case with many early towns, Main Street was the first road to be built. It has a north-south orientation. This photograph from 1888 shows the early city looking like a classic Western frontier town. Note that the street is dirt, which created quite a mess in inclement weather. The first electrical lines were also strung along Main Street that year. (Umatilla County Historical Society, 1981.001.0291.)

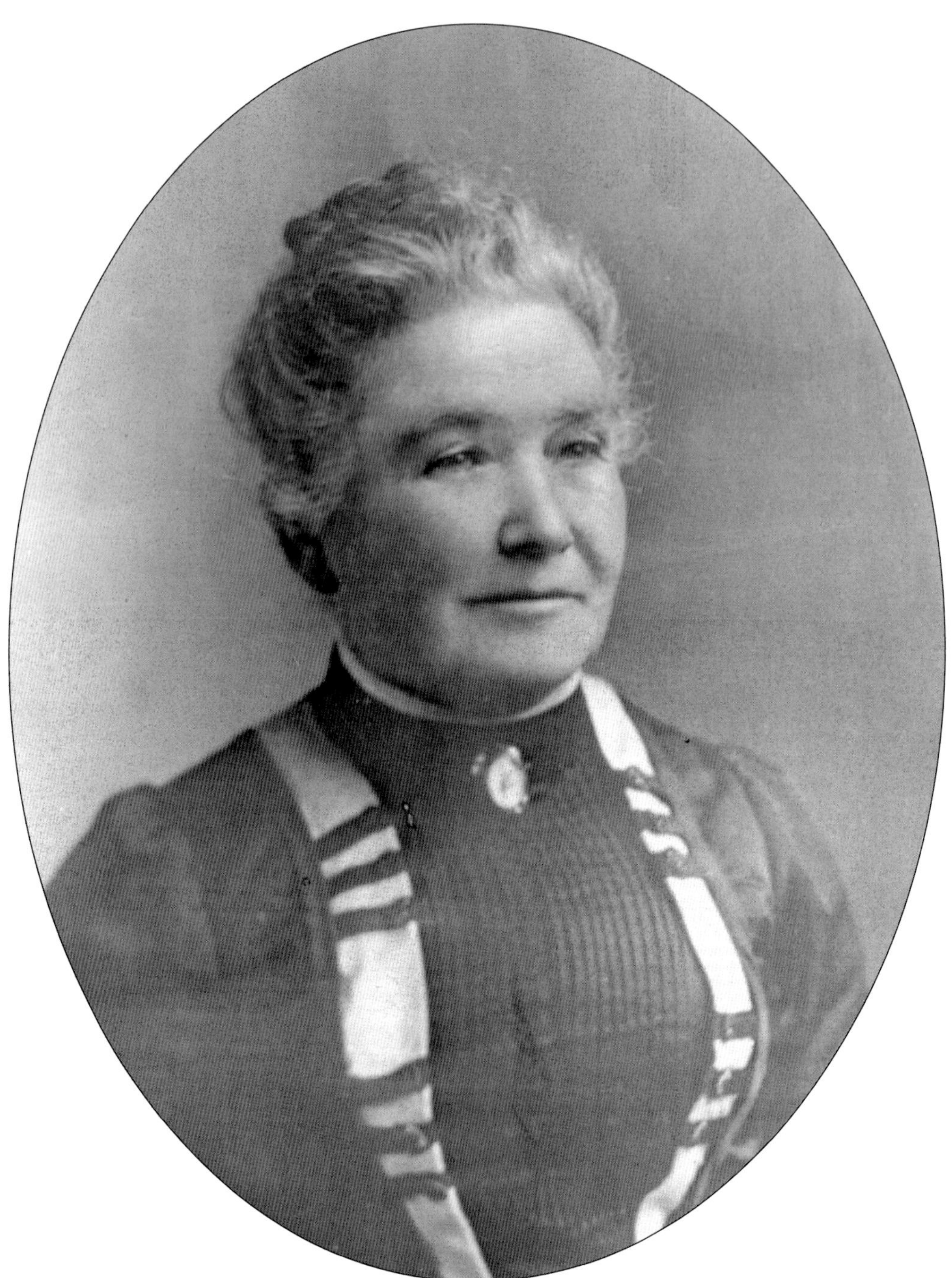

Aura M. Raley is considered the mother of Pendleton. She was the wife of Moses Goodwin, the first homesteader in the Pendleton area. They migrated to the west from Wisconsin in the 1850s. They lived near Vancouver, Washington, until moving again to Umatilla County in 1864. They were headed to Boise but could not get their herd over the Blue Mountains, so they staked a claim in Pendleton and operated the Pendleton Hotel. The couple had three children. After Moses died in 1871, Aura remarried in 1872 to Henry J. Raley. They had one child. Aura died in 1913 at the age of 84. (Umatilla County Historical Society, 2008.100.2000.)

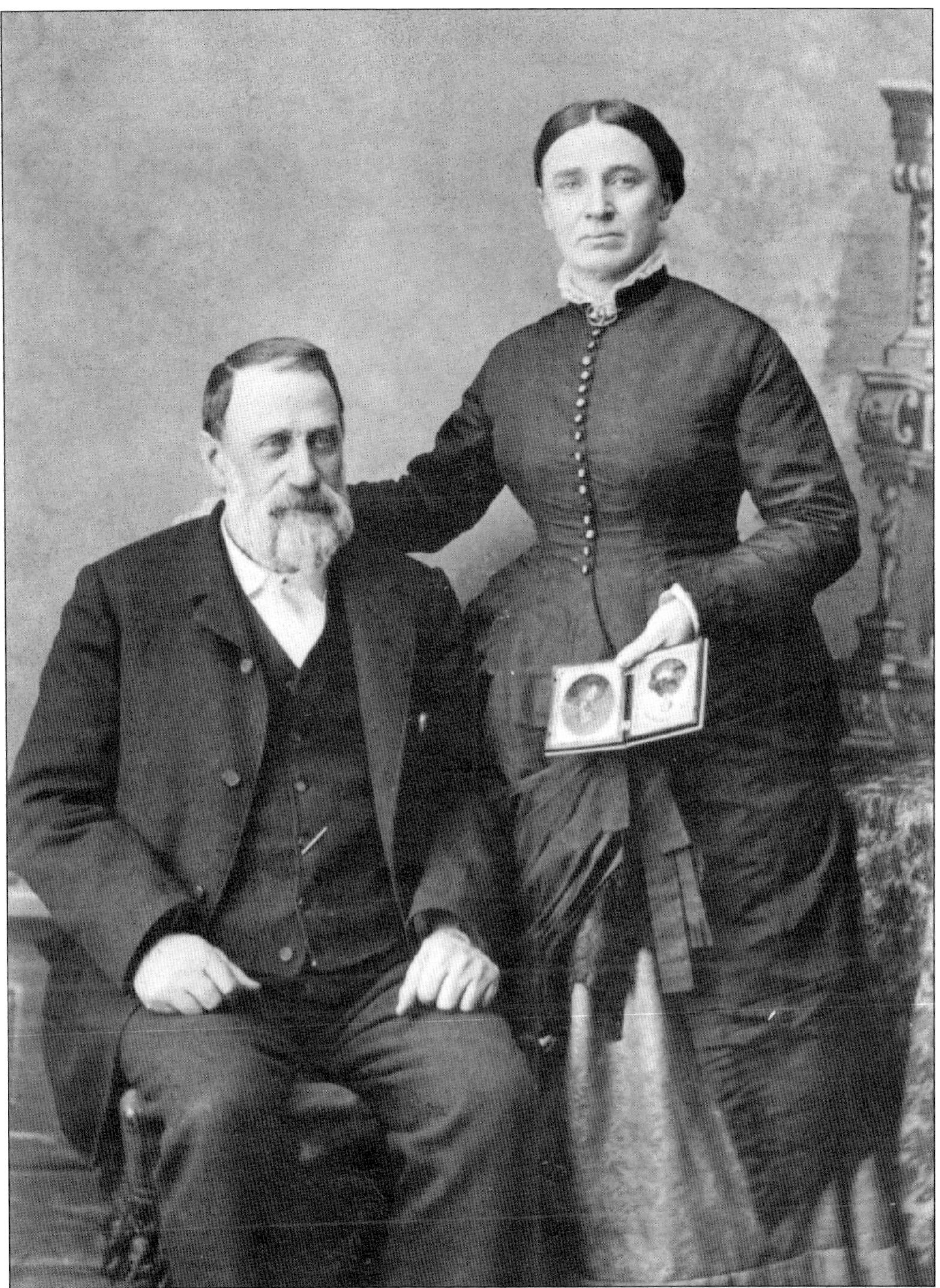

Judge William Martin came west from West Virginia in the 1840s. He had several adventures as a soldier, hunter, gold miner, and rancher in the Pacific Northwest. He met his wife during his days in California. He arrived in Pendleton in 1880. He was elected sheriff of Umatilla County that year and then reelected in 1882 and 1884. He did not run for reelection in 1886, instead winning the election for mayor of Pendleton. In 1888, he served as a county judge. He died in 1899. (Umatilla County Historical Society, 1981.001.4902.)

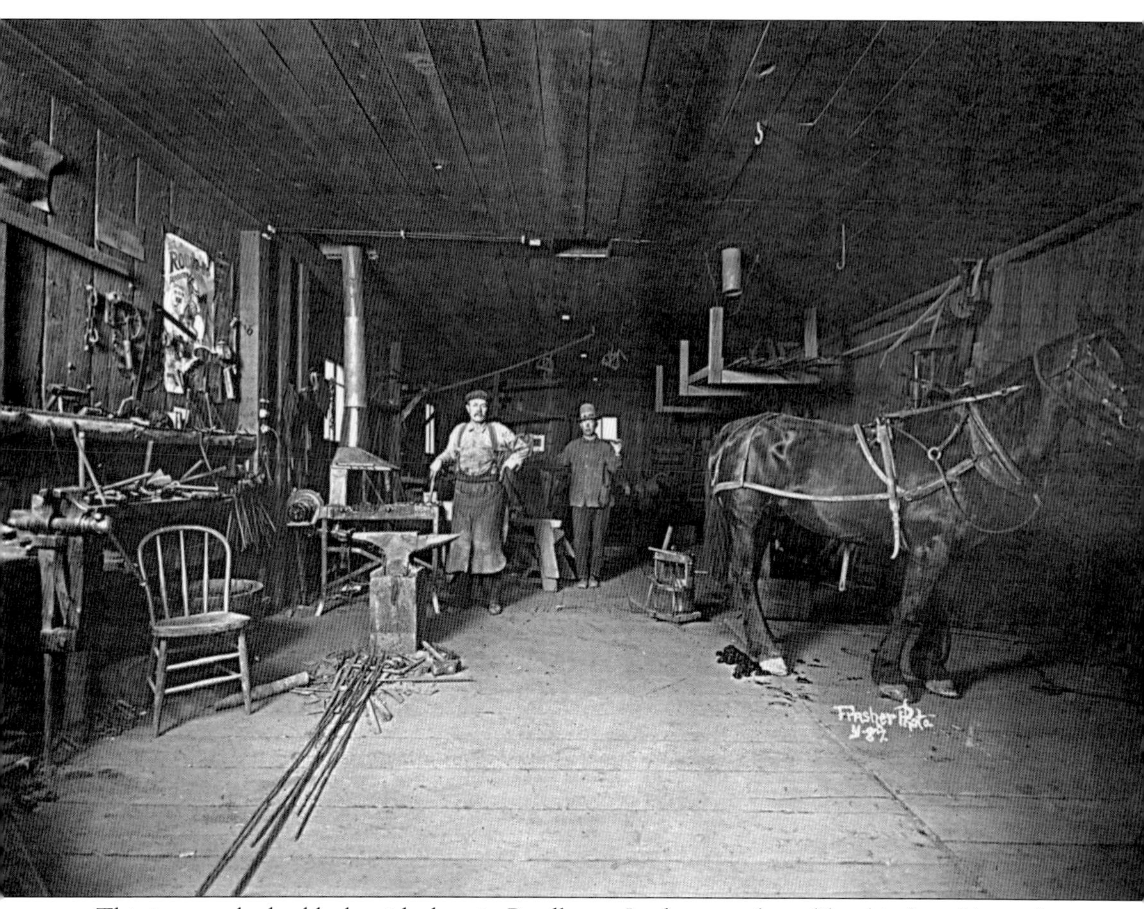

This is an early-day blacksmith shop in Pendleton. In that era, shops like this forged horseshoes for horses. They also fabricated sculptures, tools, agricultural implements, decorative and religious items, cooking utensils, and weapons. The presence of the horse suggests that this man is in the process of making horseshoes. Generally, the shoes were made by a blacksmith but installed by a farrier, though sometimes blacksmiths provided both services. (Yakima Valley Museum.)

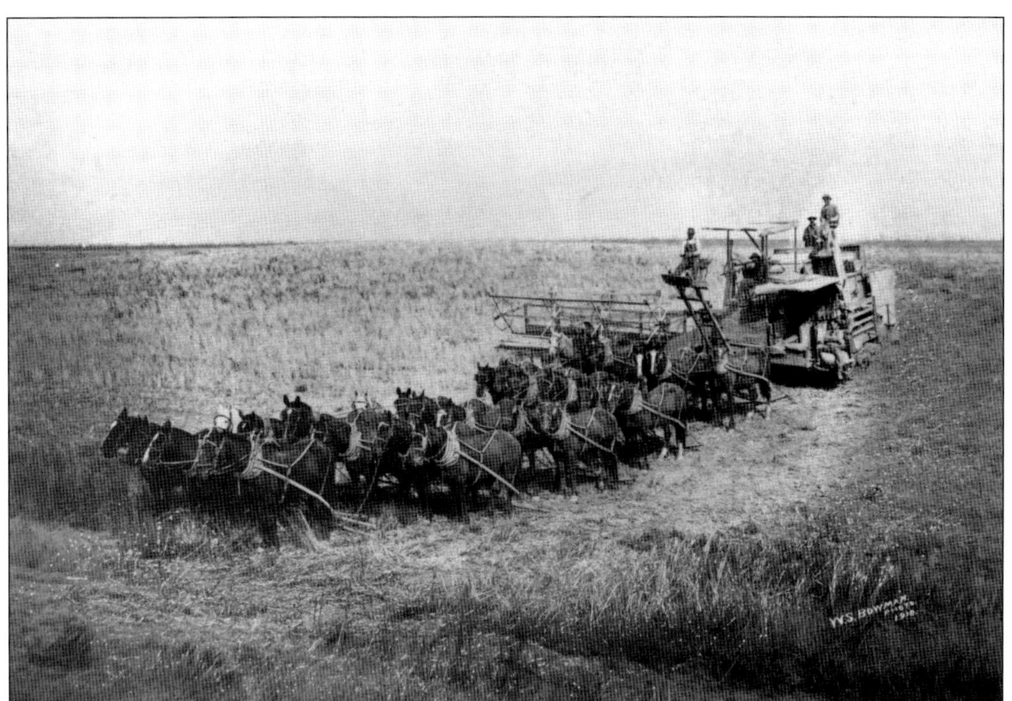

By 1890, Umatilla County was the state's largest producer of wheat. Teams such as these harvested about one-third of the state's wheat, accounting for about 15 million bushels. The harvest required large teams of animals and men. Some teams required 100 men. Some of the land harvested was located on the Umatilla Reservation. (Tamástslikt Cultural Institute.)

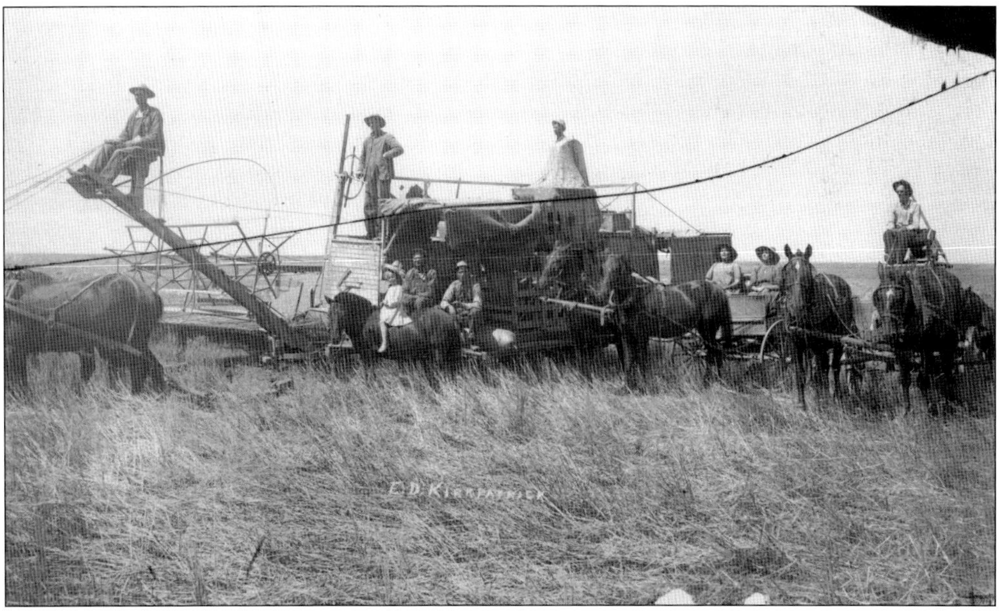

Wheat was big business throughout Umatilla County. Some of the land harvested was owned by Oliver Purl Bowman, who owned 4,000 acres throughout the area. Much of the grain supplied the area's flour mills. It also led to future business such as Pendleton Grain Growers. (Tamástslikt Cultural Institute.)

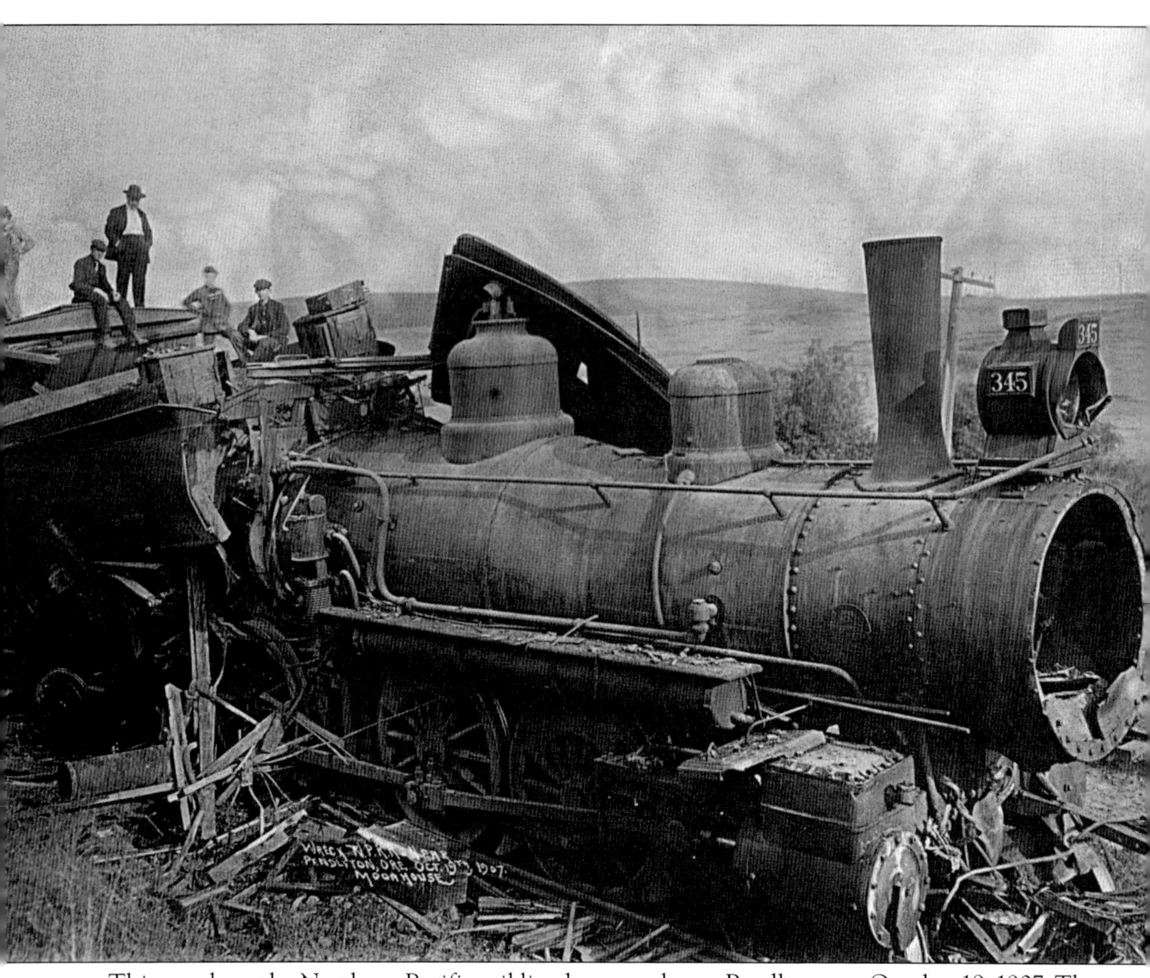

This wreck on the Northern Pacific rail line happened near Pendleton on October 19, 1907. The wreck occurred between a light engine and a passenger train traveling east from Pasco, Washington. The wreck was blamed on James Howe, who was driving the light engine. His mission was to take an engine back to Pasco for repair. He got his days confused and thought he was moving the engine on Friday when it was actually Saturday. The Northern Pacific also ran late that day, leading to Howe's confusion. Fireman Charles Burnett was killed in the collision. Engineer G.W. Wise suffered a concussion but survived. Express messenger Pringle of Seattle received only slight cuts. No passengers were injured in the collision. (Yakima Valley Museum.)

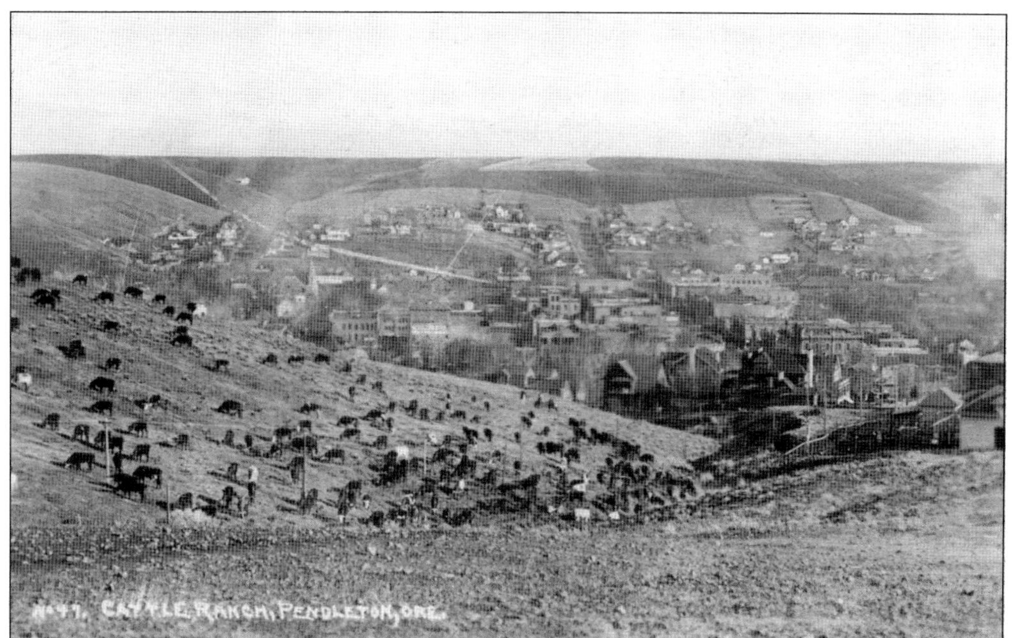

As with many towns with lots of grazing land, Pendleton grew a lucrative cattle ranching industry. In the photograph above, a large herd grazes on the north hill overlooking downtown Pendleton. (Elizabeth Gibson.)

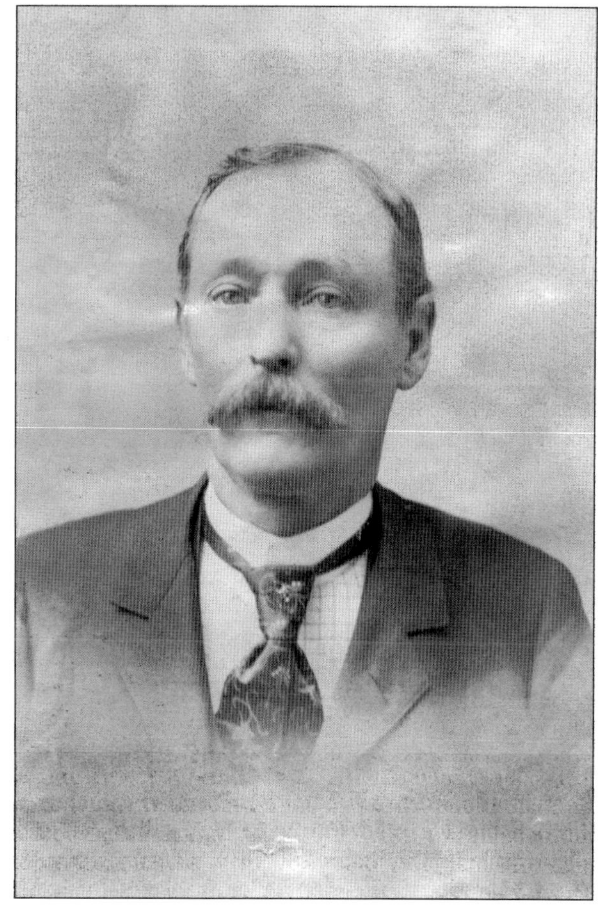

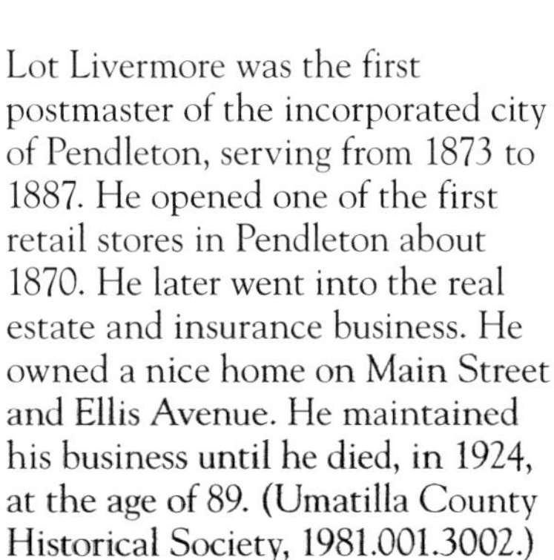

Lot Livermore was the first postmaster of the incorporated city of Pendleton, serving from 1873 to 1887. He opened one of the first retail stores in Pendleton about 1870. He later went into the real estate and insurance business. He owned a nice home on Main Street and Ellis Avenue. He maintained his business until he died, in 1924, at the age of 89. (Umatilla County Historical Society, 1981.001.3002.)

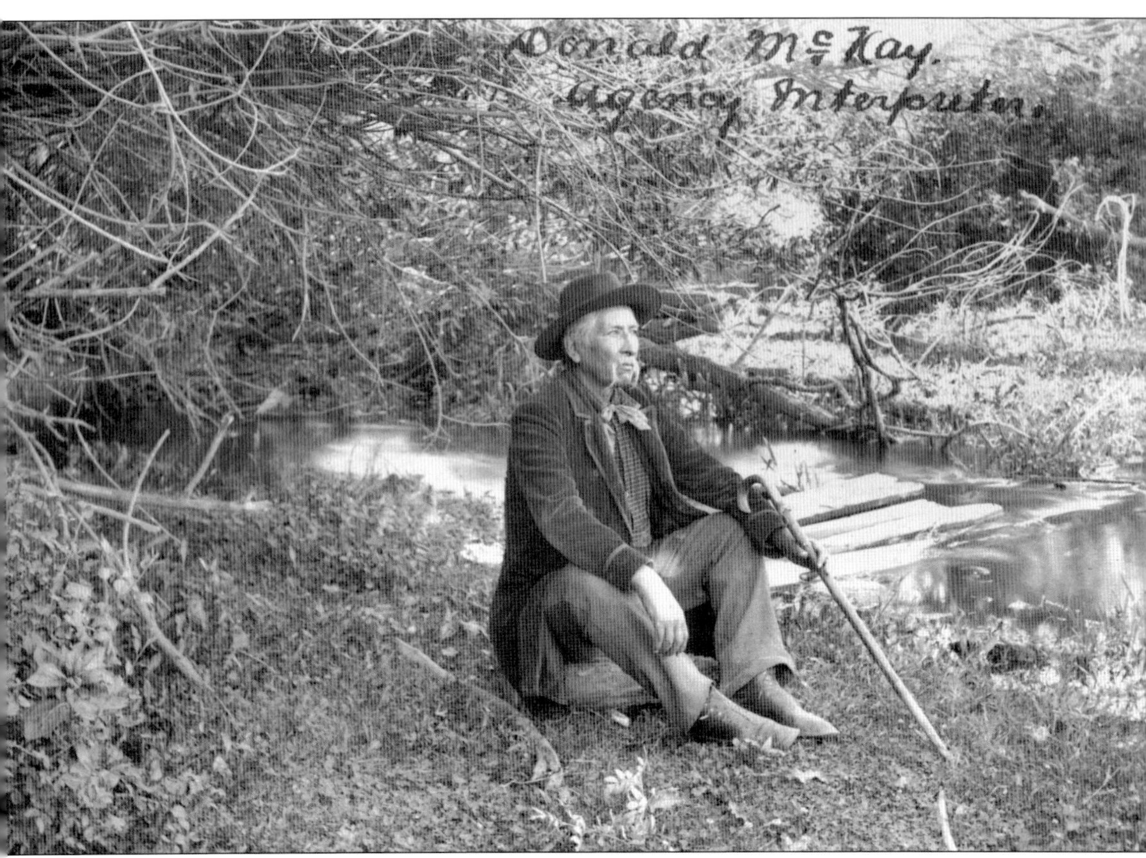

Agency interpreter Donald McKay served as the interpreter at the Umatilla Indian Reservation. He served as a government scout during the Modoc War in northern California. He spoke fluently in English, French, and several Indian languages. He married a Warm Springs Indian woman, with whom he had one daughter. McKay died at his home on the Umatilla Reservation around 1900. (National Museum of the American Indian, Smithsonian Institution [P27384]; photograph by Lee Moorhouse.)

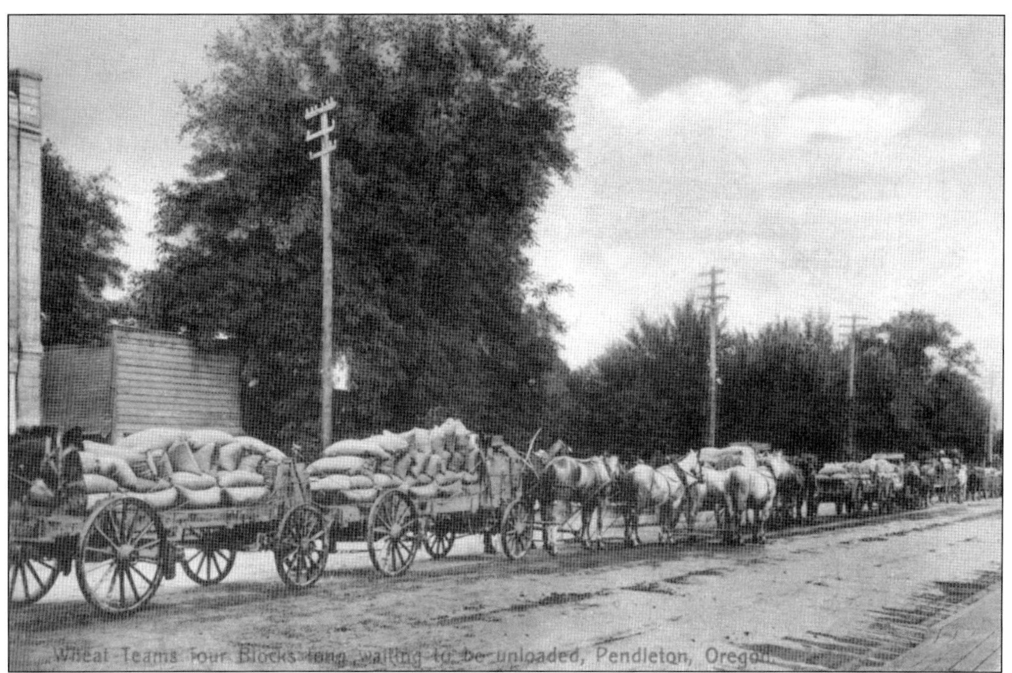

Pendleton farmers grew wheat since the earliest days. The first of several flour mills opened in 1875. This photograph, dated 1910, shows farmers bringing the finished product to town for sale or shipping to other parts of the state. (Glen Thiesfeld.)

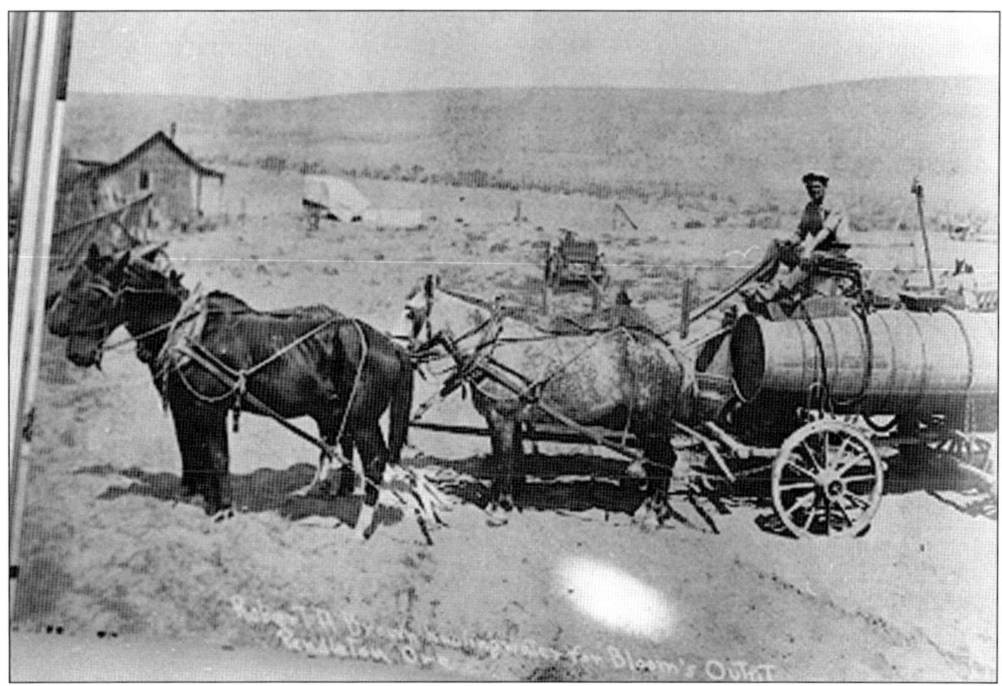

Robert A. Brown drives a horse-drawn water truck for a Pendleton farm. Before the land was irrigated, these types of conveyances were common. (Fort Walla Walla Museum.)

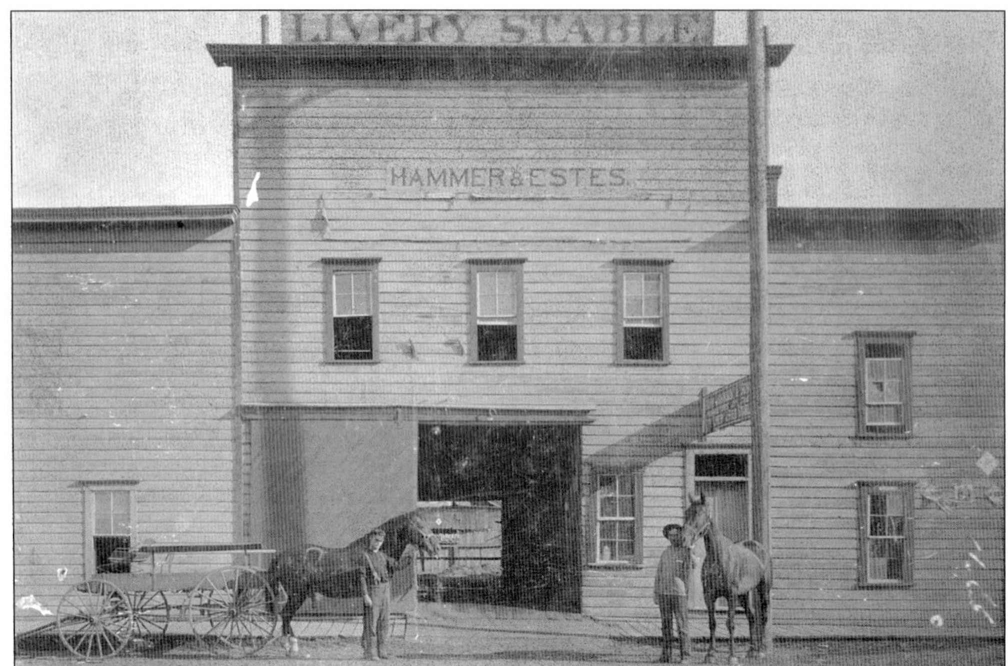

This old livery stable was located near the original city hall building. Such businesses offered overnight boarding of visitors' horses. Some of them also offered horses and teams for hire. The sign on the building reads, "Burr Johnson & Son, Proprietors of the Day Livery Feed Stable." (Umatilla County Historical Society, 1981.001.2123.)

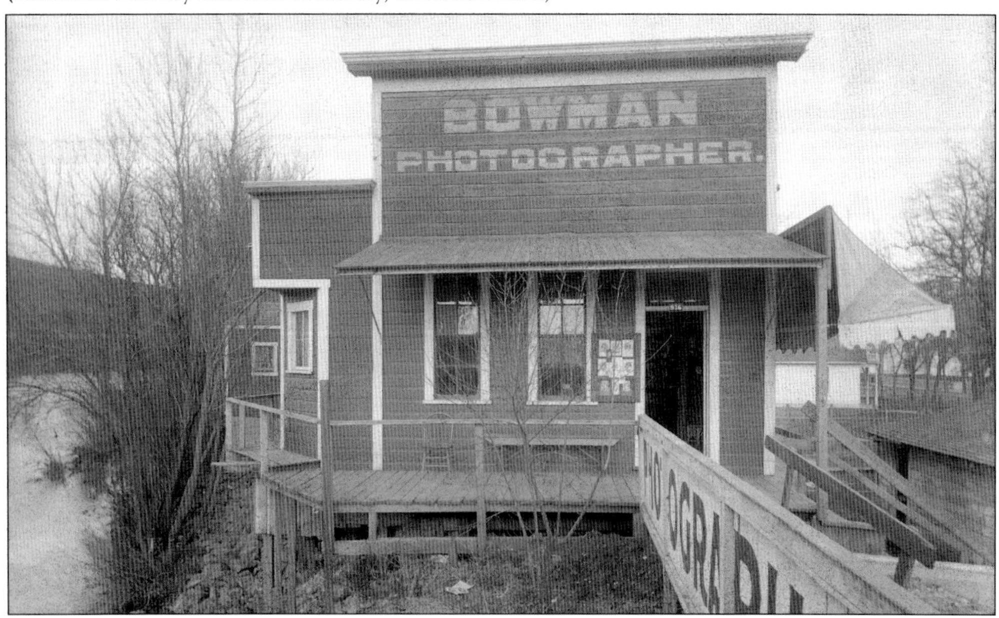

Walter S. Bowman lived and worked in the Pendleton area his whole life. This is the first of two photography studios he used when he developed and printed photographs. It was built in approximately 1887. He took many photographs, documenting places and events in Pendleton, especially the Pendleton Round-Up. He died in a car accident in 1938. (Lee Moorhouse Collection [PH036 6687], Special Collections and University Archives, University of Oregon.)

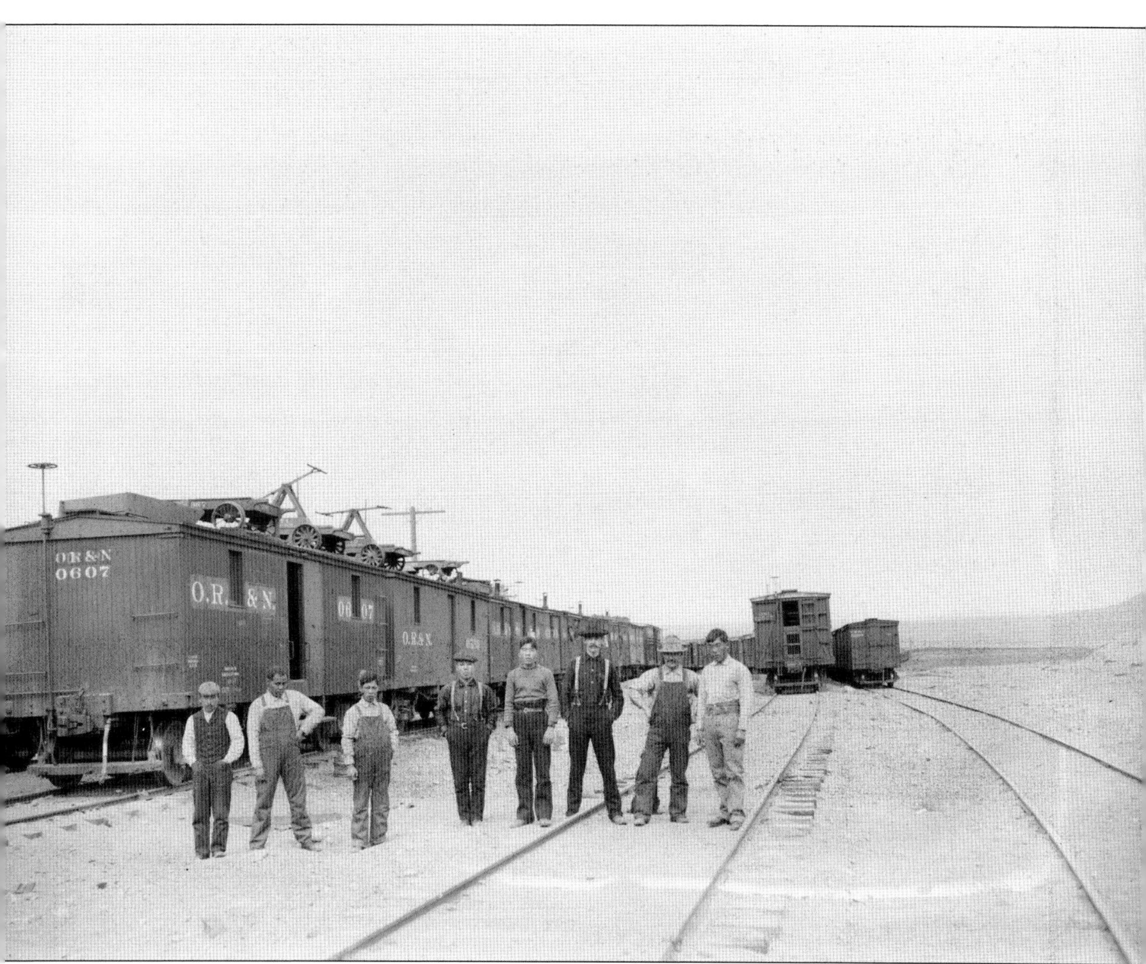

This photograph shows the rail yard at Pendleton. Though these cars are marked "O.R.&N.," the Oregon Railway & Navigation Company had been absorbed by the Union Pacific by 1900. The railcar on the right marked "OSL 12527" is a cattle car on the Oregon Short Line, which was also a subsidiary of the Union Pacific. These Chinese workers were likely descendants of the men who came to the area in the previous century to build railroads and mine for gold. (Lee Moorhouse Collection [PH036 1025], Special Collections and University Archives, University of Oregon.)

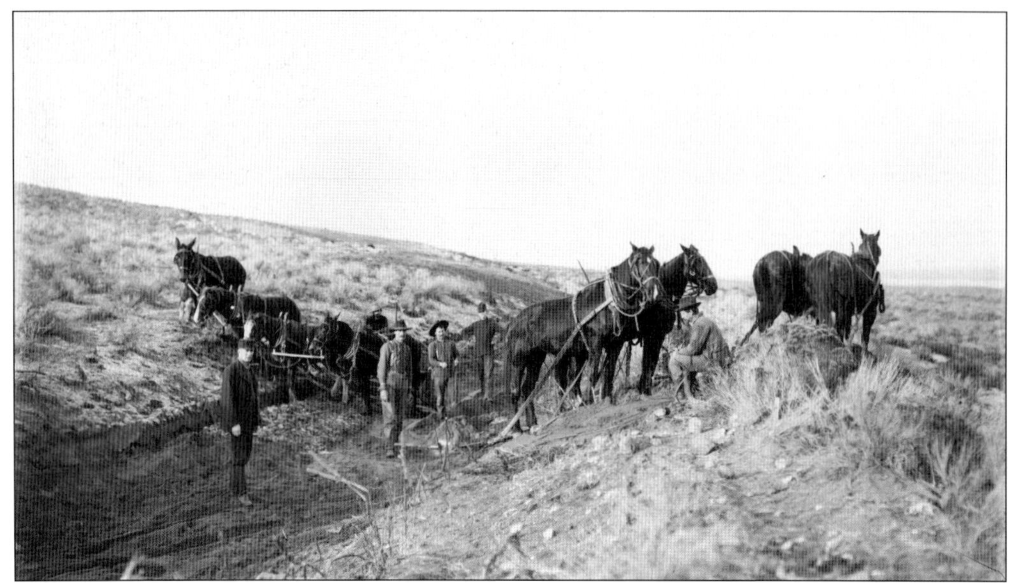

This photograph, taken about 1907, shows a six-man, eight-horse team clearing land for a new irrigation canal. They are pulling scrapers to form the canal. The land was part of the holdings of Joseph T. Hinkle, a local businessman, attorney, and newspaperman. At one time, Hinkle owned 400 acres of alfalfa. (Lee Moorhouse Collection [PH036 1399], Special Collections and University Archives, University of Oregon.)

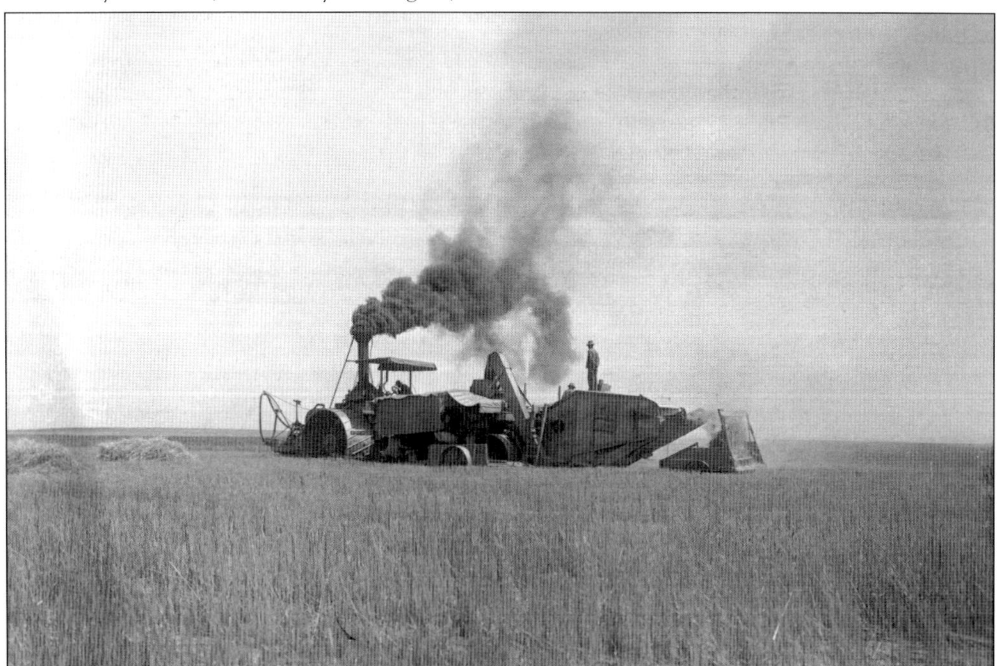

As time went on, harvesting was done by mechanized equipment. The earliest equipment came on the scene about 1911. The equipment required far fewer men and animals. Farmers increased their acreage to justify the expensive equipment. Many small farmers were bought out by larger ones. By 1920, the county was producing one percent of the country's wheat. (Tamástslikt Cultural Institute.)

Ezra Meeker came west on the Oregon Trail in 1852. He was a successful hop farmer and the mayor of Puyallup, Washington. Later, he became concerned that the original Oregon Trail was being lost to development. He was in his 70s when he went on the road, traveling the trail and promoting its preservation. There are several markers in Pendleton commemorating the Oregon Trail. (Library of Congress.)

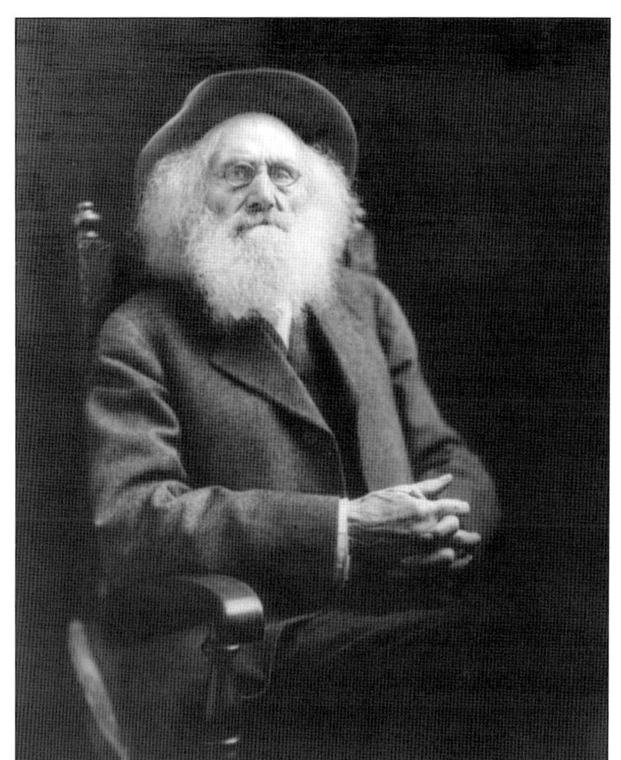

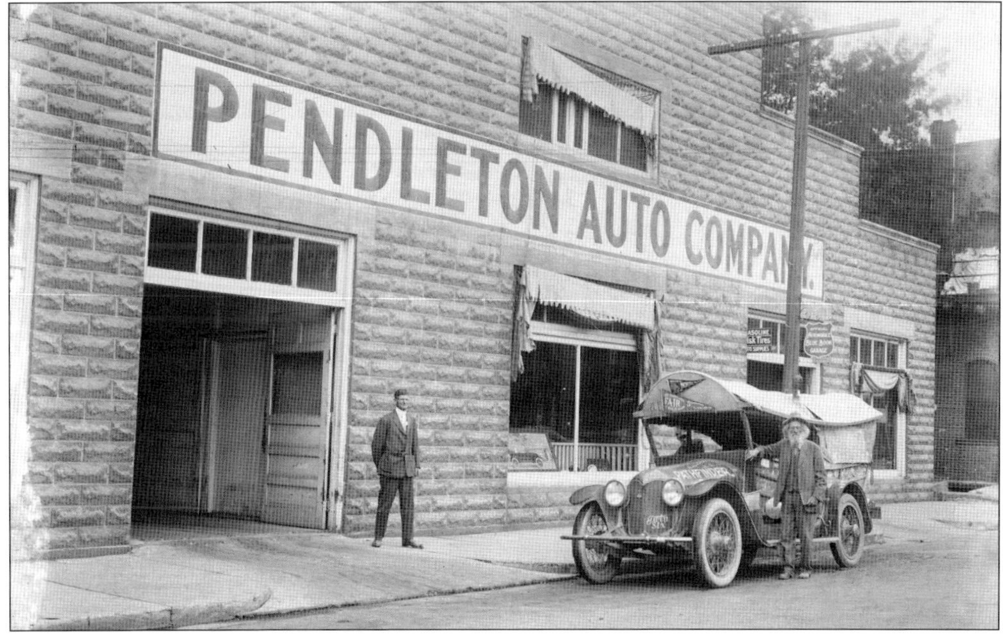

Ezra Meeker poses outside of the Pendleton Auto Company with his specially equipped "Twin Six" Packard, which was loaned to Meeker as a publicity stunt. This unique V-12 engine came out in 1916 and was a huge hit with the American public. Meeker toured in the car that year while promoting the idea of creating a national highway. (Lee Moorhouse Collection [PH036 1101], Special Collections and University Archives, University of Oregon.)

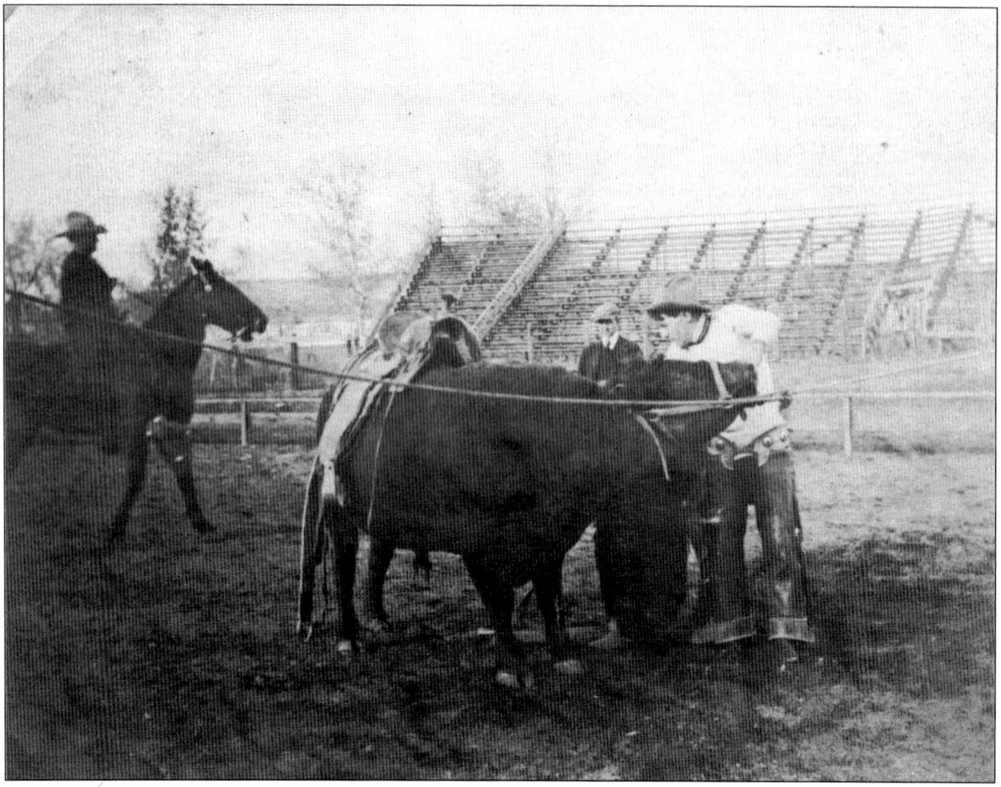

Major League baseball player Dick Hoblizell toured through Pendleton around 1914 for exhibition games put on in small towns. Hoblizell played for the Reds and the Red Sox from 1907 to 1917. While on tour, he extensively documented the places he visited in photographs. This photograph was taken at the Round-Up grounds, as can be seen by the grandstand in the background. (Elizabeth Gibson.)

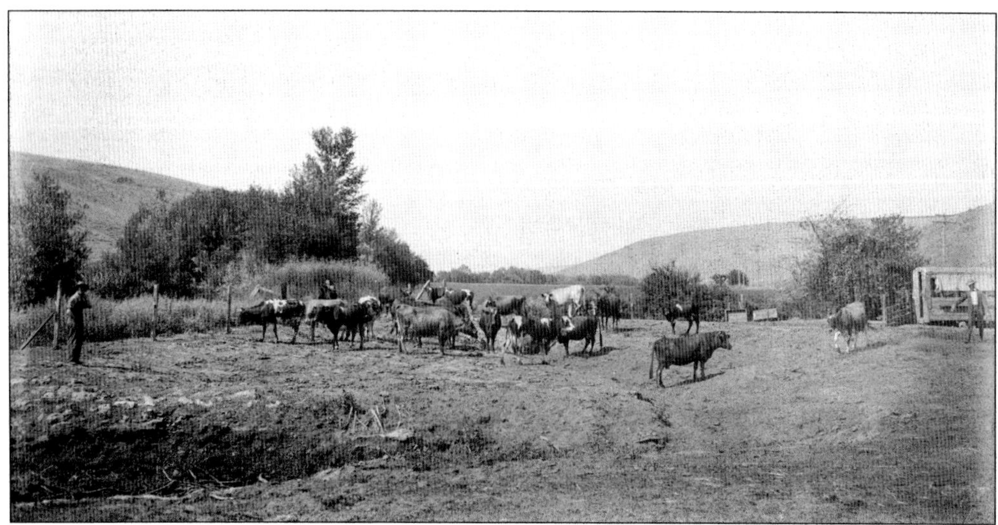

This is an early dairy farm in the area. Early dairies served the immediate needs of the population and eventually grew into large, family-owned businesses. (Lee Moorhouse Collection [PH036 0547], Special Collections and University Archives, University of Oregon.)

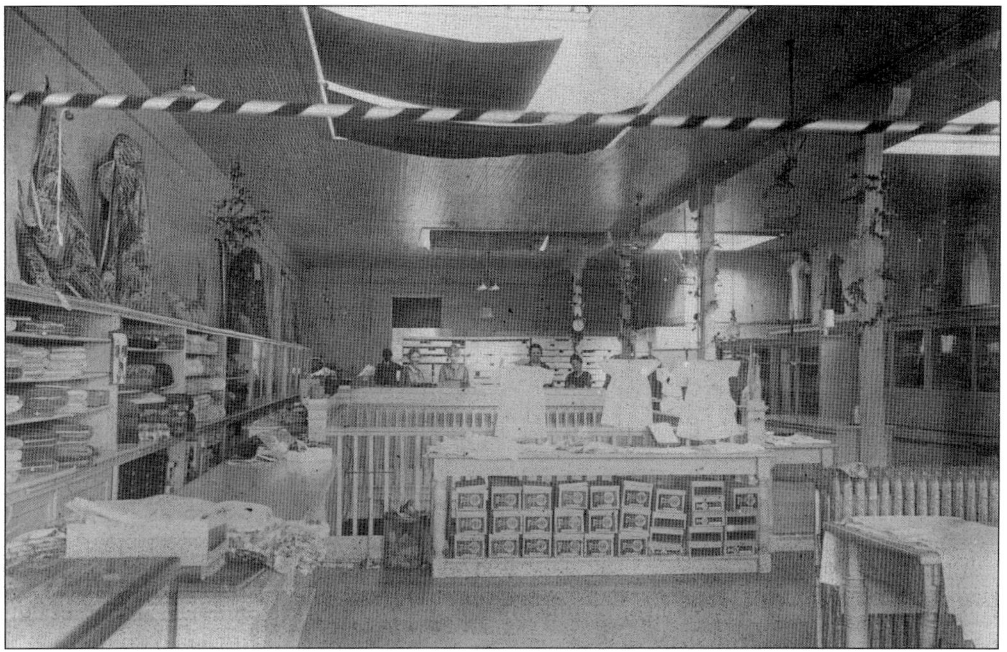

This dress shop was an early business in downtown Pendleton. It is unknown exactly where it was located. Note the many bolts of cloth on the shelves on the left side of the shop. Several employees stand ready to assist customers with cutting and measuring. (Elizabeth Gibson.)

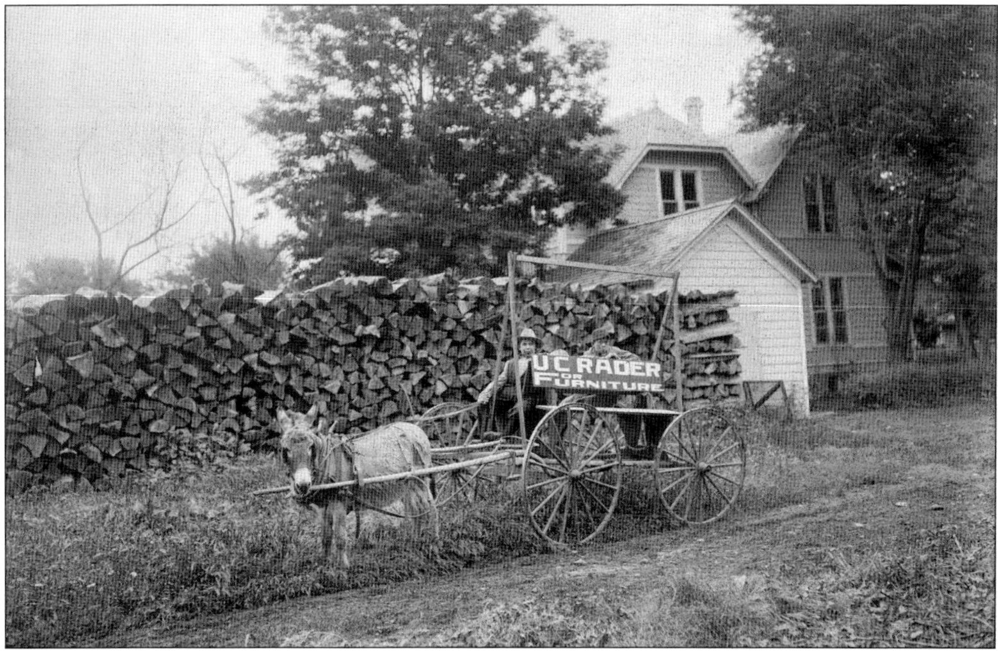

The M.A. Rader furniture store was located on Main and Webb Streets in the early 1900s. The store carried everything from wooden rockers to carpets. The owner also operated a funeral parlor. These two young people towed this advertising conveyance long before businesses paid to have their names painted on the sides of cabs and buses. (Lee Moorhouse Collection [PH036 2572], Special Collections and University Archives, University of Oregon.)

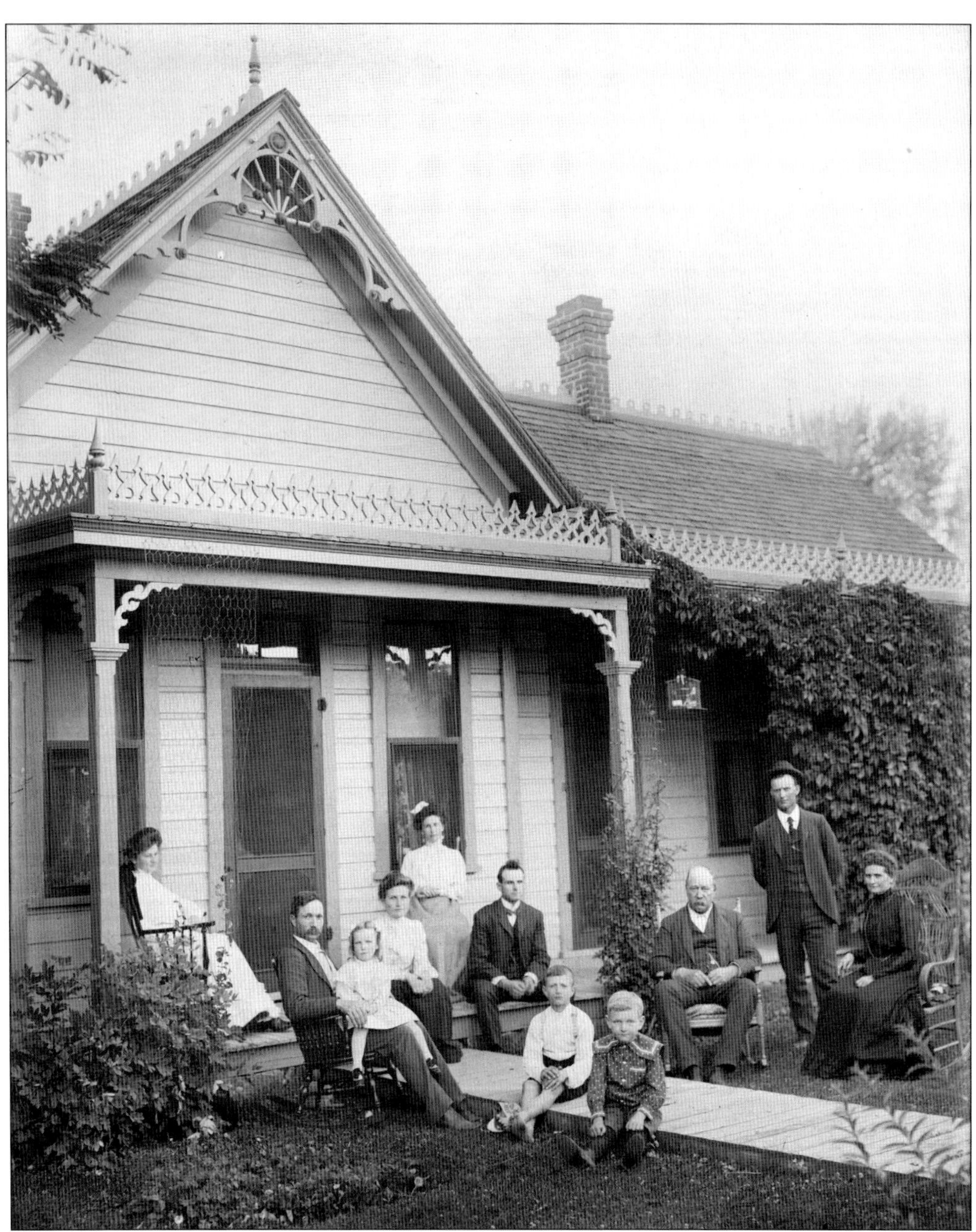

The Moorhouse home, at 400 Water Street, is seen here. Lee Moorhouse used his home as his studio. He collected a large number of Indian artifacts that he used in his photographs as props. Moorhouse died at his home on June 1, 1926, after a month-long illness. His daughter Lessie Moorhouse Cornelison inherited his photographs and later donated them to the Smithsonian Institute and the Umatilla County Public Library. The Indian artifacts are owned by the city. Lee Moorhouse married Sara Ella Willis in 1878, and they had three daughters—Celestine "Lessie," Augusta "Gussie," and LaVelle—and a son, Mark. (Lee Moorhouse Collection [PH036 2563], Special Collections and University Archives, University of Oregon.)

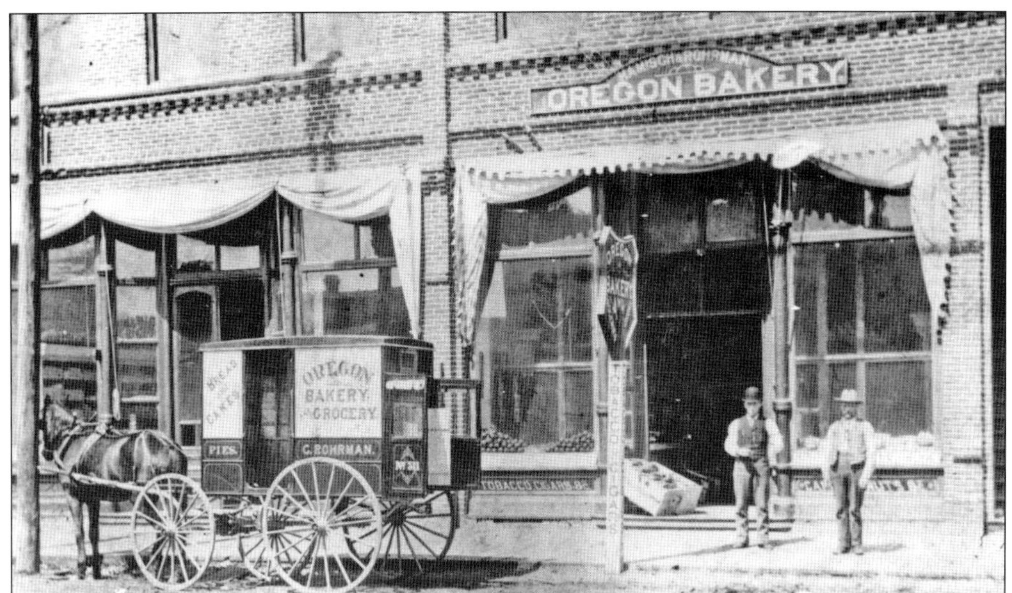

The Oregon Bakery, on Court Street near Southeast Second Street, was operated by Charles Rohrman and his partner Mr. Hamlisch. Rohrman opened his first bakery in a small wooden building near today's courthouse. He later moved to this larger building, which also contained a grocery store. This store operated from approximately 1888 to 1910. Rohrman retired in 1916. (Umatilla County Historical Society, 2008-100-2172.)

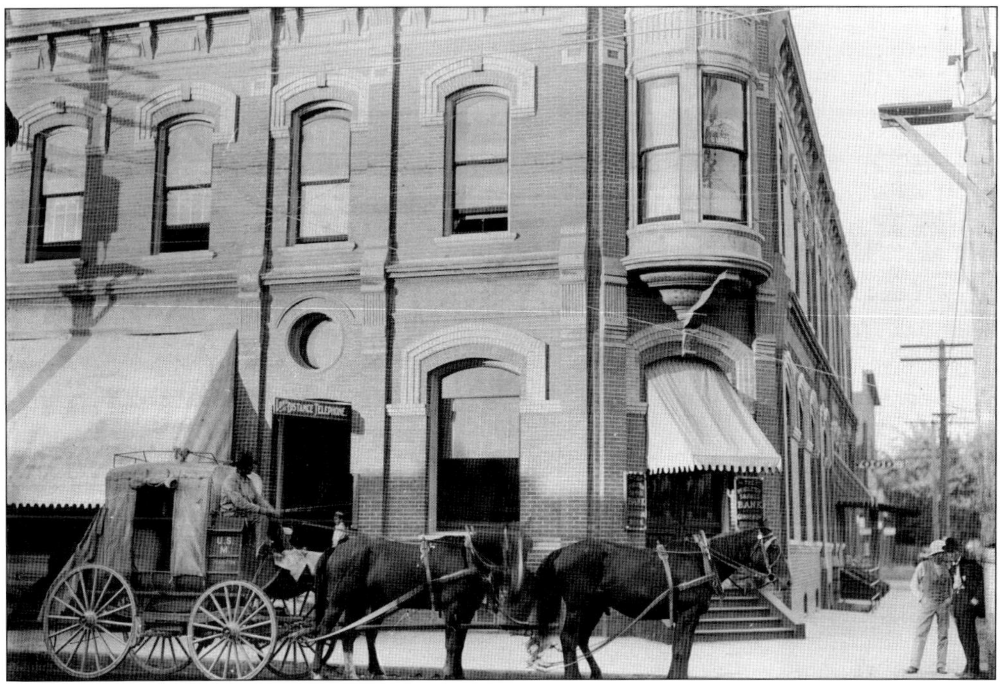

This typical stagecoach ran on the Pendleton-to-Ukiah stage line. Ukiah was a small town about 50 miles south of Pendleton. The building in the background housed the Pendleton Savings Bank, one of the older banks in town, which was established prior to 1890. It was closed by 1921. (Lee Moorhouse Collection [PH036 2988], Special Collections and University Archives, University of Oregon.)

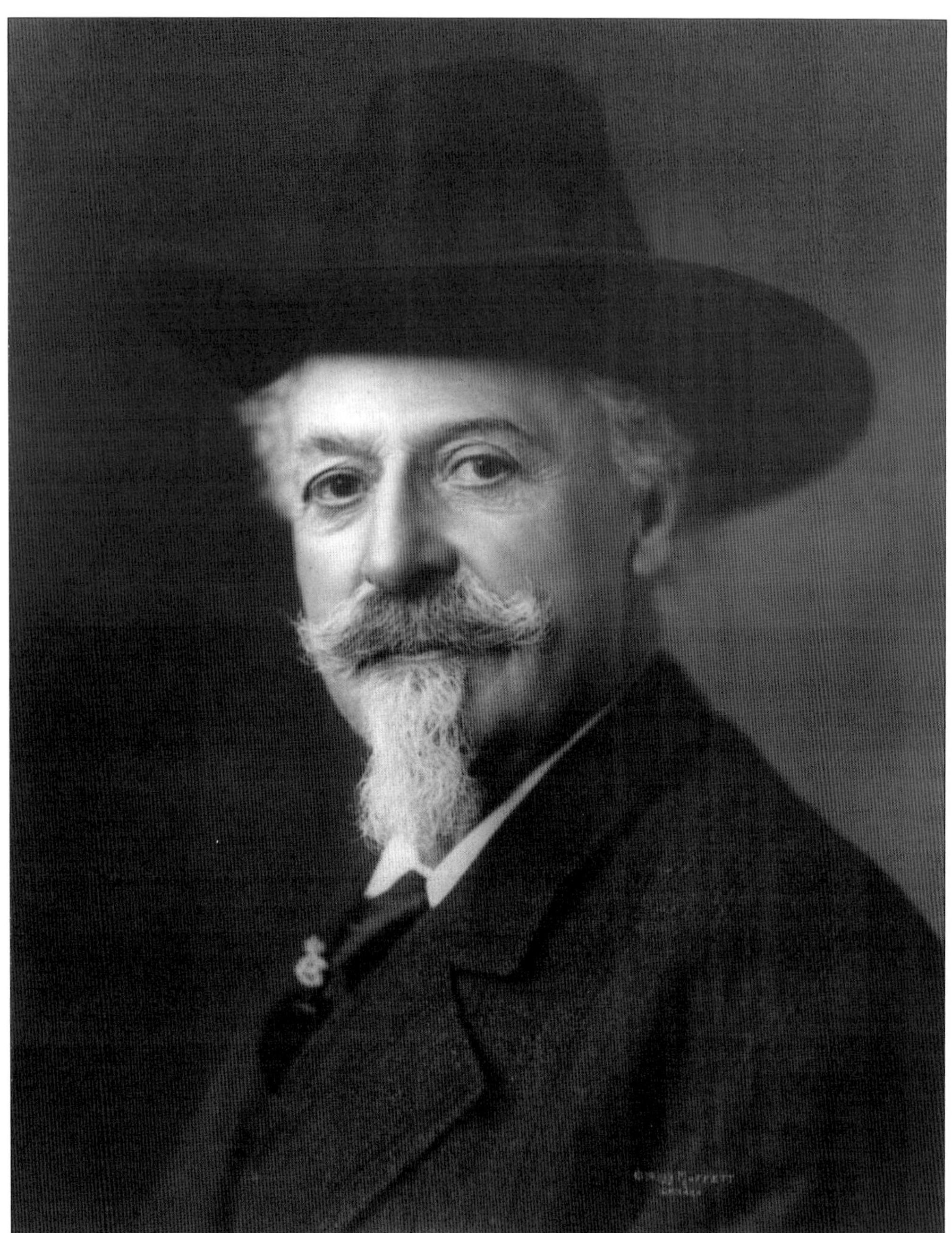

William F. Cody, also known as Buffalo Bill, was notorious for his time as an Army scout in the 1860s. He supplied buffalo meat to the army. Later, he formed Buffalo Bill's Wild West Show and took it across the country. On August 20, 1902, he brought his show to Pendleton. The event was chronicled by local photographer Walter S. Bowman. Sharpshooter Annie Oakley toured with the show that year, as well as some Sioux Indian chiefs. The group performed a historic reenactment of the famous taking of San Juan Hill in Cuba. The cost of admission was 50¢ for adults and 25¢ for children under nine. Residents found it amusing since they were still living in the "Wild West." (Library of Congress.)

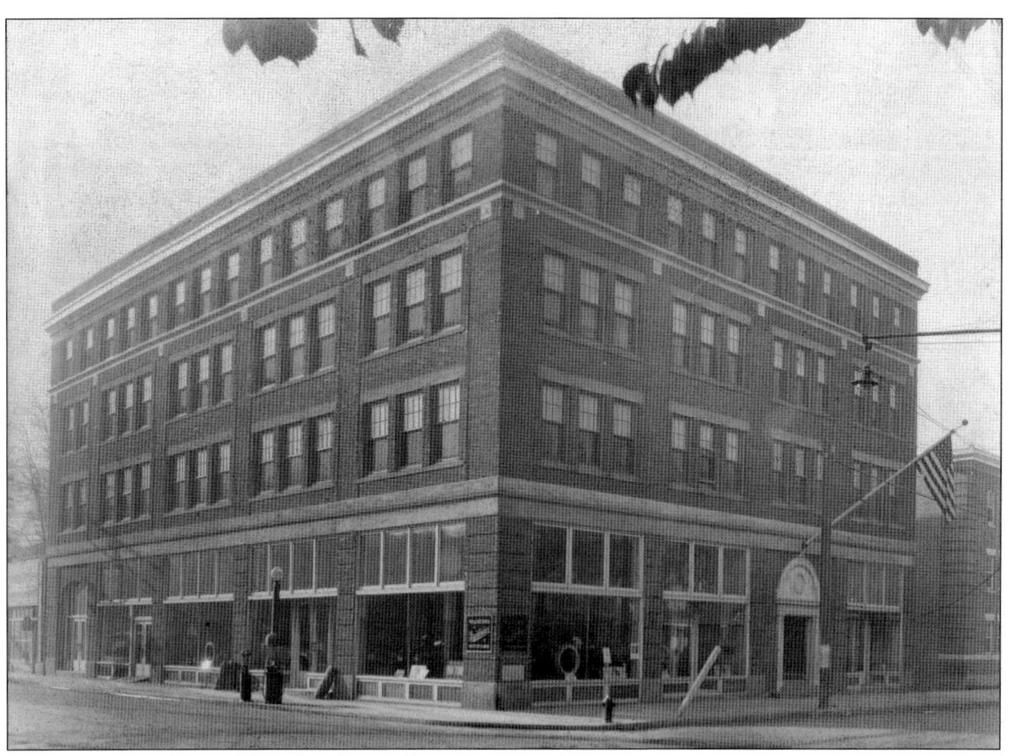

The Brown Building (above) is located on Court and Southwest First Streets. It was built in 1919 by the Elks lodge. The ground floor was used for commercial purposes, and the lodge used the second and third floors. At one time, there was a pool and a bowling alley in the basement. The Elks left the building in the 1960s, and the remaining floors were converted into apartments. (Umatilla County Historical Society, 2008.100.2171.)

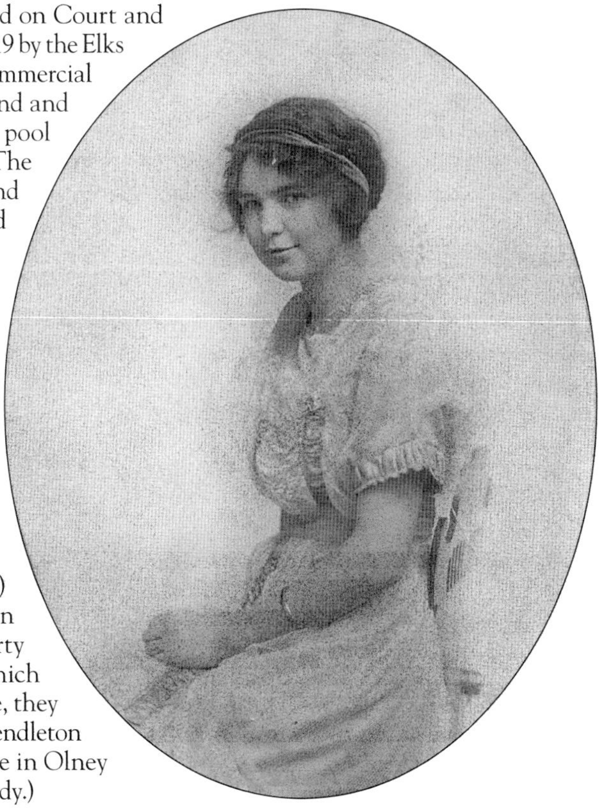

Margaret Louise Hampton (1896–1992) married Lycurgus William "L.W." Owen (1882–1964). The family owned property on the northeast hill of Pendleton, which was known as Owen's Hill. At one time, they operated a dairy there. The longtime Pendleton residents found their final resting place in Olney Cemetery in Pendleton. (Nina Kennedy.)

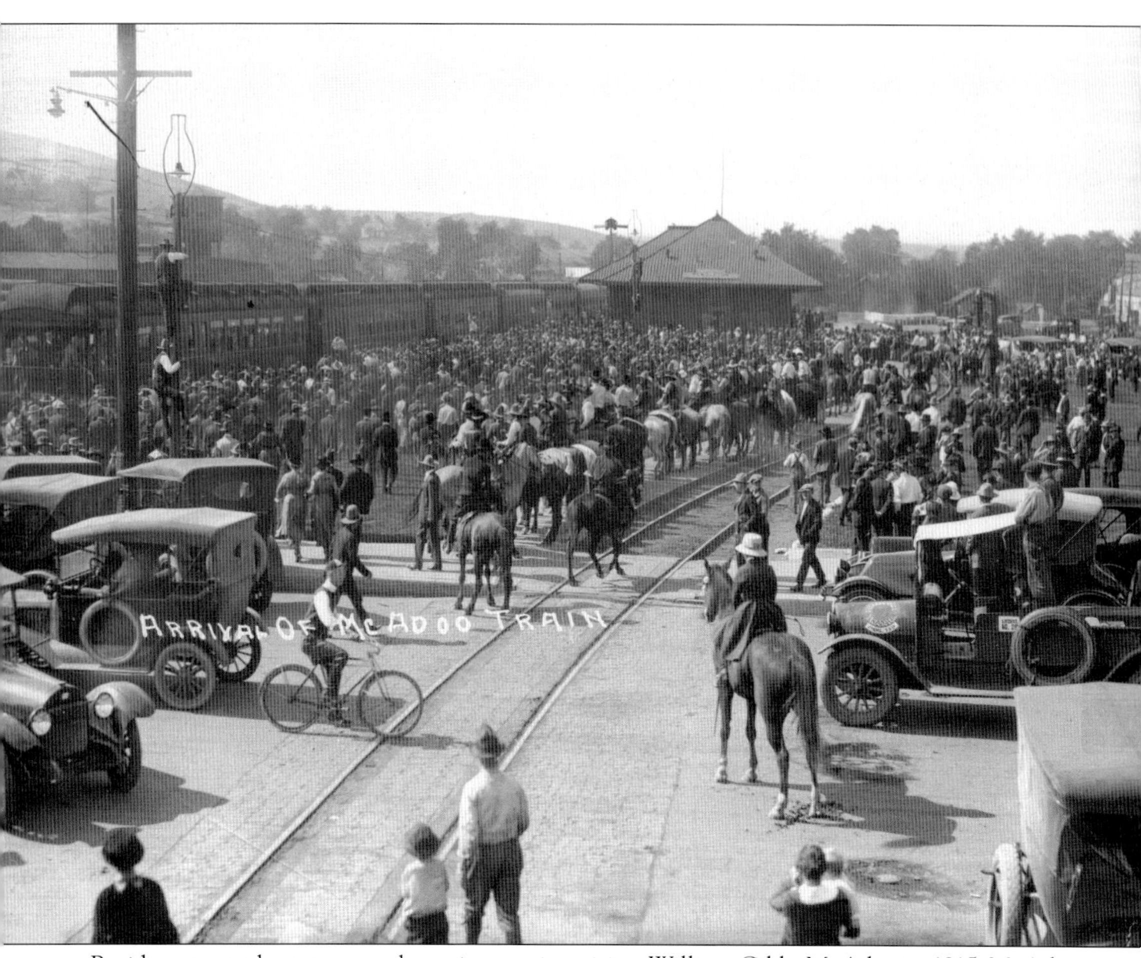

Residents turned out to greet the train carrying visitor William Gibbs McAdoo in 1915. McAdoo was the secretary of the treasury under Pres. Woodrow Wilson. He came to Pendleton to dedicate the new post office that was being built. (Umatilla County Historical Society, 2008.100.017.)

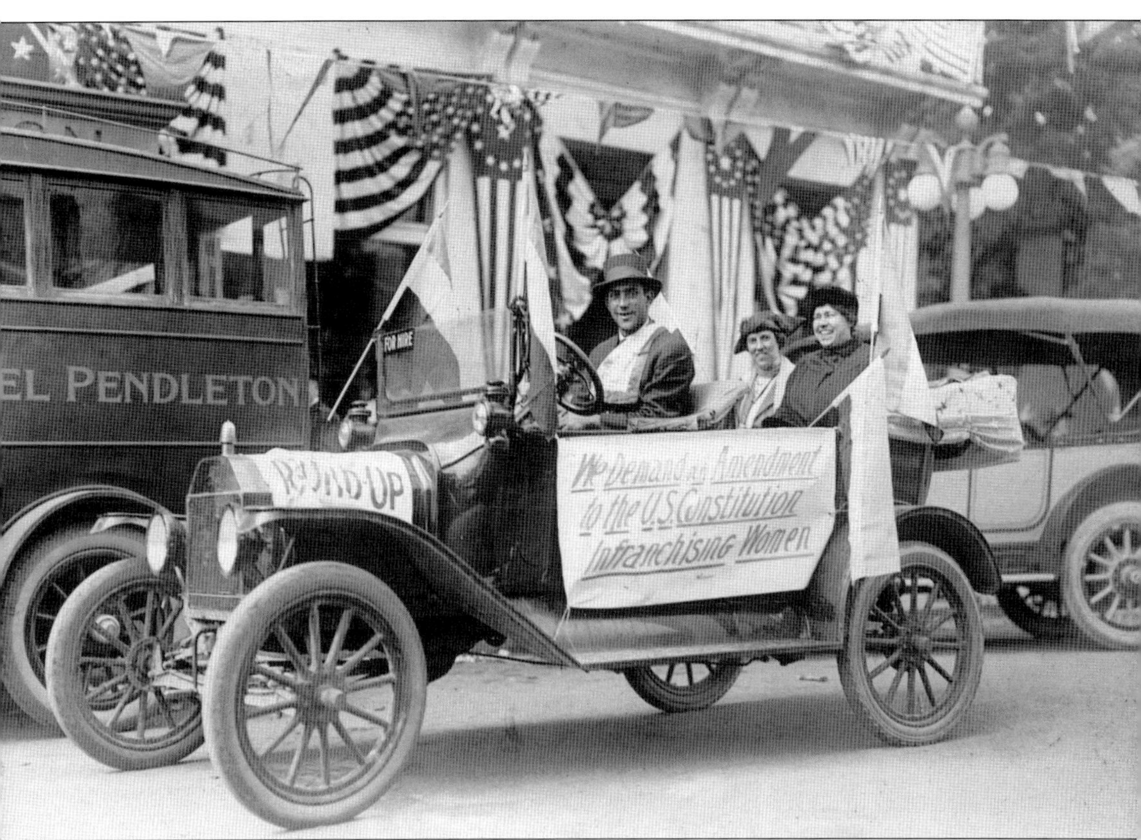

Mary G. Fendall (left) and Margaret Whittemore (right) are seen here campaigning for the women's right to vote in Pendleton on September 23, 1916. The banner on the car reads, "We Demand an Amendment to the U.S. Constitution Infranchising Women." Whittemore was the National Woman's Party congressional union organizer for election campaigns in Washington State in 1914 and 1916. Fendall was the representative for Oregon. (Women of Protest: Photographs from the Records of the National Woman's Party, Manuscript Division, Library of Congress.)

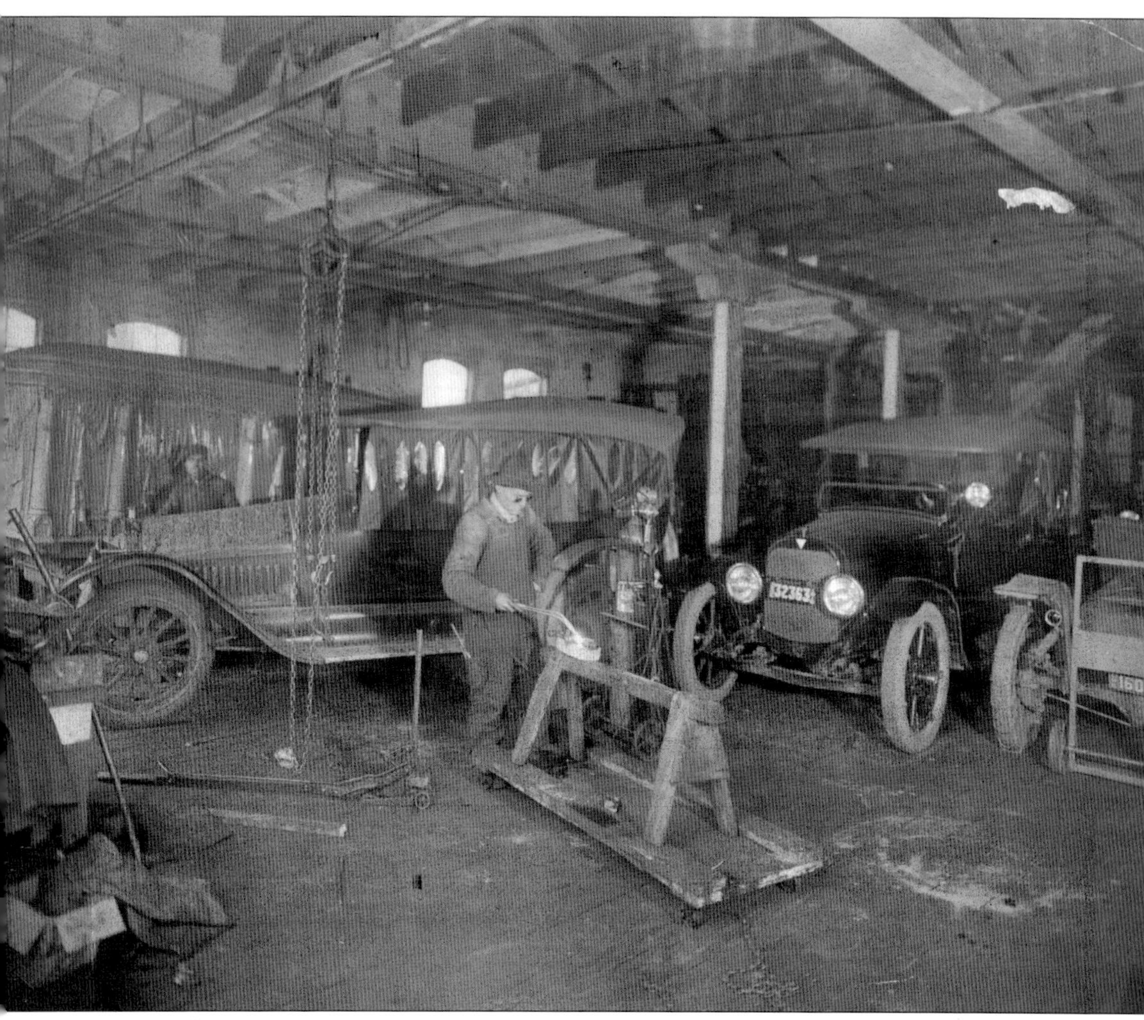

This building was originally Neagle's blacksmith shop. When residents began acquiring cars, the old livery was used as a garage. Many of the tools came in handy for meeting the new demands of car repairs. In fact, many blacksmiths became the first mechanics. The shop was located near Main and Byers Streets. G. Blanchett (center) is seen here in the shop. (Umatilla County Historical Society, 1981.001.4941.)

Three

Pendleton Woolen Mills

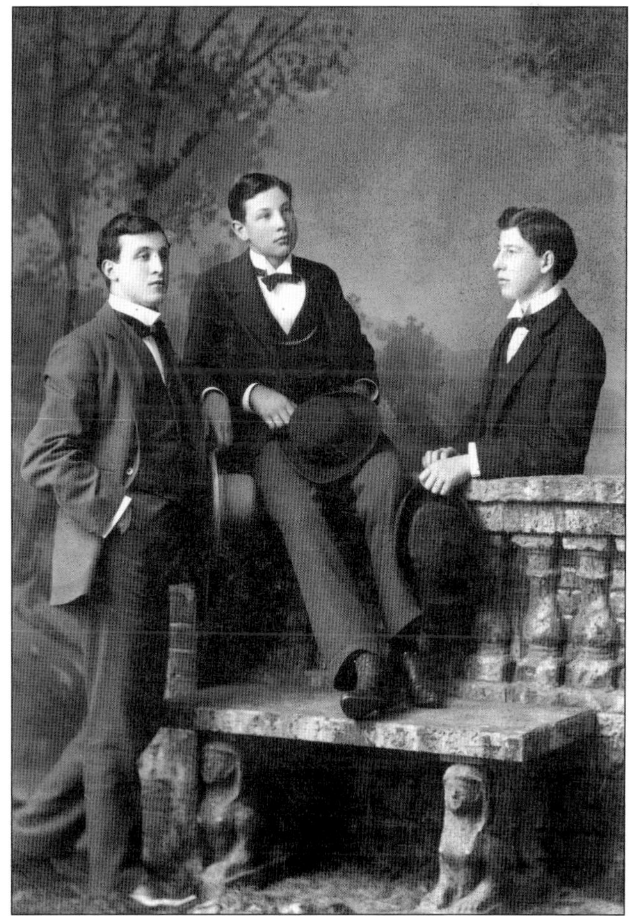

Seen here from left to right are the Bishop brothers: Clarence, Chauncey, and Roy. The three brothers purchased a defunct mill in Pendleton in 1908. Their father, C.P. Bishop, owned a retail clothing store, and their mother was Fannie Kay, the daughter of Thomas Kay, an English weaver and the owner of Thomas Kay Woolen Mills in Salem. Clarence and Roy attended a textile school on the East Coast so the brothers would be well prepared for a career in wool. (Pendleton Woolen Mills.)

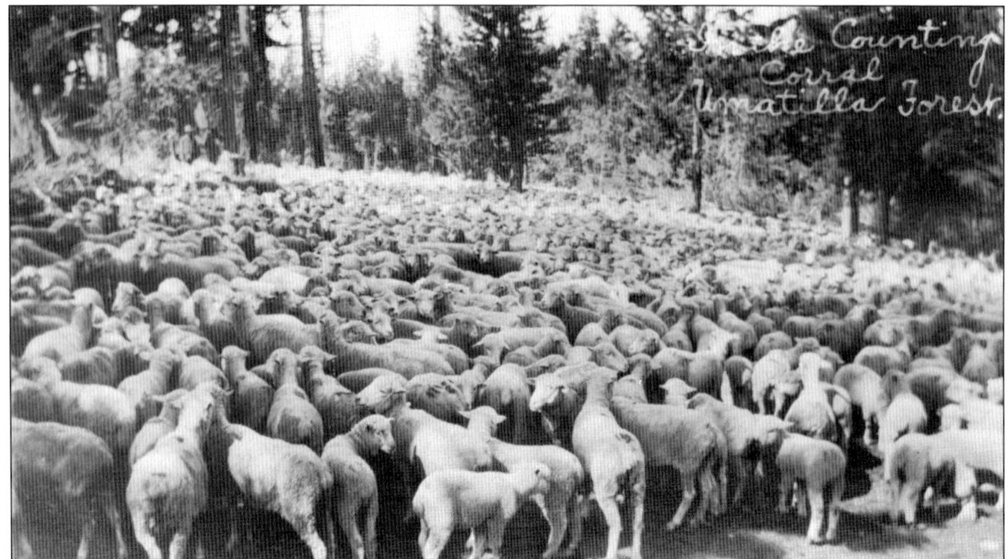

Many early sheep herds used in the industry were grazed in the nearby Umatilla National Forest. Herds could be quite large, as seen here. One early sheep rancher in the area was Jacob Frazer, who brought his herds from the Willamette Valley, on the other side of the state. Oliver Purl Bowman was another area sheep rancher. (Elizabeth Gibson.)

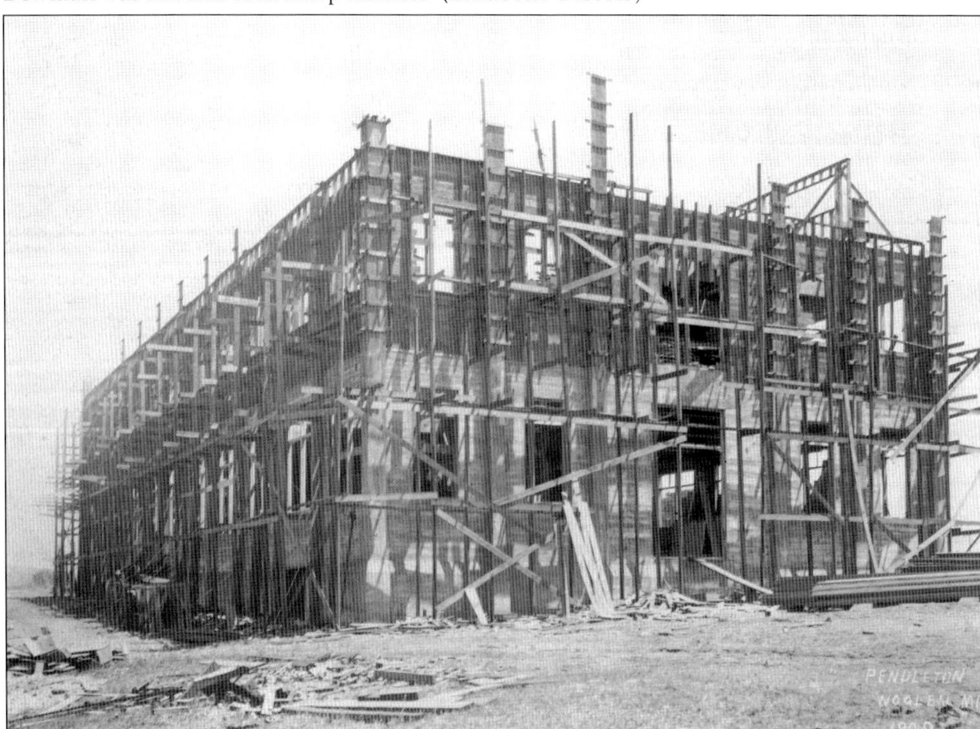

The Pendleton Woolen Mills are seen here under construction before their 1909 opening. The Bishop family, with local support from a bond issue, specialized in weaving Jacquard-design Indian blankets. The blankets were popular with the local Umatilla, Cayuse, and Walla Walla tribes. (Pendleton Woolen Mills.)

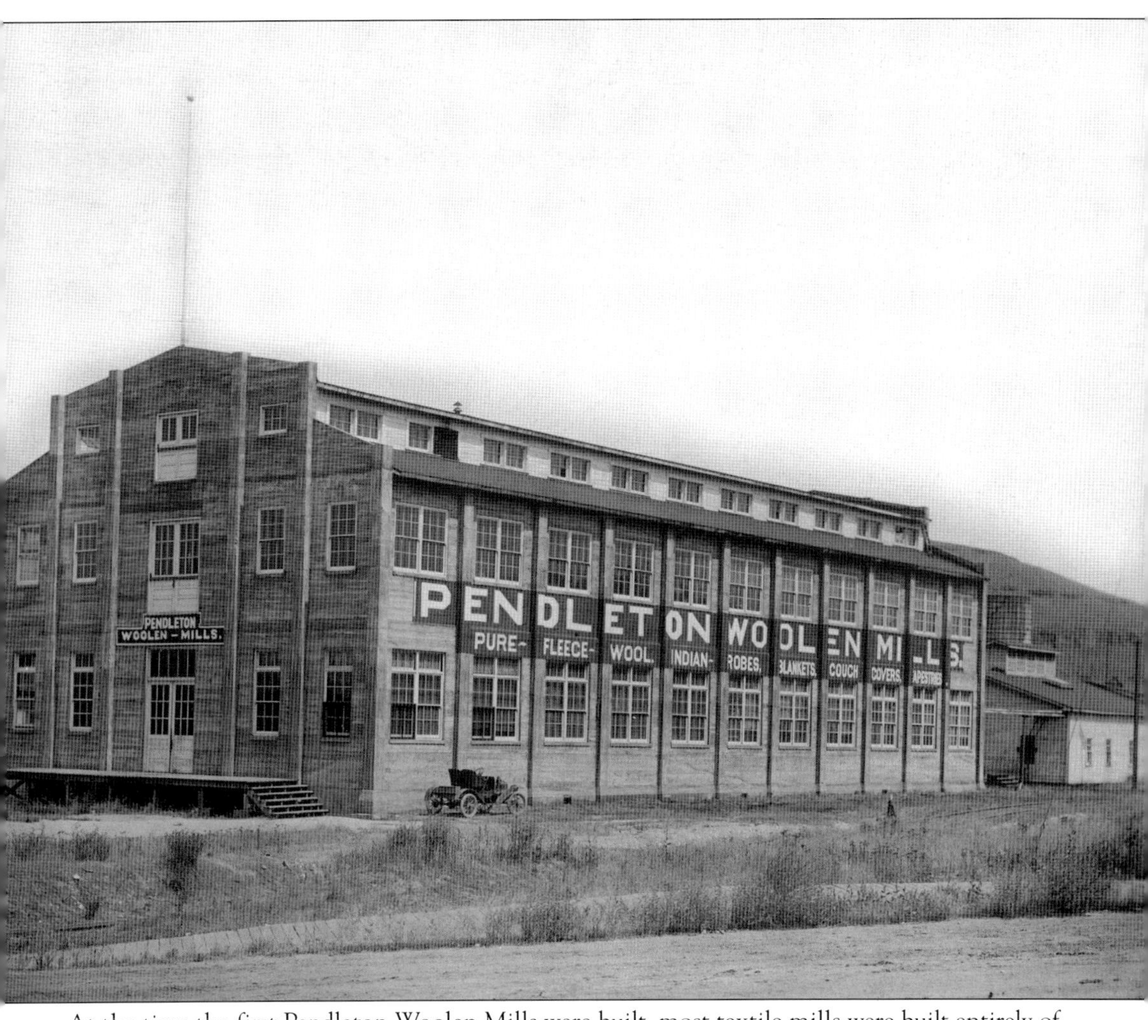

At the time the first Pendleton Woolen Mills were built, most textile mills were built entirely of wood. However, founder Thomas Kay had experienced many woolen mill fires throughout his career, so he designed the Pendleton mill to have concrete walls, an innovative idea for the day. (Pendleton Woolen Mills.)

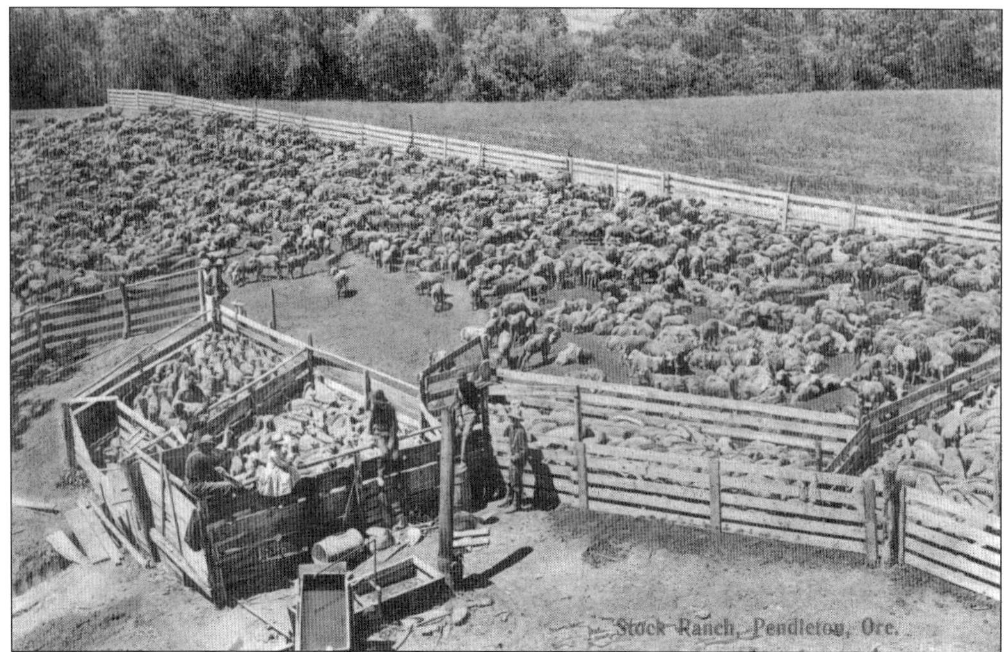

This is a typical sheep ranch in the Pendleton area. Wool manufacturing at Pendleton generally used wool from Rambouillet or Columbia sheep. The wool from these types of sheep has a finer diameter, which produces a softer and more comfortable cloth. Some early ranches in the area included the Cunningham Sheep Company, Krebs Livestock, and Hay Creek Ranch. (Elizabeth Gibson.)

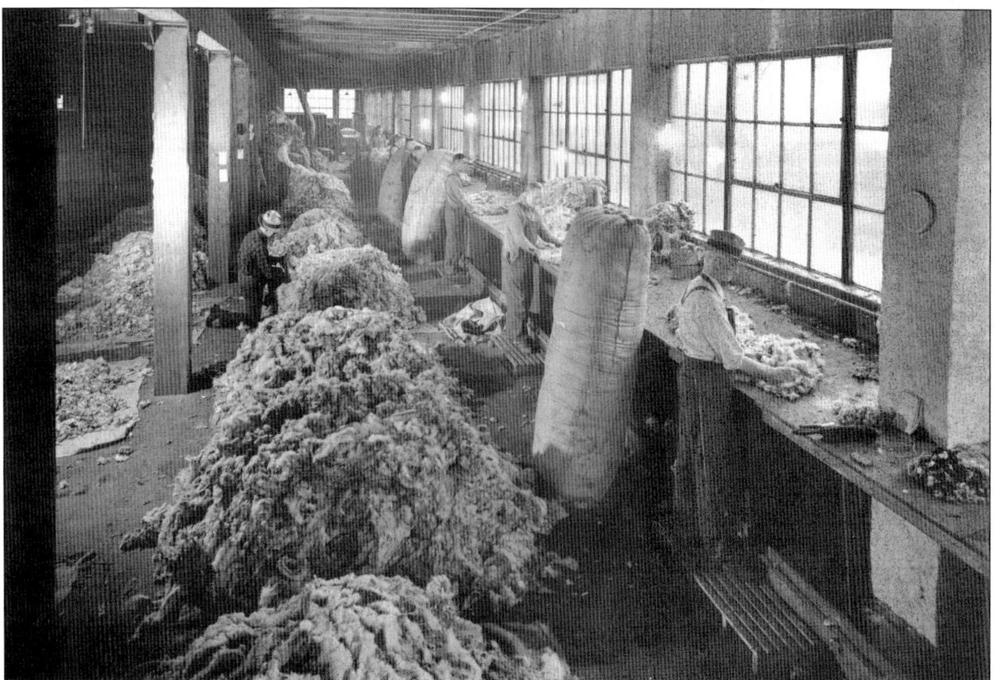

Before being processed, the wool was graded. The wool graders look for length of crimp, overall quality, and fineness. Damaged or stained fibers are removed. Not all wool products require the same grade level of wool. (Pendleton Woolen Mills.)

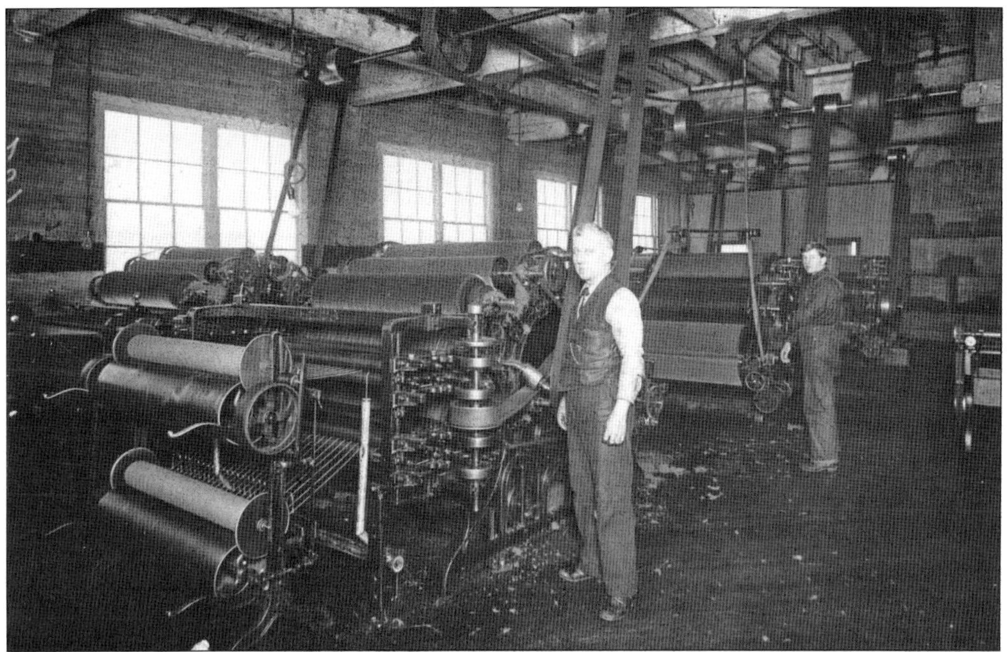

Wool is then washed and dyed. Depending on the cloth, different colored fibers or wool lots might be mixed. Then the fibers are run through a carding machine like this one. The rollers are covered with fine wires that lengthen and straighten the wool fibers in long, continuous strands. The carded fleece is wound on a large spool as roving, which is very weak and must be spun to strengthen the yarn. (Pendleton Woolen Mills.)

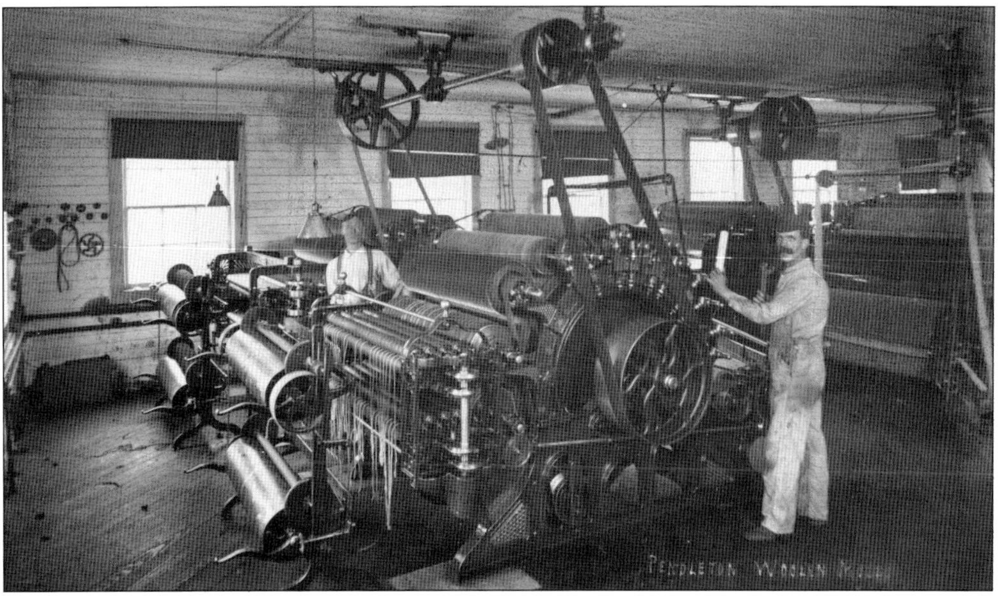

This is another view of a carding machine. Early drum carders were hand-cranked. Later, electric motors were added. More sophisticated cottage carders pass the fibers through the machine for additional processing by other machines. Besides straightening the fibers, the carding machine also loosens the fibers, removes the dust, and removes shorter fibers for a stronger yarn. (Pendleton Woolen Mills.)

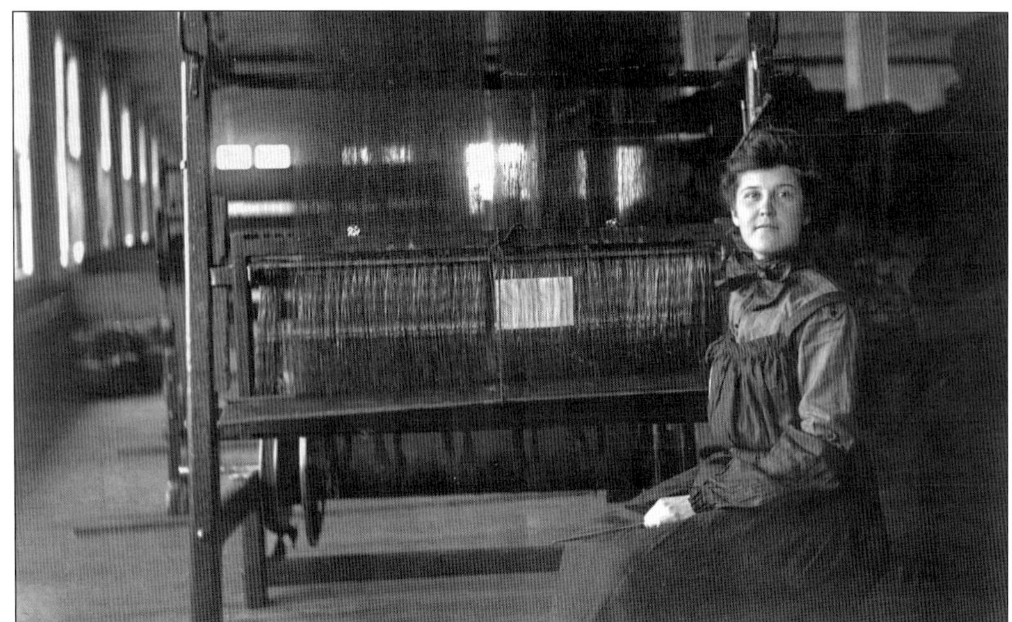

The roving is spun through rollers to even it out and give it the right amount of twist. The yarn is then wound onto bobbins. This hand-operated loom dates from the 1900s. Looms weave the yarn strands into cloth or fabric. The fabric is made from two sets of yarns that interlace at right angles to each other. Looms were quickly mechanized to improve speed and the quality of the fabric produced. (Pendleton Woolen Mills.)

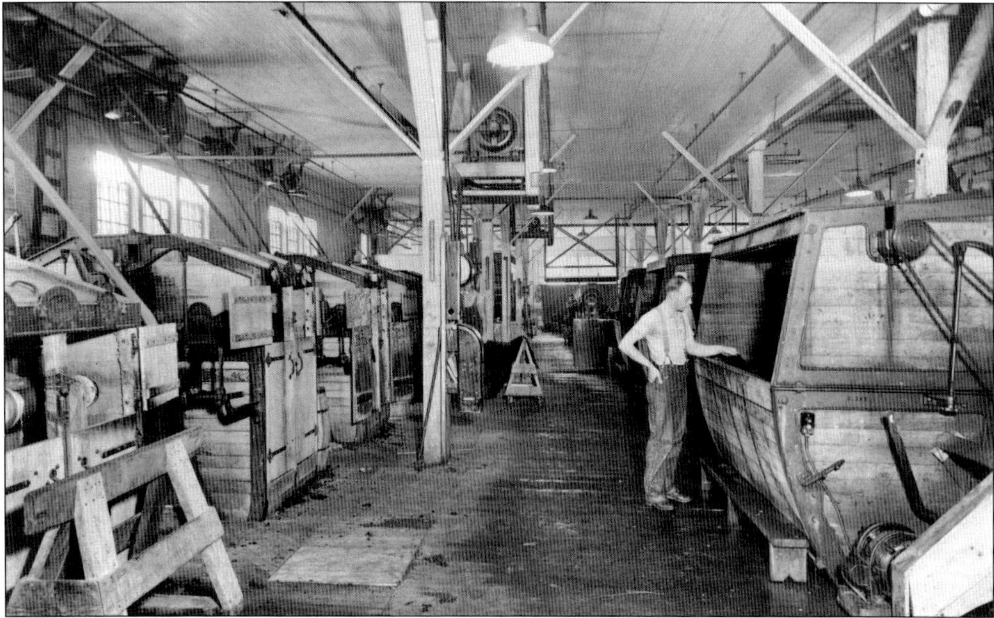

Next, the fabric goes through the fulling process, which helps control the shrinkage of the loomed fabric. Soap, heat, and friction are applied to cause the material to shrink a determined amount in length and width. The amount depends on the weight of the fabric and the finished effect desired. Afterward, the fabric is washed to remove the soap and oil used in the process. (Pendleton Woolen Mills.)

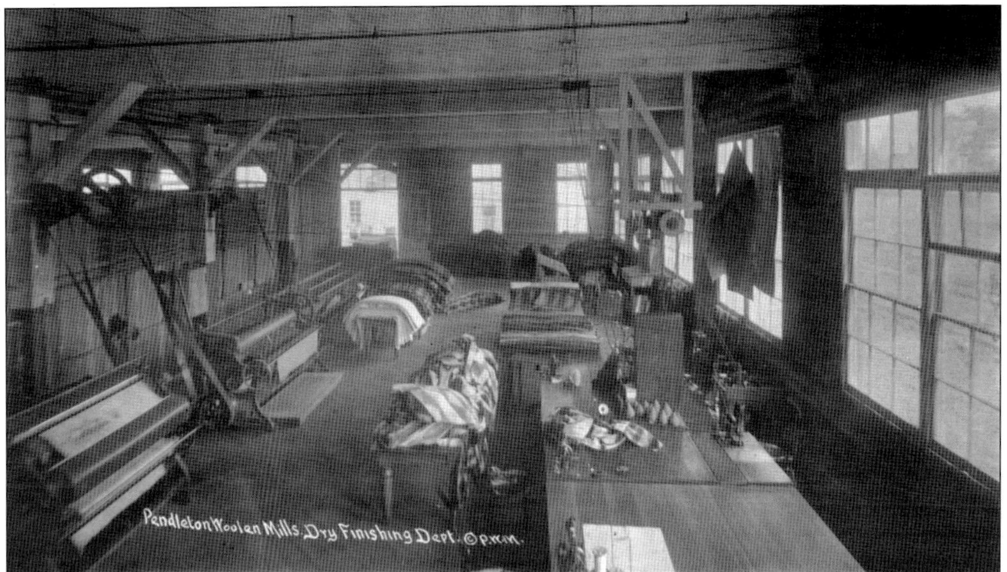

The finishing machine binds edges to fabric and sews on labels. The fabrics may be treated by brushing, shearing, or pressing. In later years, fabrics would be treated for machine washability at this time. Employees also inspect the finished product for quality. (Pendleton Woolen Mills.)

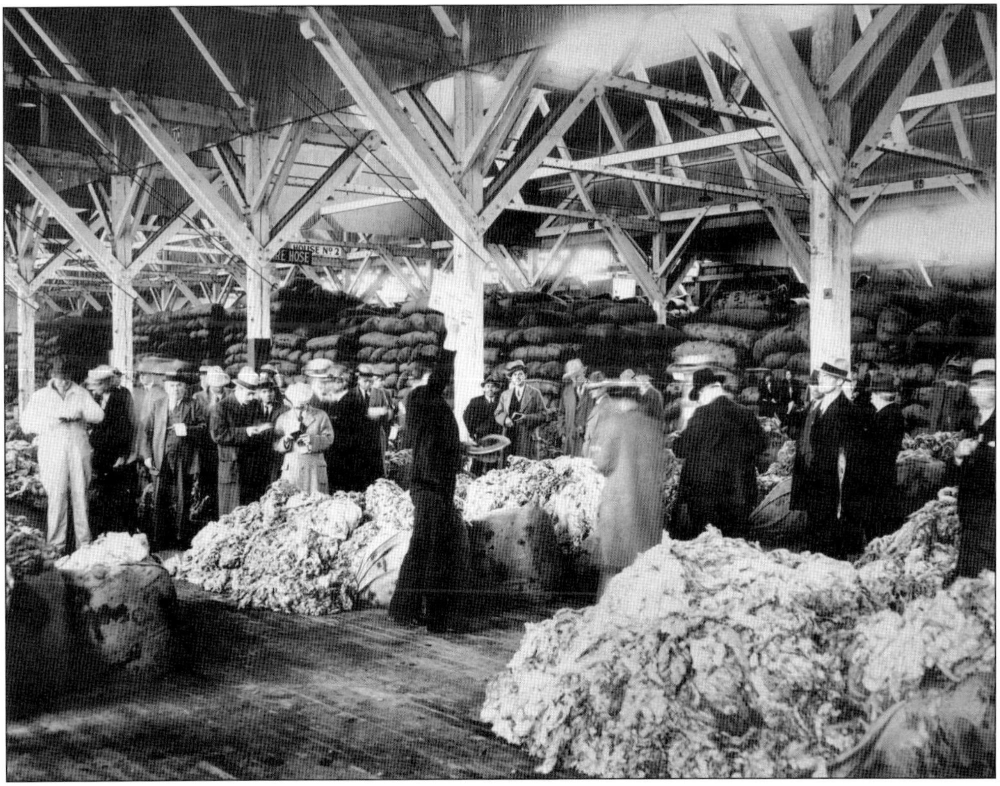

This photograph was likely taken at a wool auction. In the old days, bids were written down and thrown into a hat. Those bidding would have to be able to judge the wool in front of them and know what price to offer. (Pendleton Woolen Mills.)

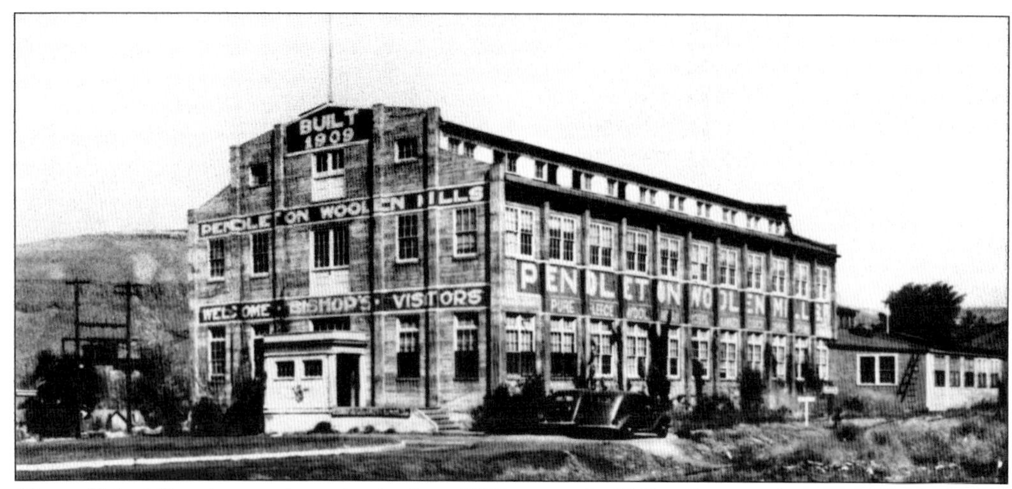

The mill building is seen here in the late 1920s or early 1930s. During this time, the mill was expanding its lines and produced a full line of men's virgin wool sportswear. Times were lean during the Depression years, but business boomed again when the mill was contracted to supply blankets to troops during World War II. (Pendleton Woolen Mills.)

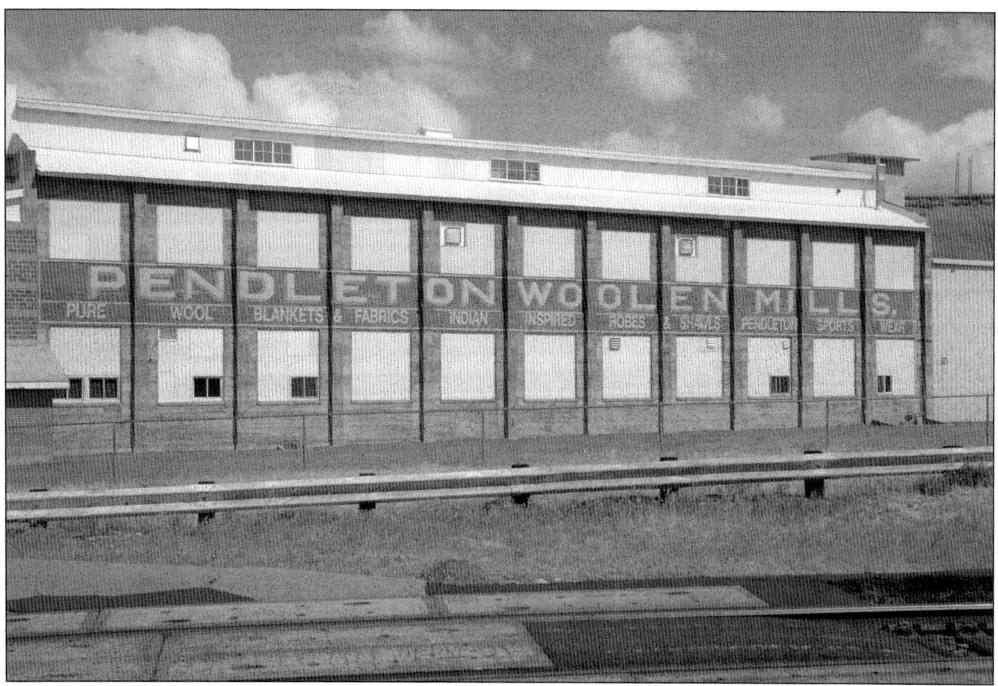

The woolen mill is seen here in the late 1970s. By then, the company was using national advertising campaigns. At one time, actress and model Cheryl Tiegs modeled Pendleton skirts. The mill supplied clothing for the directors of the Pendleton Round-Up and Happy Canyon Associations. The mill also offered reasonably priced women's clothing to the Round-Up and Happy Canyon courts. (Pendleton Woolen Mills.)

Four

Churches and Schools

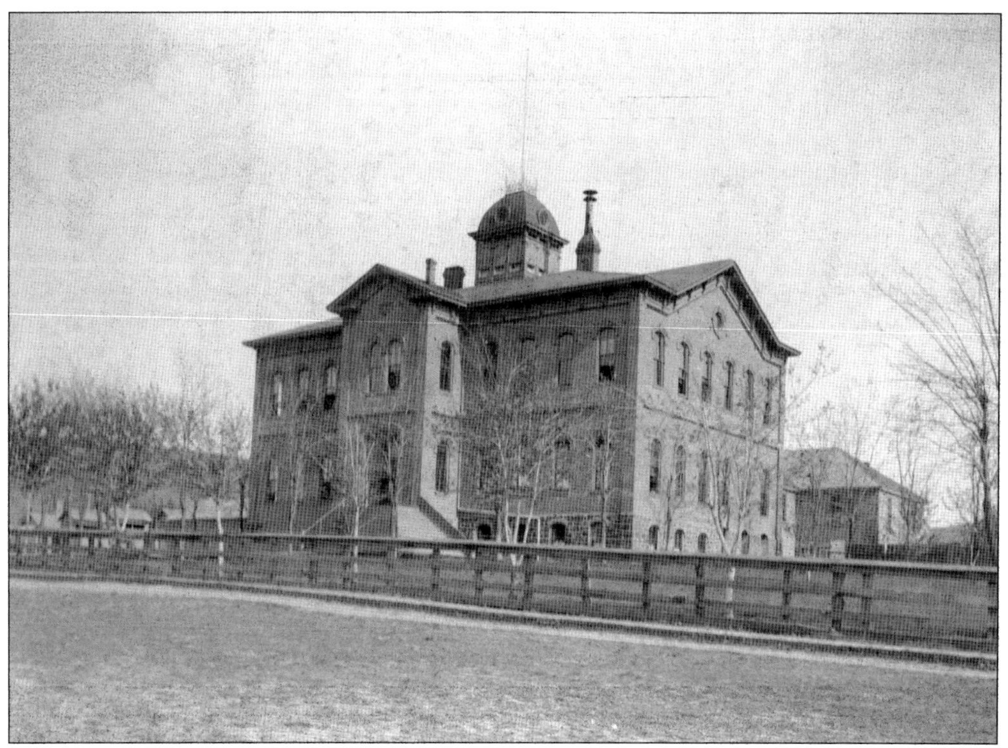

The first public high school, built in 1888, was made of brick and cost $20,000. It could hold 750 students. (Umatilla County Historical Society, 1995.027.033.)

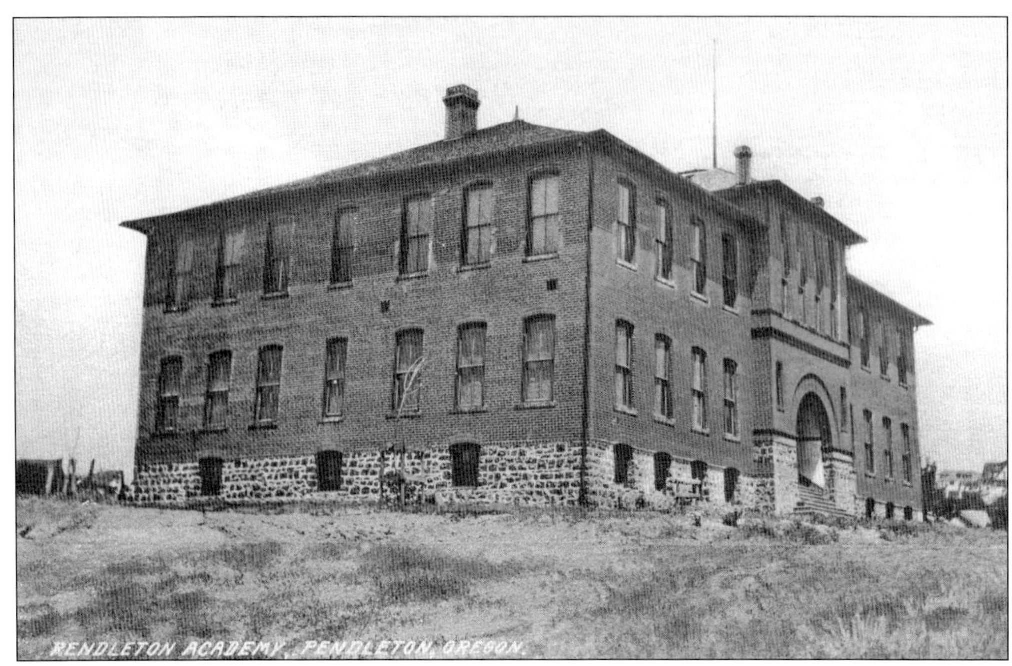

The Pendleton Academy was built in 1903 near the Main Street Bridge over the Umatilla River. It was a coeducational school with boys' and girls' dormitories and offered 12 years of education. It was founded by Jessie Vert and Rev. T.M. Boyd, a Presbyterian minister. The building was destroyed by fire in 1914. (Elizabeth Gibson.)

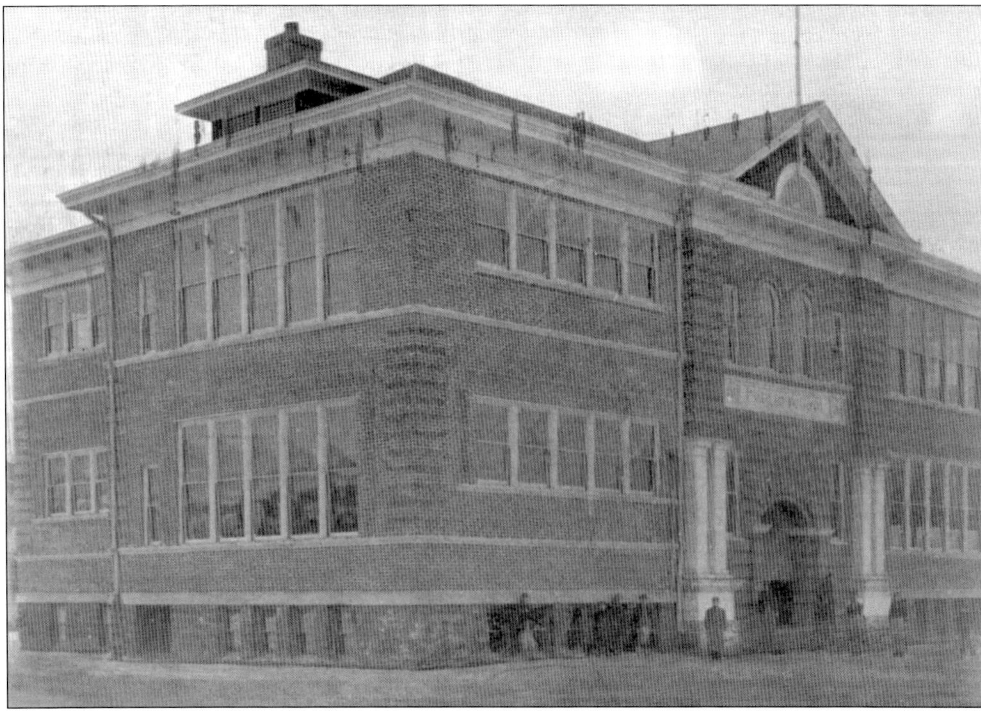

This early public school served Pendleton in the early 1900s. Seen here in approximately 1906, it is uncertain exactly where the school stood. (Elizabeth Gibson.)

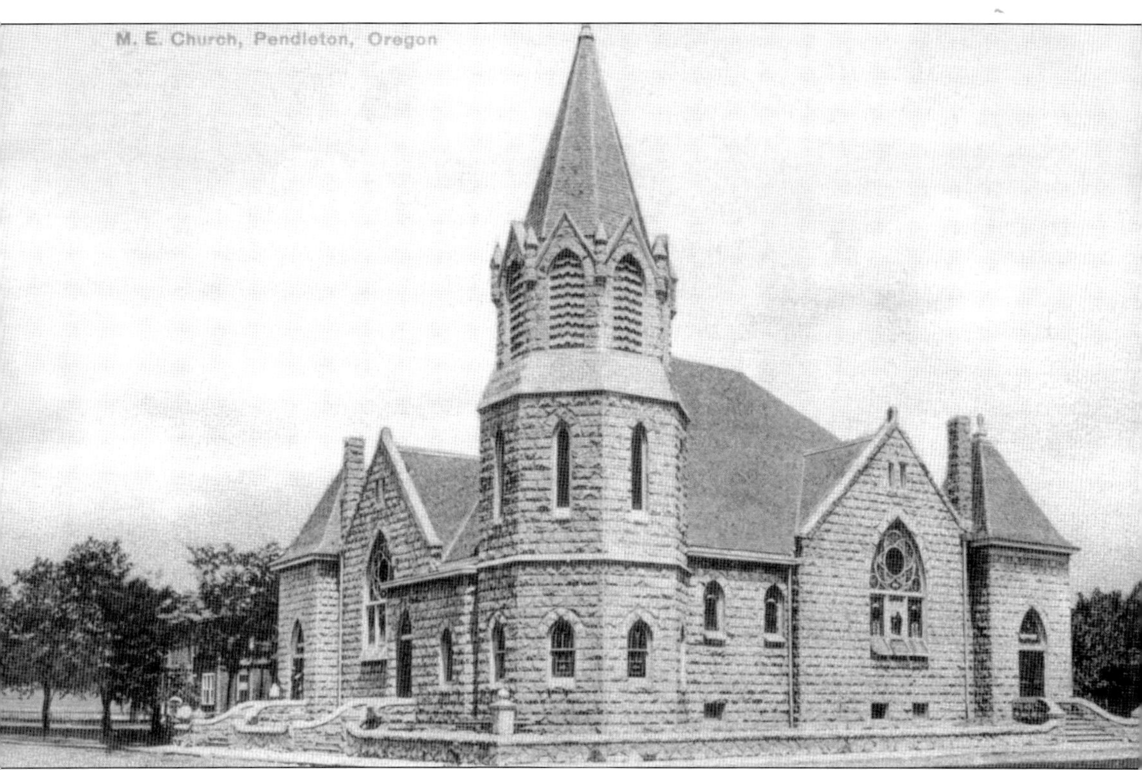

The new Methodist church was dedicated on June 2, 1907. This building, on Southeast Second Street, replaced an earlier building on Thompson Street (now Southeast Third Street) that was built in 1874. This building cost about $30,000 and was made of stone shipped by railcar from Baker City. The building was damaged twice by fires, in 1954 and 1977. In 2004, the roof was replaced and the stained glass windows were restored. (Elizabeth Gibson.)

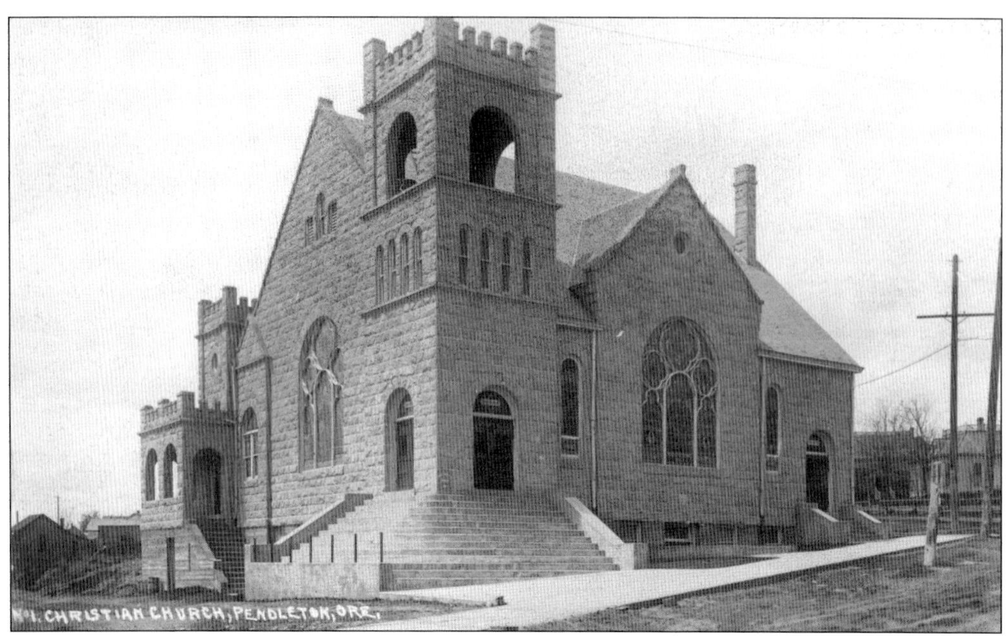

The Christian church was located at the corner of Second Street and Byers Avenue. When the original wooden church burned down in 1908, the congregation built this new stone building, which was completed in 1910, at the north end of the Main Street Bridge. (Elizabeth Gibson.)

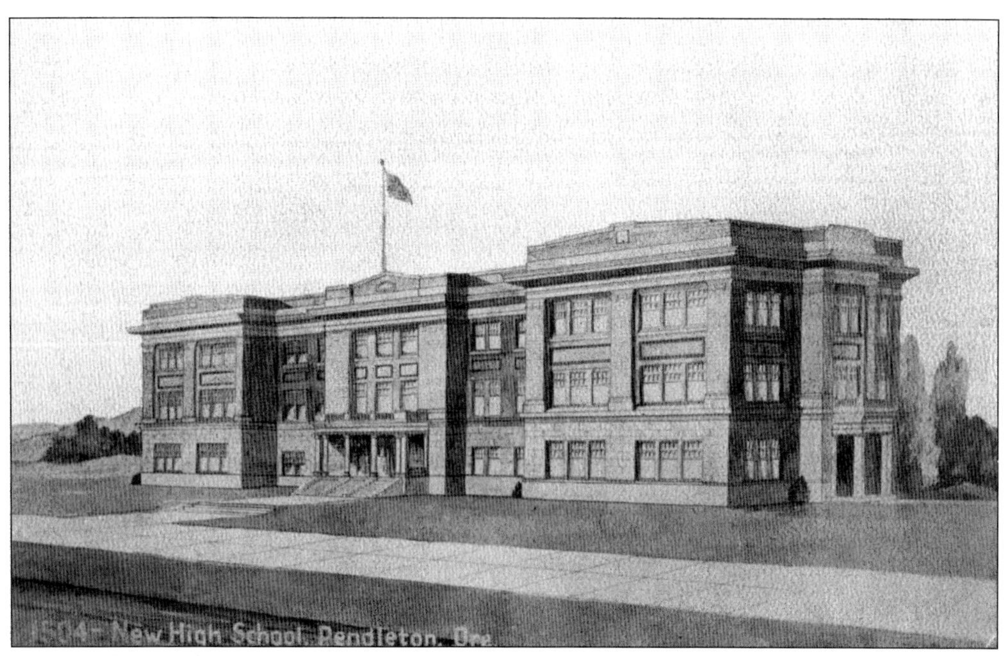

The population of the town quickly outgrew the old high school, so this new stone structure of over 50,000 square feet was built in 1914. The new building was called the John Murray Building and was constructed on the same site as the original facility on South Hill. The high school relocated to a new building in 1954. (Elizabeth Gibson.)

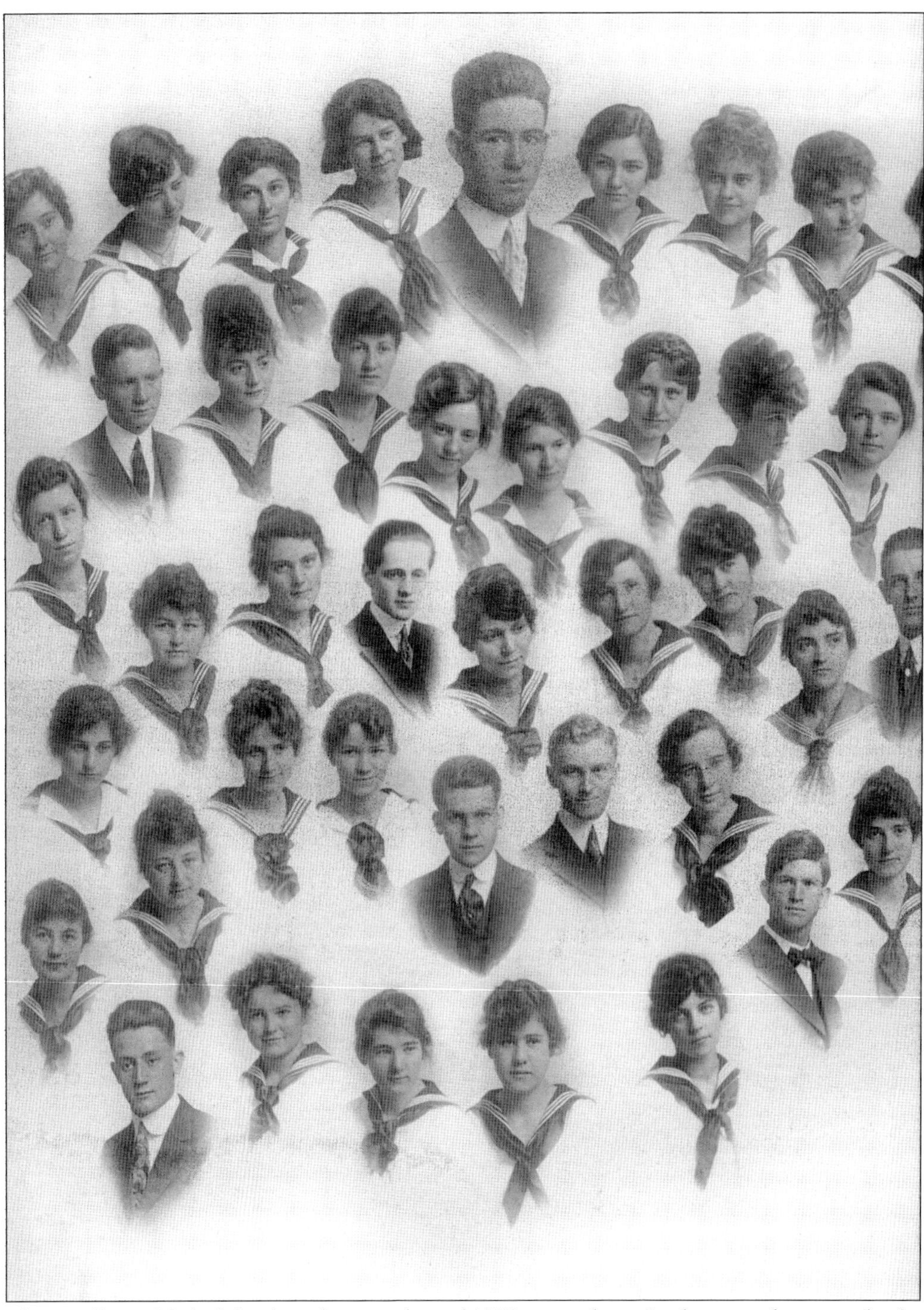

The Pendleton High School graduating class of 1915 is seen here. In the second row on the far right is Margaret Louise Hampton. (Nina Kennedy.)

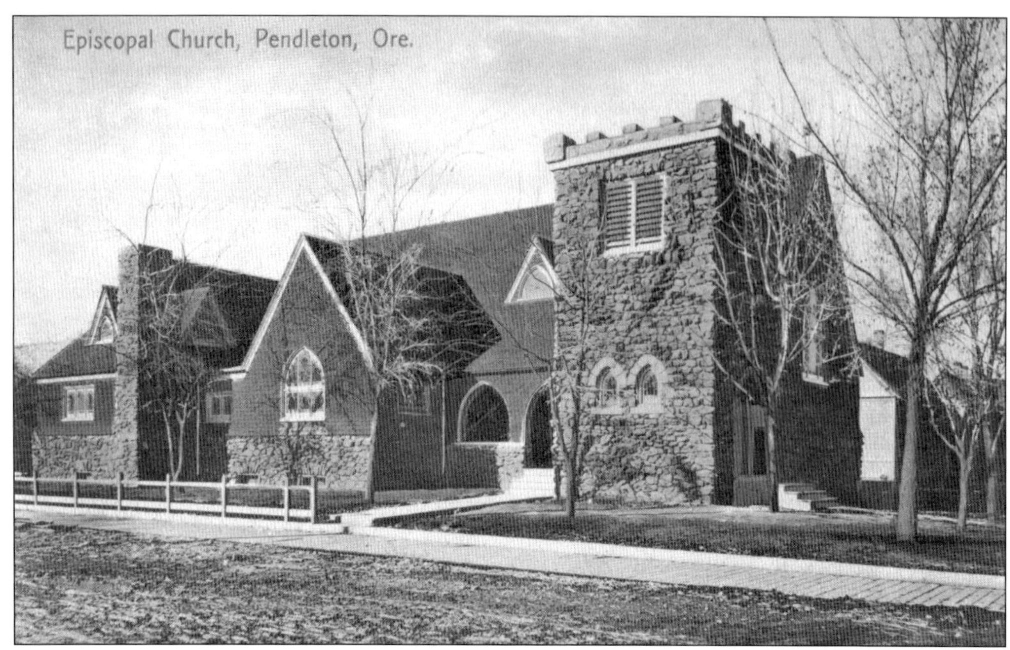

The cornerstone was laid for the Episcopal church in 1897. The church was built of stone and cedar shingles. Rev. W.E. Potwine served the church at this time. A parish house was built next door in 1939, and the basement was renovated in 1949 for Sunday school. The church still stands today on Southeast Second Street. (Elizabeth Gibson.)

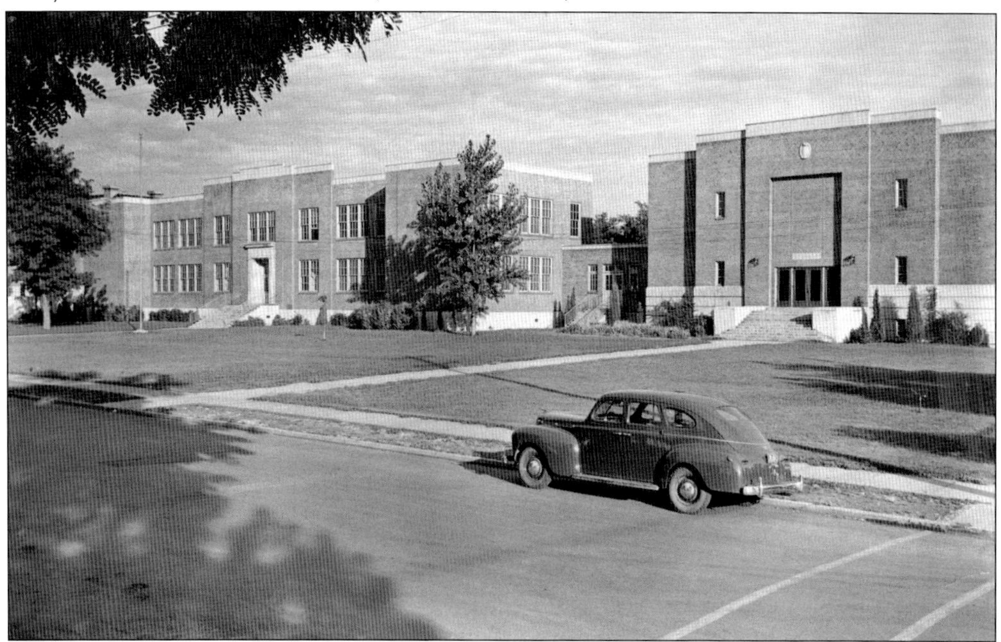

This building was the original Pendleton Junior High School, built in 1936. The school was renamed Helen McCune Junior High School in remembrance of the school principal, who died in a car accident. The city offices moved into the second floor of this building in 1996, and the library moved into the first floor. The parks and recreation department occupies the building to the west. (Umatilla County Historical Society, 1981.001.2114.)

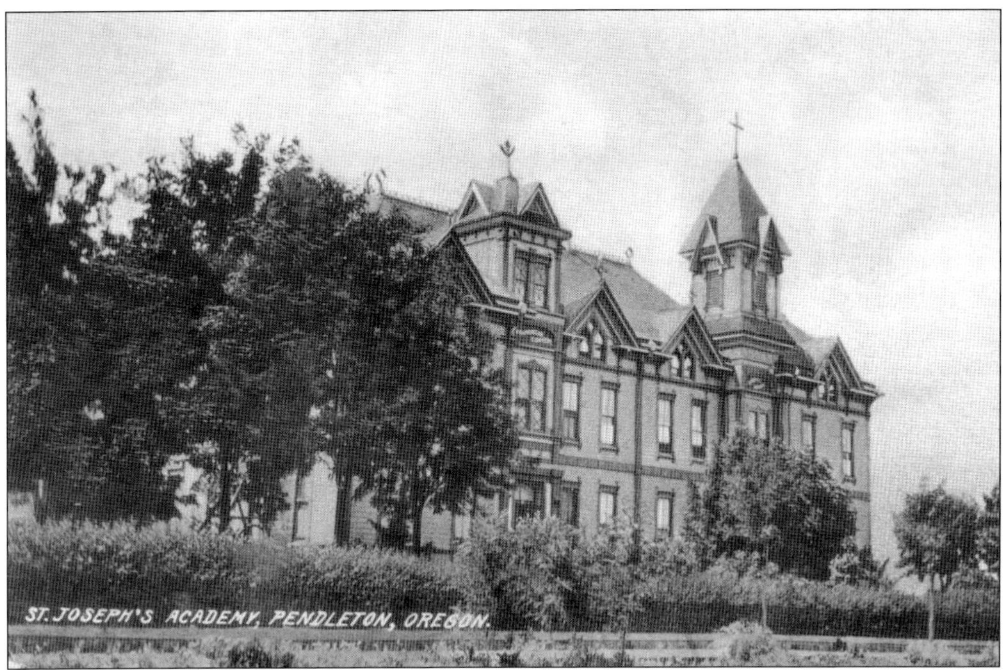

St. Joseph Academy was first established by the Catholic Sisters of Mercy in 1884. In 1887, the Sisters of St. Francis took over operation of the school. The building was originally made of wood, and a second addition was added in 1896. A third building, made of brick, was added in 1918. It was located at Southeast Court Place and Fourteenth Street. (Elizabeth Gibson.)

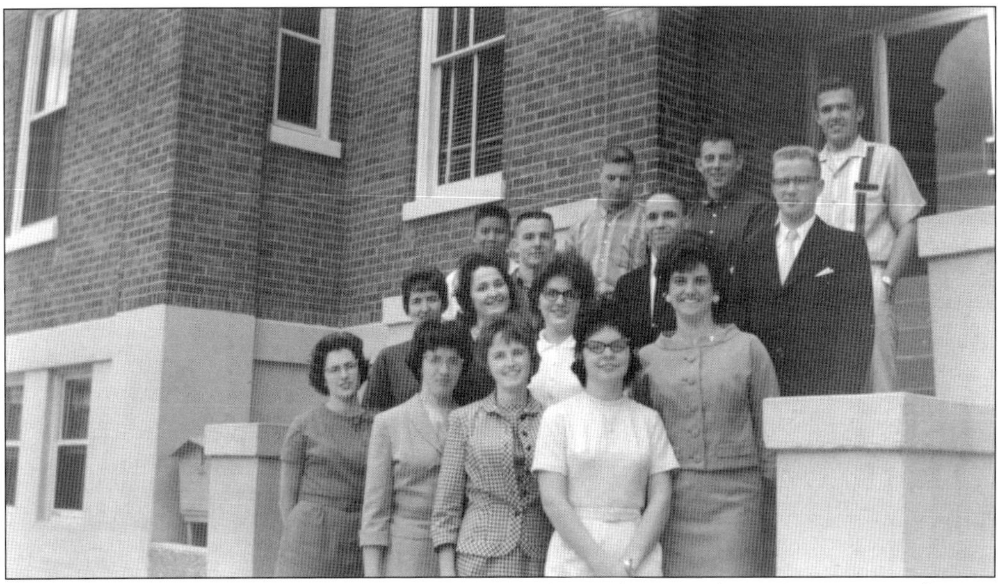

These young people stand on the steps of St. Joseph Academy in the 1950s. In 1956, the two original wooden buildings burned down. School continued to be held in the remaining brick structure, making classrooms very crowded. (Elizabeth Gibson.)

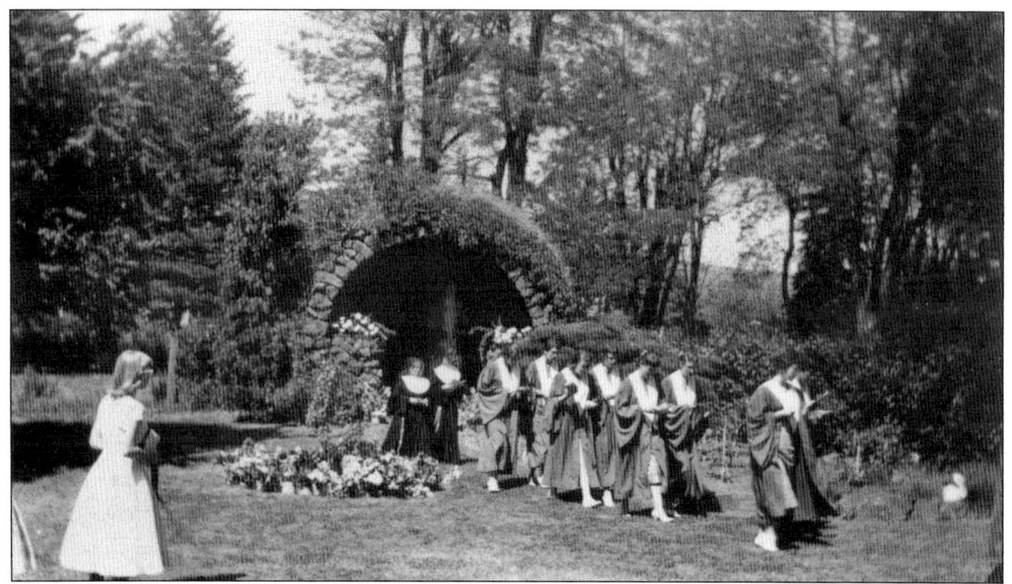

This scene from St. Joseph Academy shows a May Day celebration in the 1950s. The holiday is celebrated in various ways, but the traditional Catholic celebration honors the Virgin Mary, mother of Jesus, for the month of May. Catholic schools honor her with skits, special artwork, and the crowning of a statue with flowers. (Elizabeth Gibson.)

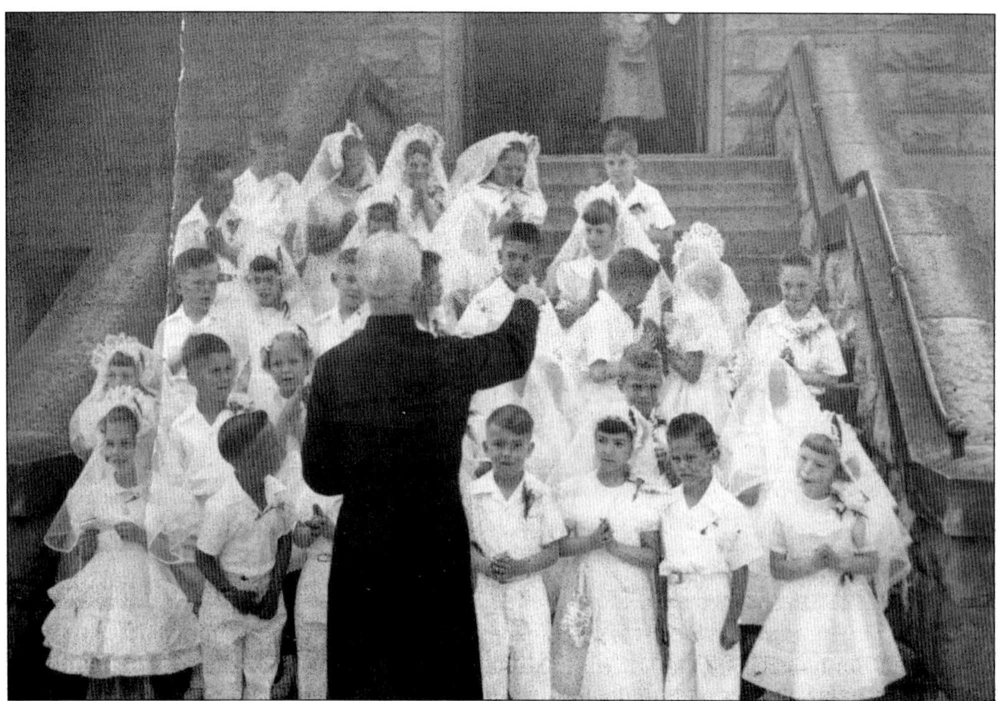

Students celebrate their first communion at St. Joseph Academy in the 1950s. The school was still expanding then, and, in 1957, the sisters moved into a new convent. In 1962, a gymnasium and a classroom were added to the original 1918 building. (Jim Knight.)

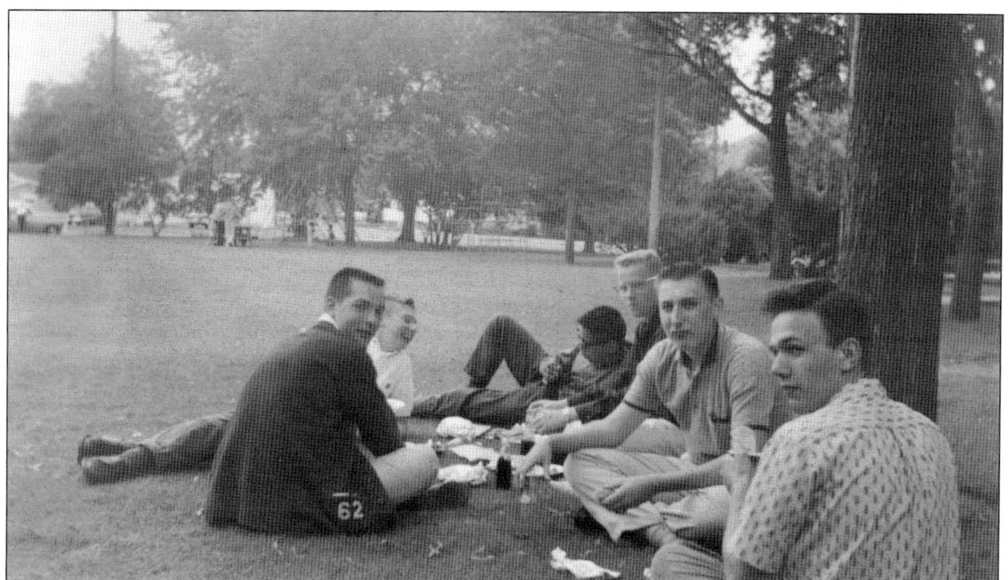

This photograph shows a group of alumni relaxing on the grounds of St. Joseph Academy. In 1962, the high school portion of the school was closed due to declining enrollment. In 1974, the school was closed completely. The last of the old buildings were demolished in 1997. (Jim Knight.)

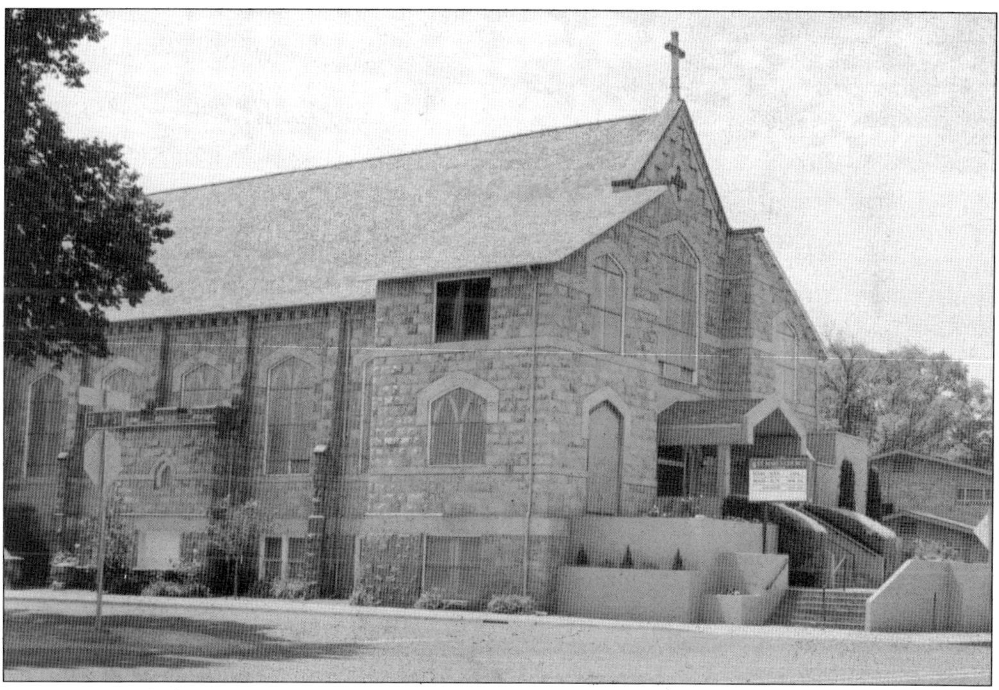

St. Mary's Catholic Church is located on Southeast Court Street. Two Catholic churches preceded it, one on Fourth Street and Emigrant Avenue and another on Eighth Street and Emigrant. Construction began on this church in 1912, and it was dedicated in 1916. It was made from volcanic tuff quarried near Baker City. Murals were added in 1948, a rectory was built in 1956, and other remodeling occurred in the 1960s and 1970s. (Elizabeth Gibson.)

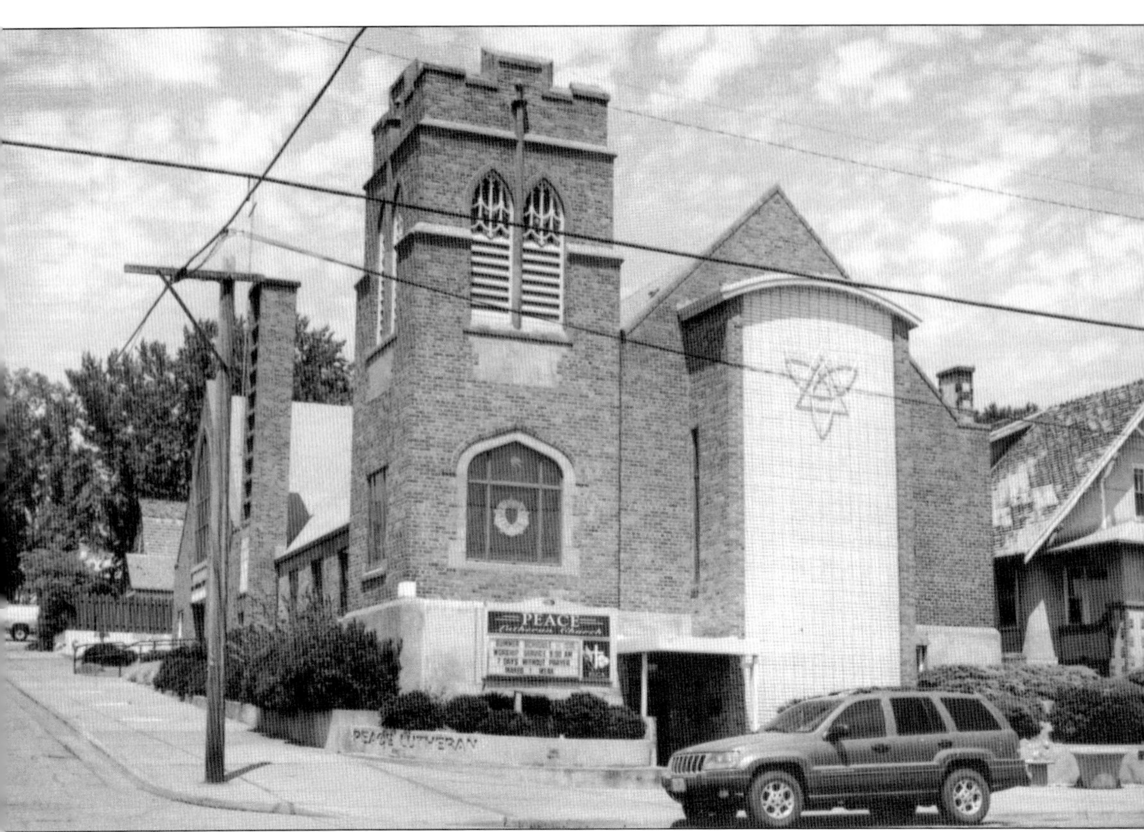

Peace Presbyterian Church is located on Southwest Ninth Street. There has been a Presbyterian presence in Pendleton since 1885. (Elizabeth Gibson.)

Five

Pendleton Round-Up

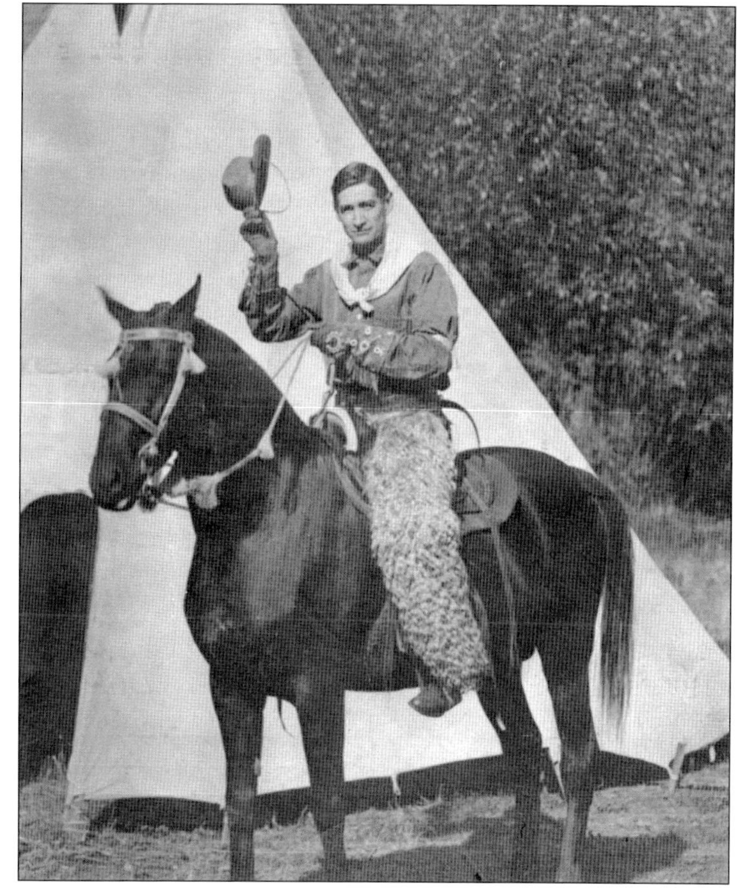

The first year of the Pendleton Round-Up was 1910, the same year this photograph was taken. Roy Raley, seen here, was the president of the first Round-Up. In 1913, Raley came up with the concept of the Happy Canyon pageant, which was added to the Round-Up in 1916. He was also a lawyer, serving as the city attorney and the president of the Oregon State Bar Association. (Umatilla County Historical Society, 1981.001.3002.)

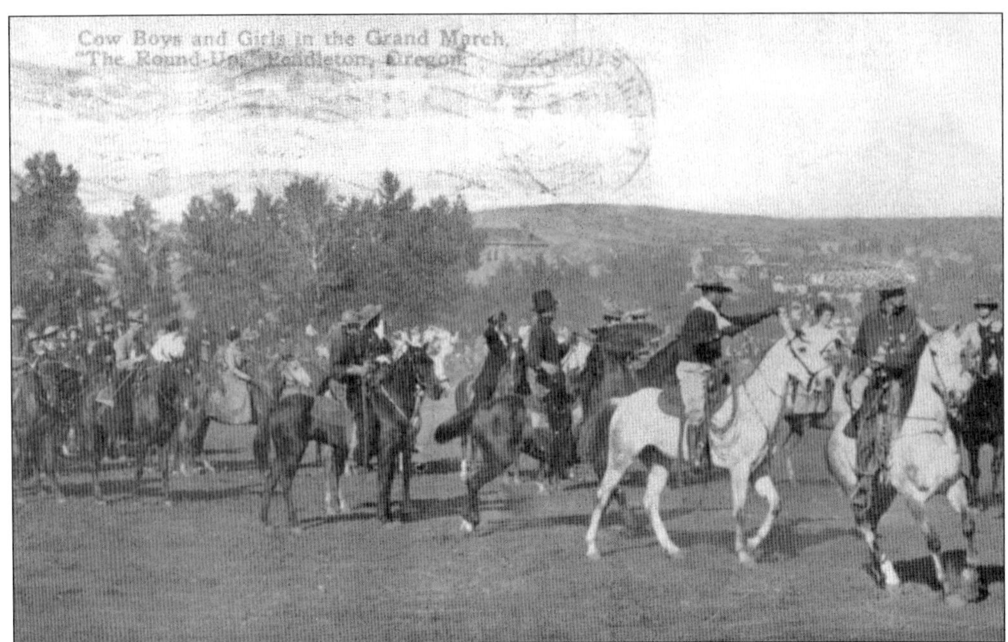

The grand parade has been part of the Pendleton Round-Up since the early days. The first parade was organized by Paul Sperry and named Westward Ho. Participants dressed in vintage 1880s clothing, though that was still common attire in 1910. The parade typically starts on the Friday morning prior to the start of the Round-Up. (Elizabeth Gibson.)

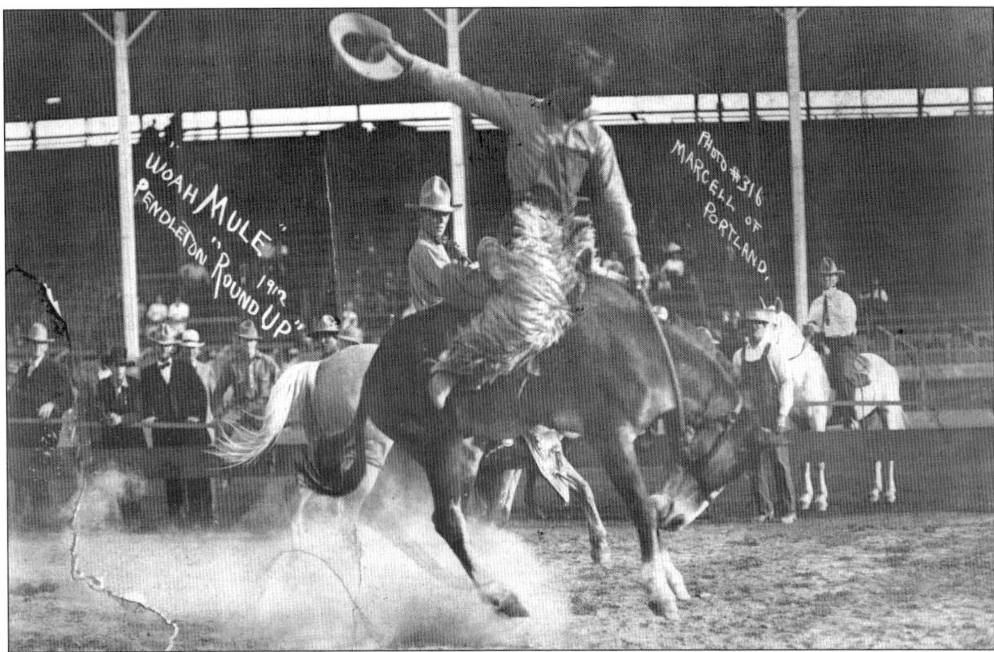

The early years of the Round-Up featured 28 different events, including a mule ride, as seen here. This photograph was taken at the 1912 Round-Up, one of the earliest ones. It appears that the mule is not any happier than a horse to have a man on his back. (Fort Walla Walla Museum.)

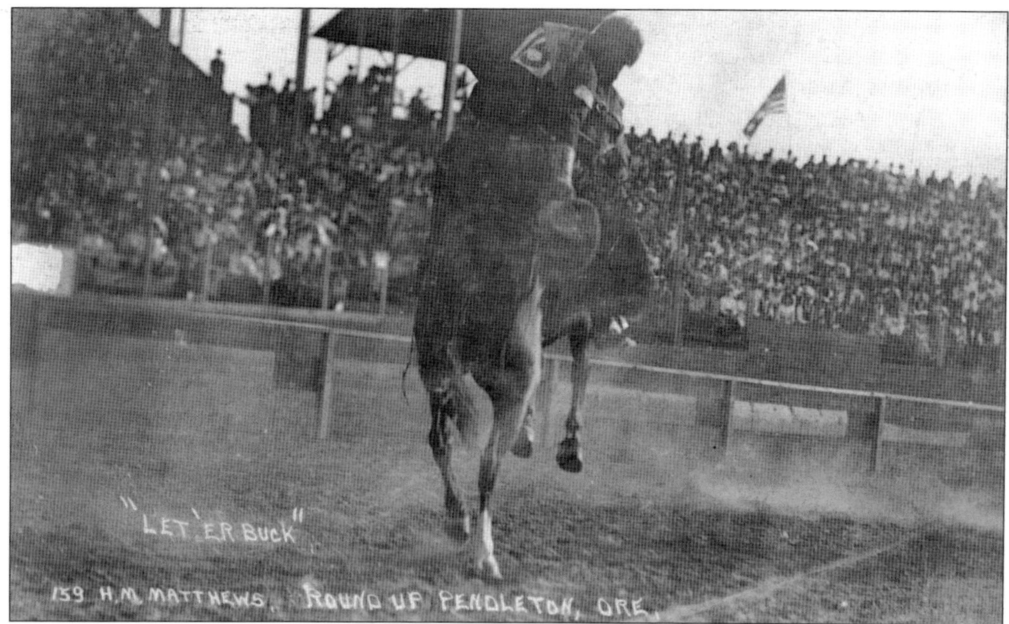

This photograph shows H.M. Matthews bronc riding in 1919. This event traces its origins back to the days when cowboys broke wild horses. The Round-Up featured both saddled and bareback events. Saddle bronc events began when the Round-Up began in 1910. Bareback bronc riding was added in 1948. (Elizabeth Gibson.)

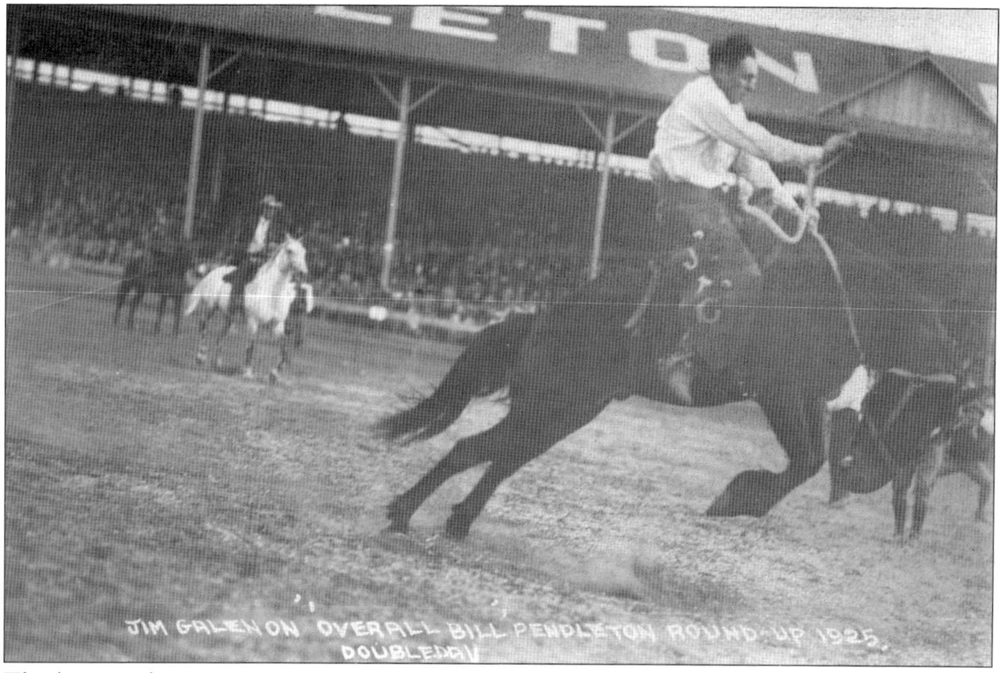

The bronc riding competition has been part of the Pendleton Round-Up since its inception in 1910. Bob Askins led the 1925 event, but Jim Galen, seen here riding on Overall Bill, was another tough competitor that year. The horses' names were almost as colorful as their owners. (Glen Thiesfeld.)

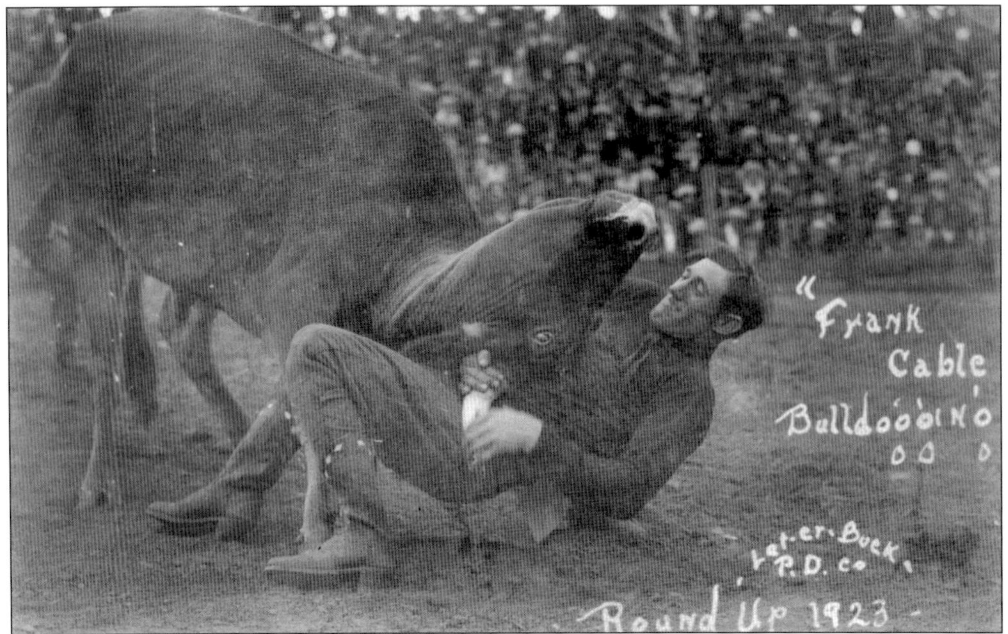

Bulldogging was also one of the earliest events at the Round-Up, starting in 1911. Frank Cable is seen here bulldogging in 1923. In the bulldogging event, a rider jumps from a galloping horse onto a running steer's head, twists the steer's head toward the sky, and wrestles it to the ground. The rider is scored by how fast he accomplishes this extremely dangerous task. (Glen Thiesfeld.)

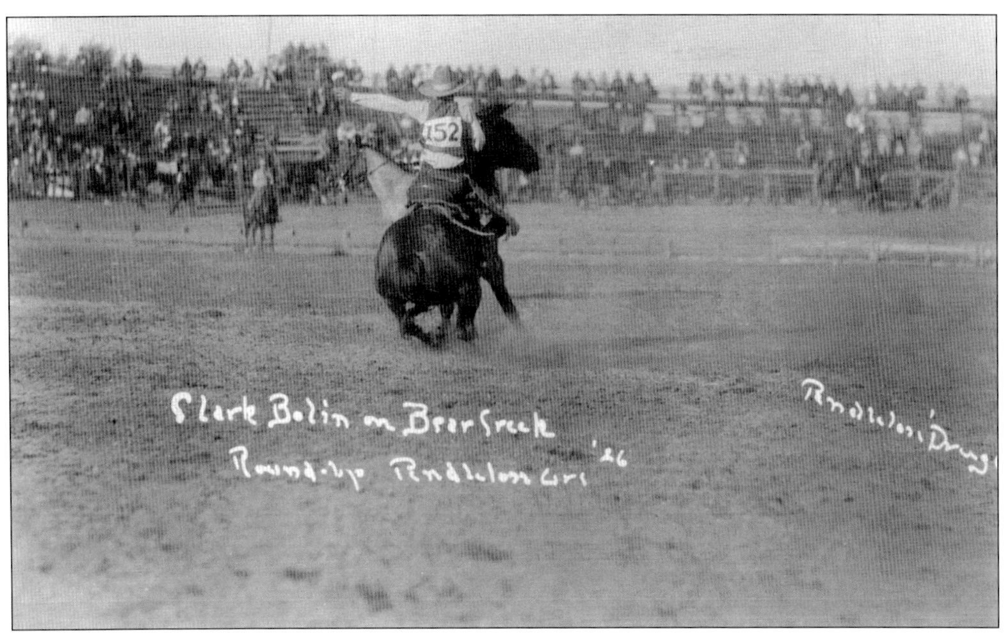

Another colorful bronc rider was Clark Bolin. He is seen here on his horse Bear Creek in 1926, when he was about 21 years old. That year, the champion was Shark Irwin. Bolin lived a long life and died in 1975. (Glen Thiesfeld.)

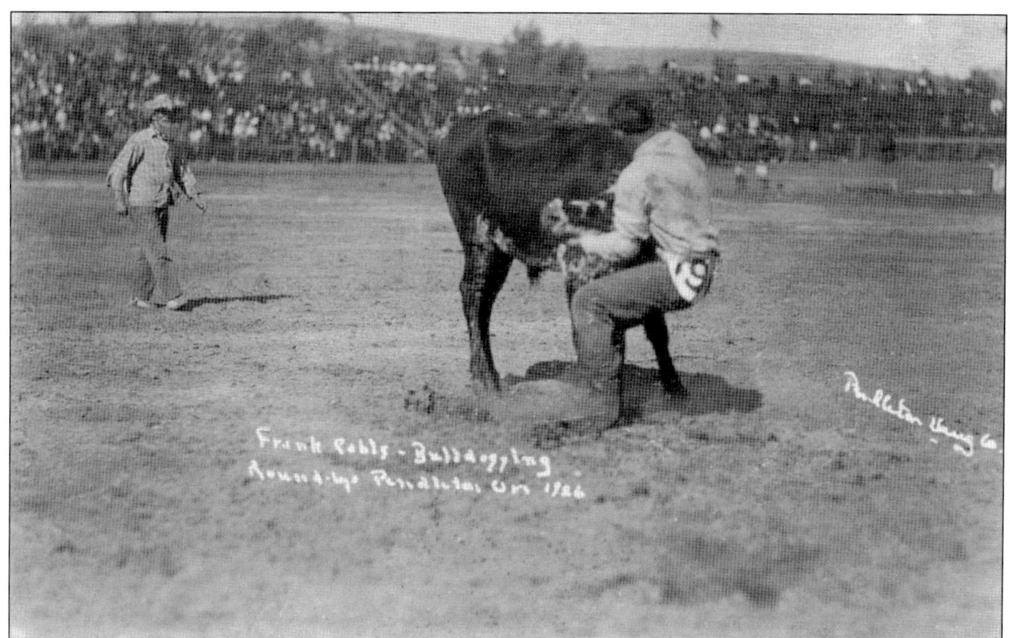

Some riders returned year after year. Frank Cable was the bulldogging champion in 1915, but he was still riding hard in this photograph, taken in 1926. Cable was also one of several riders who volunteered for World War I service in 1917. Troop D was made up of 108 volunteers and billeted at the Happy Canyon pavilion. (Glen Thiesfeld.)

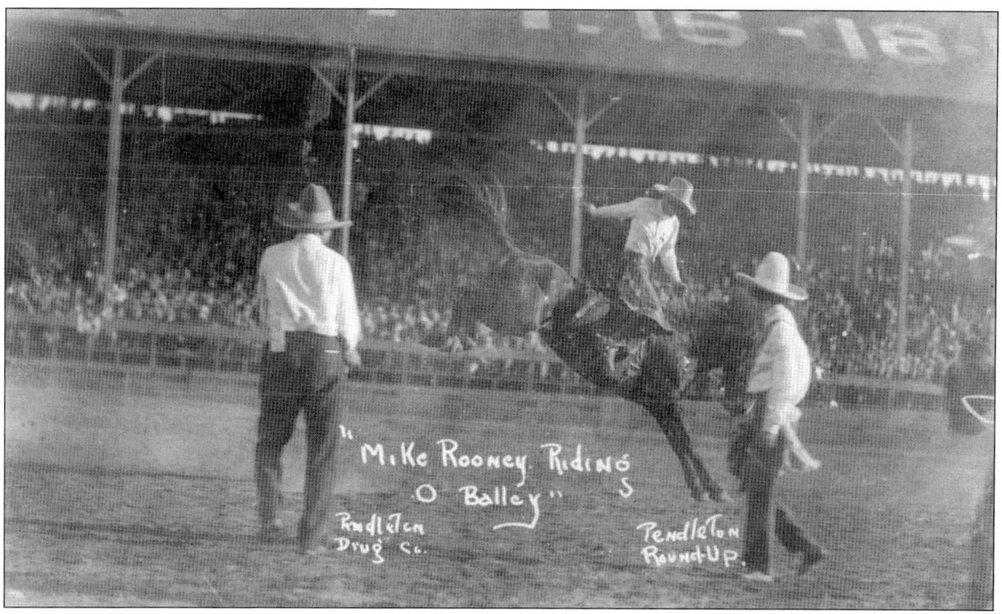

Mike Rooney loved riding his favorite horse, O Balley. It took nerves of steel and strong stamina to sit astride a bucking bronco long enough to take the championship. (Glen Thiesfeld.)

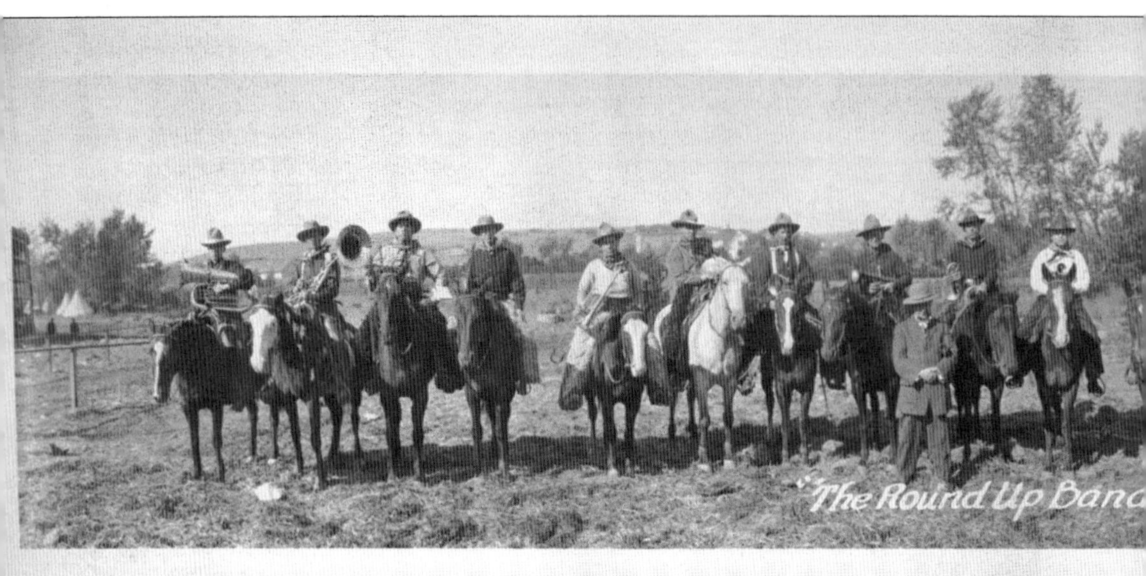

The Pendleton Round-Up Marching Band entertains the crowds at every show. This photograph dates from 1911, the second year of the Round-Up. This group is made up of 20 men playing everything from tuba to bass drum. It must have been a special challenge to play tunes on

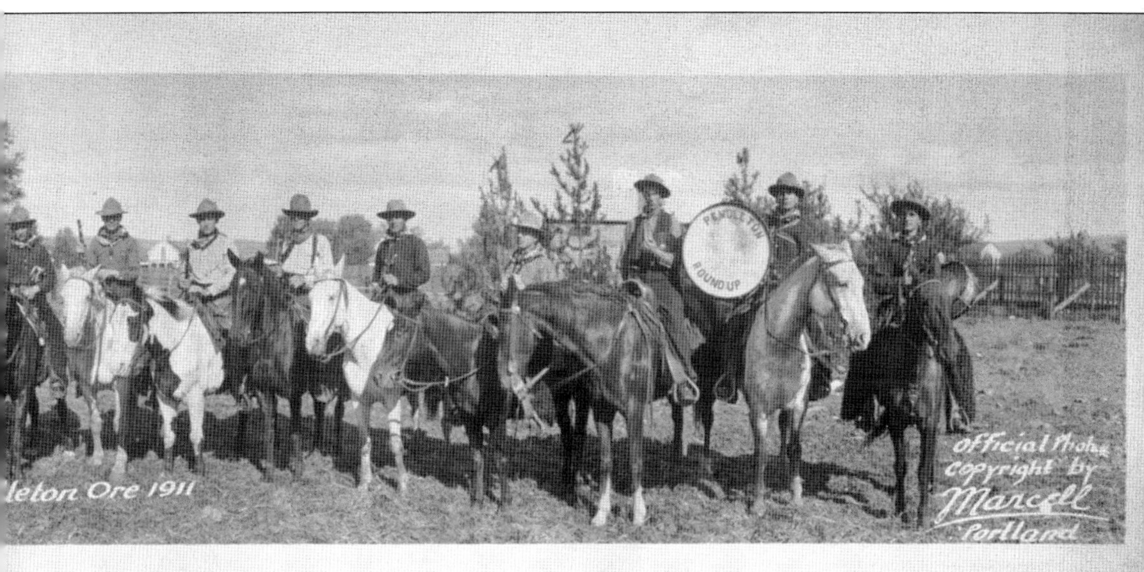

horseback. Special animals that could tolerate the noise of the musical instruments were also needed. (Library of Congress.)

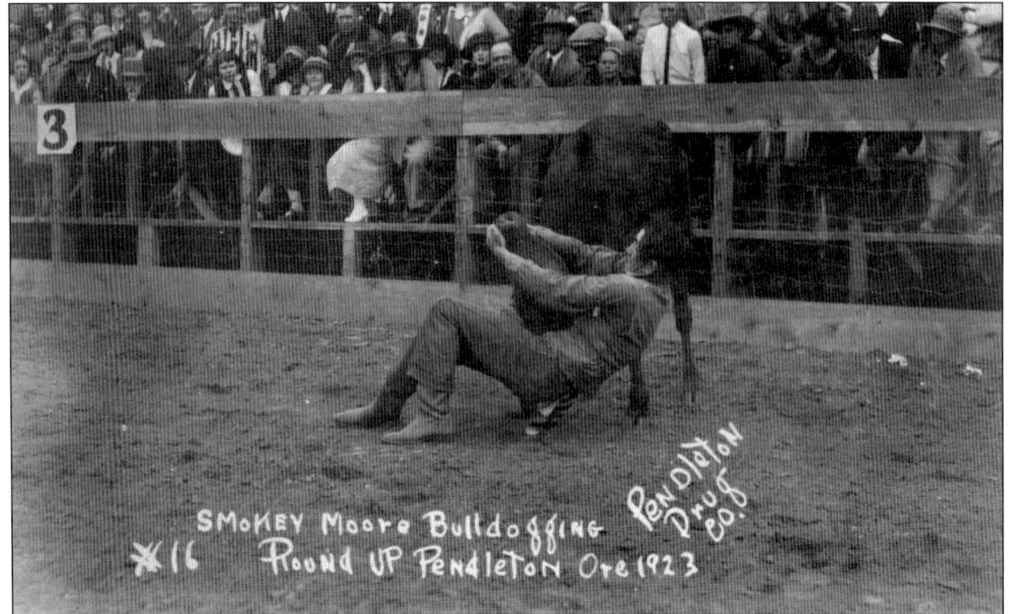

Smokey Moore entered the bulldogging competition year after year. He also entered competitions in the Ellensburg Rodeo, another famous event in the Pacific Northwest. He won third place there in 1931. His real name was Dennis Meadows, and he also had a successful career as an actor in Hollywood Westerns. (Glen Thiesfeld.)

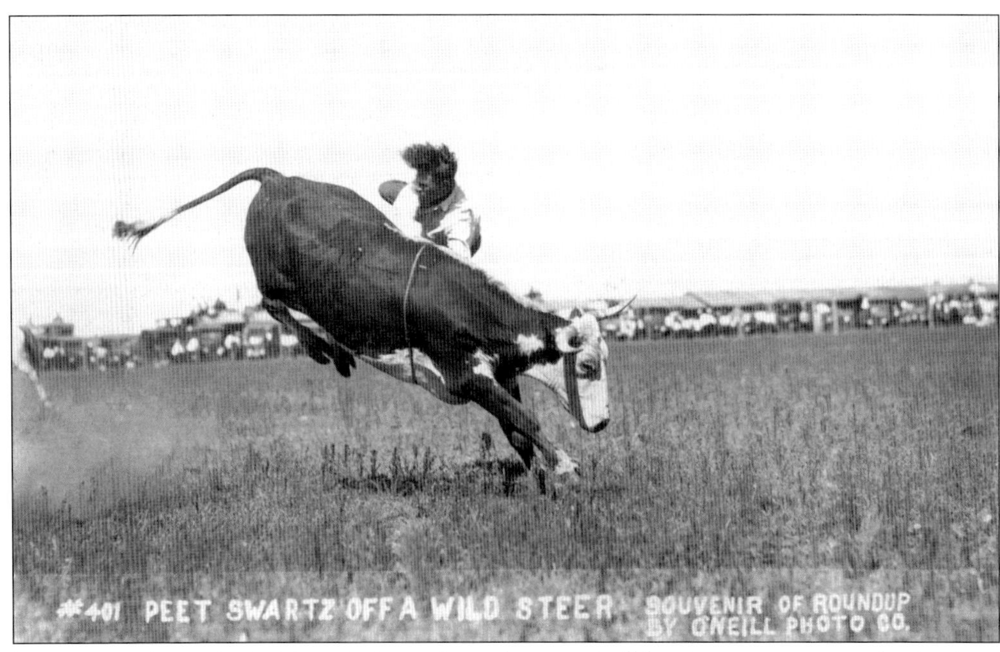

Peet Swartz also rode the Round-Up in the early years. Bulldogging was very popular in those days. Bull riding was not be added to the Pendleton Round-Up until 1944. (Glen Thiesfeld.)

This studio photograph shows two unidentified Indian cowboys in their Round-Up paraphernalia. (Fort Walla Walla Museum, Lloyd Family Collection.)

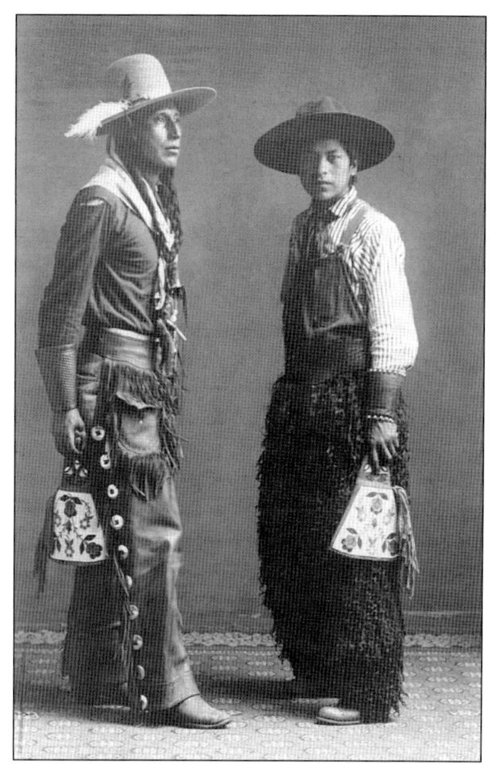

Many women participated in the Round-Up, including Vera McGinnis, who is seen below in the "drunken ride." This involved holding a whiskey bottle while pretending to be drunk and doing crazy stunts. McGinnis's career ended when a horse fell on top of her and she suffered a collapsed lung, three broken ribs, a broken hip, a broken neck bone, and five broken vertebrae. She was inducted in the Rodeo Hall of Fame in 1985. (Elizabeth Gibson.)

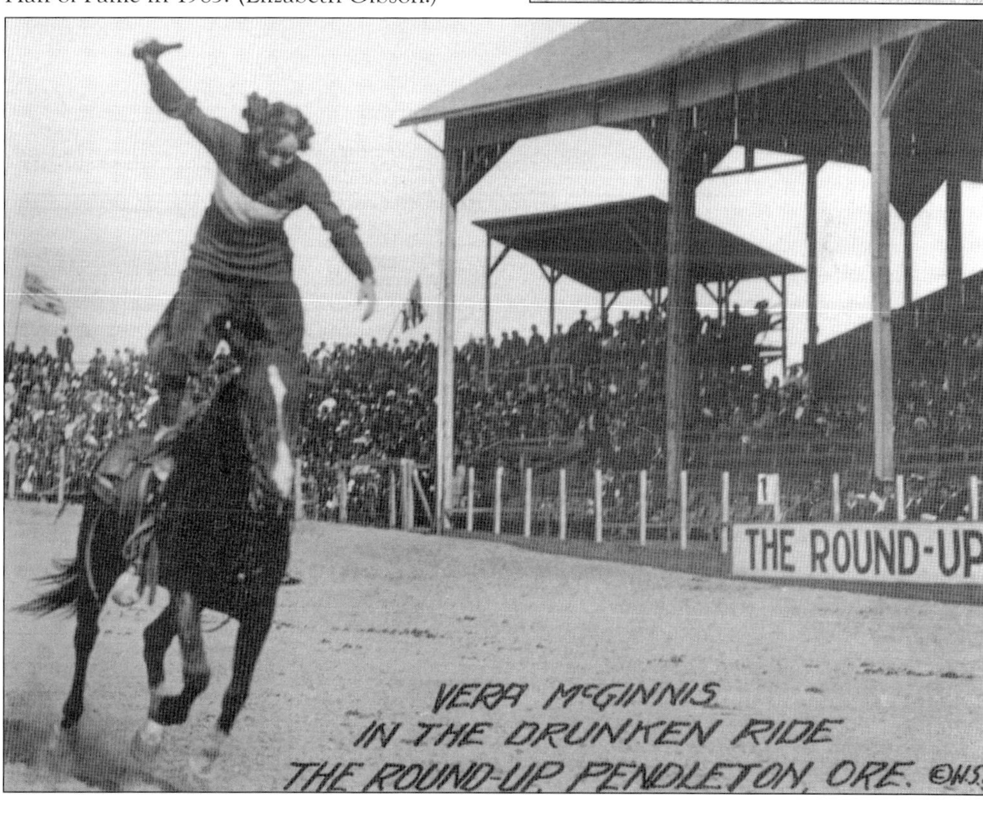

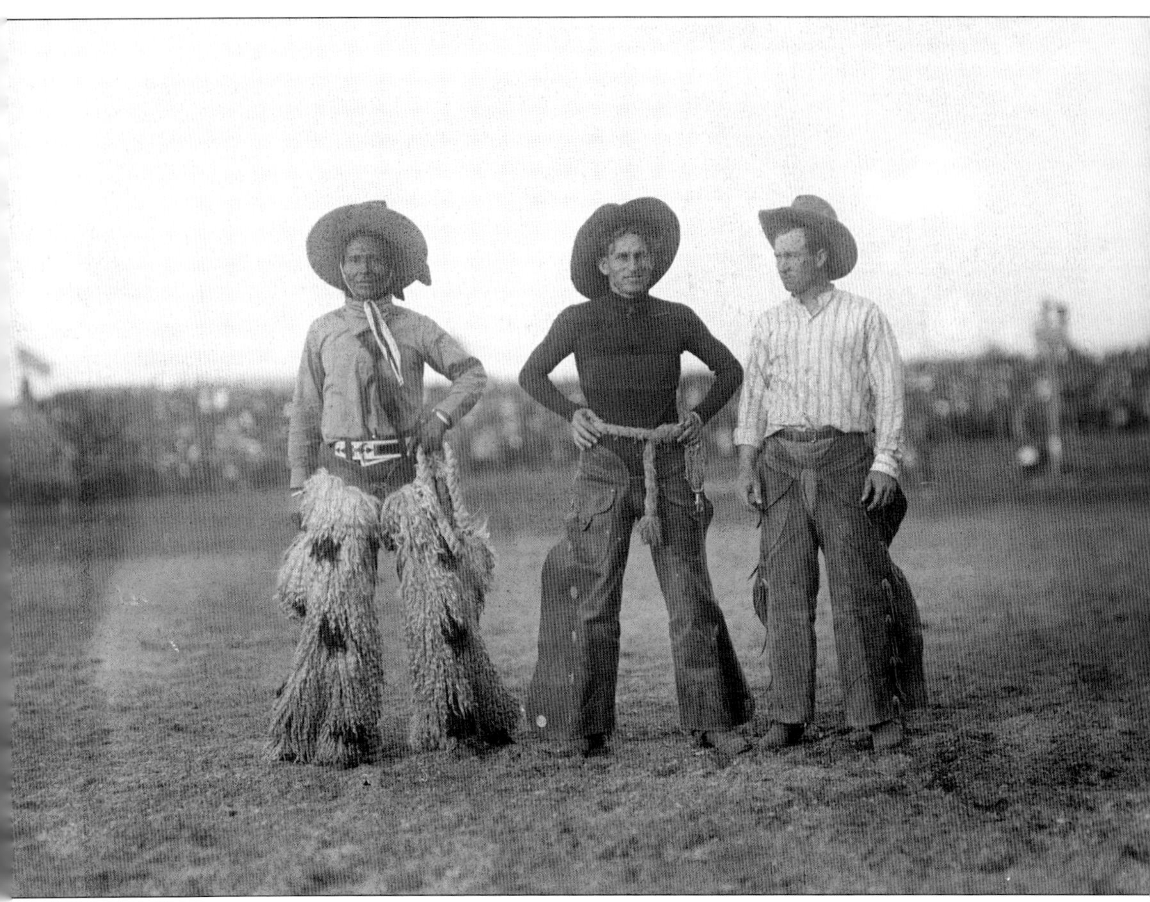

Jackson Sundown (left) was a popular Indian rider in the Pendleton Round-Up. He was born in 1863 in the Nez Perce tribe and lived in Canada for a time after the famous Nez Perce Retreat of 1877. He returned to the United States in 1910 and became a famous horseman. He won third place in bronc riding in 1915. In 1916, he won the world title in bronc riding and was voted outstanding rodeo performer of the year. In 1972, he was inducted into the Round-Up Hall of Fame. He died in 1923 of pneumonia. (Lee Moorhouse Collection [PH036 3997], Special Collections and University Archives, University of Oregon.)

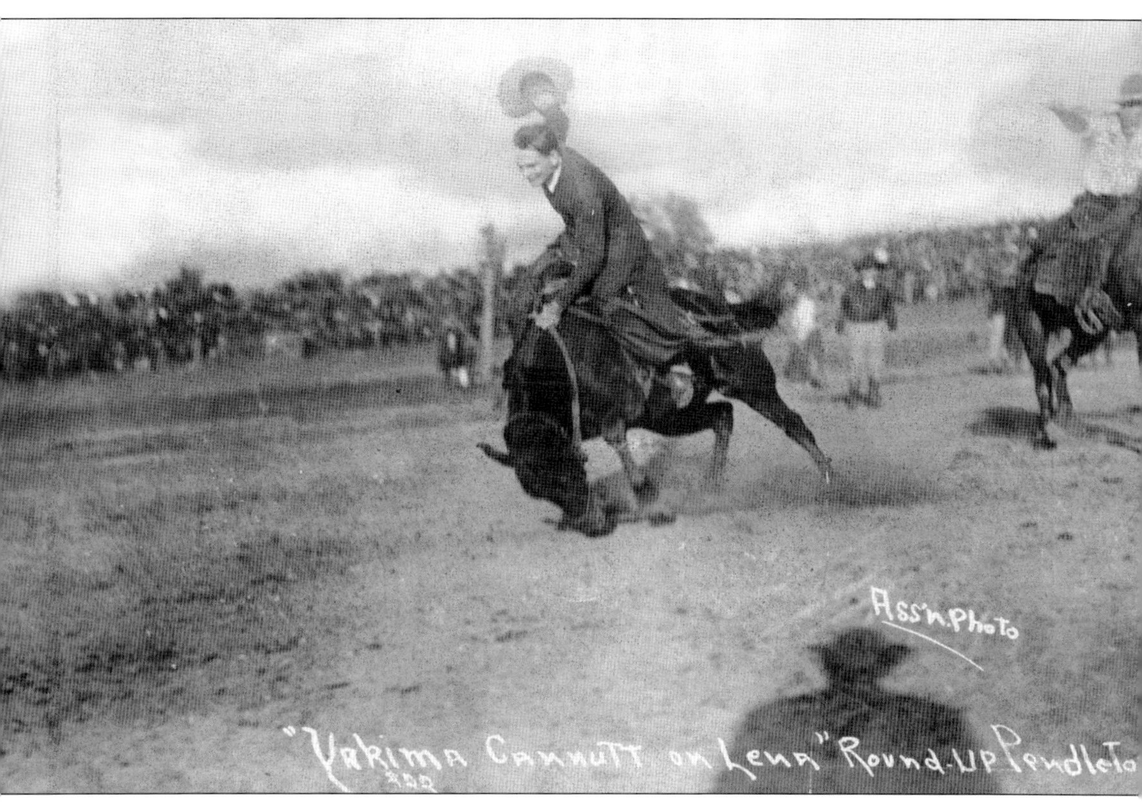

Enos Edward "Yakima" Cannutt was Hollywood's most renowned stuntman. He was born near Colfax, Washington, where he grew up riding and roping. His nickname came from the town he hailed from when he became known as a champion bronc rider and bulldogger. He appeared at the Pendleton Round-Up many times during its early years. For a short time, he was married to Kitty Wilks, a champion female bronc rider. His experience led to premier roles as a stuntman during the silent-film era. In the 1930s and 1940s, he created or refined most of the stunt techniques that would be used in Westerns and action films for many years. (Yakima Valley Museum.)

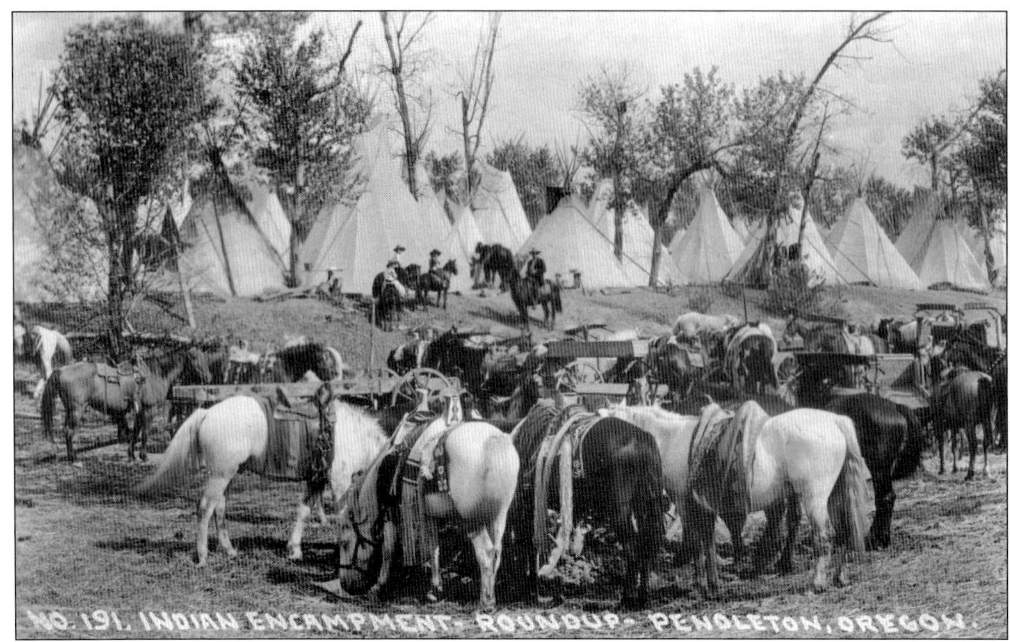

The Indian village sits on the north side of the Pendleton Round-Up arena. Many families have occupied the same sites over the decades. Gilbert Minthorn and James "Poker Jim" Burke are thought to be the first Indians to set up camp in the Indian village. The Round-Up Association supplied the tribes with basic foodstuffs and hay for their horses, a tradition that still continues today. (Elizabeth Gibson.)

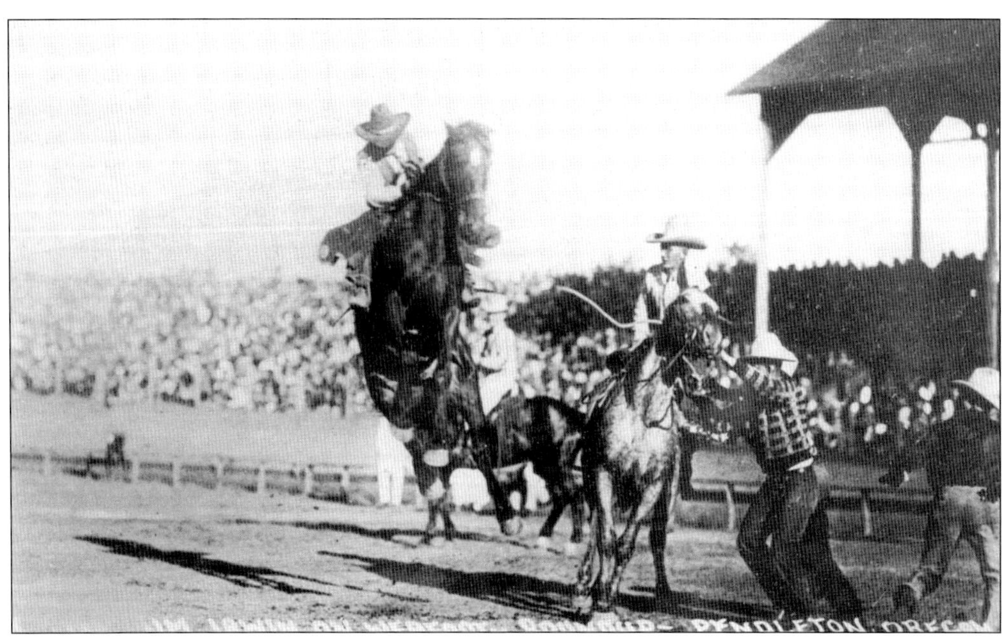

Jim Irwin rides a bucking bronco for the big prize. (Elizabeth Gibson.)

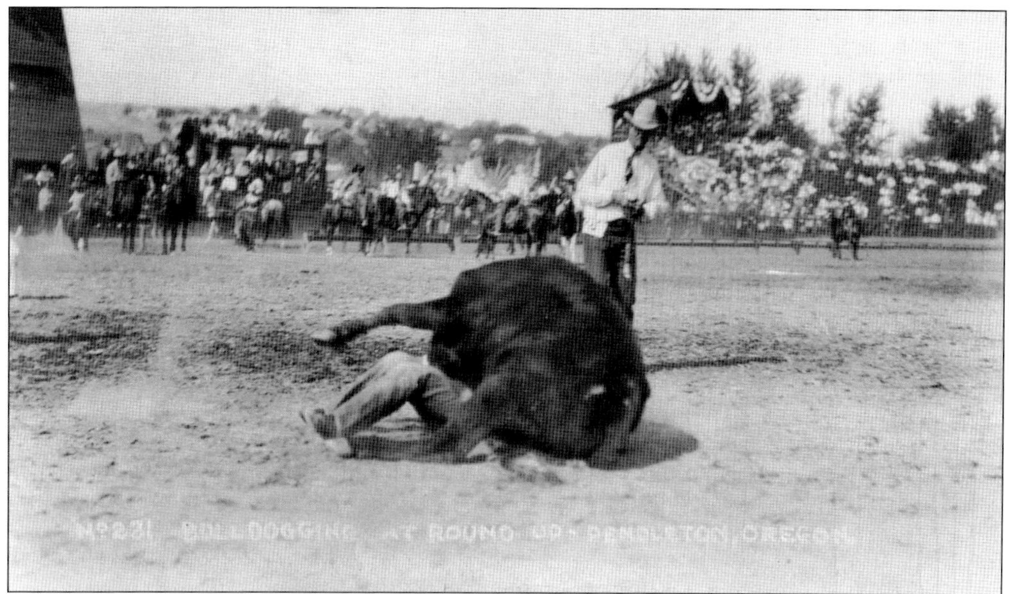

This photograph shows bulldogging gone awry, as this steer wrestler mishandled the steer and was crushed by the animal. Most of the time, riders got up without much injury beyond scratches and bruises, although they were sometimes seriously hurt. (Elizabeth Gibson.)

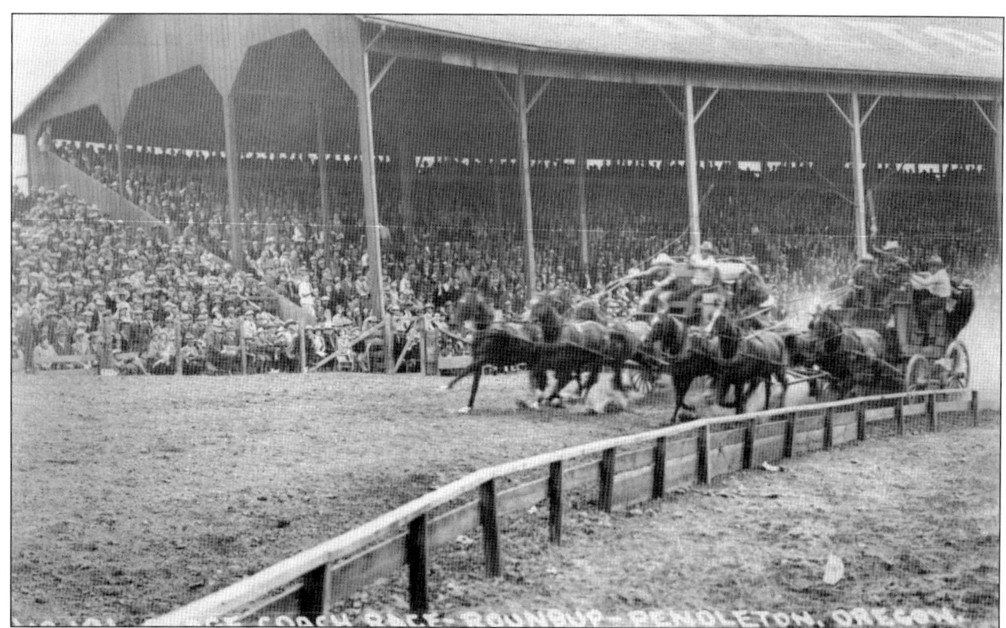

Another early event was the stagecoach race. These races were very popular with the spectators. Many such events were dropped when the Great Depression created financial strain for the Round-Up. (Elizabeth Gibson.)

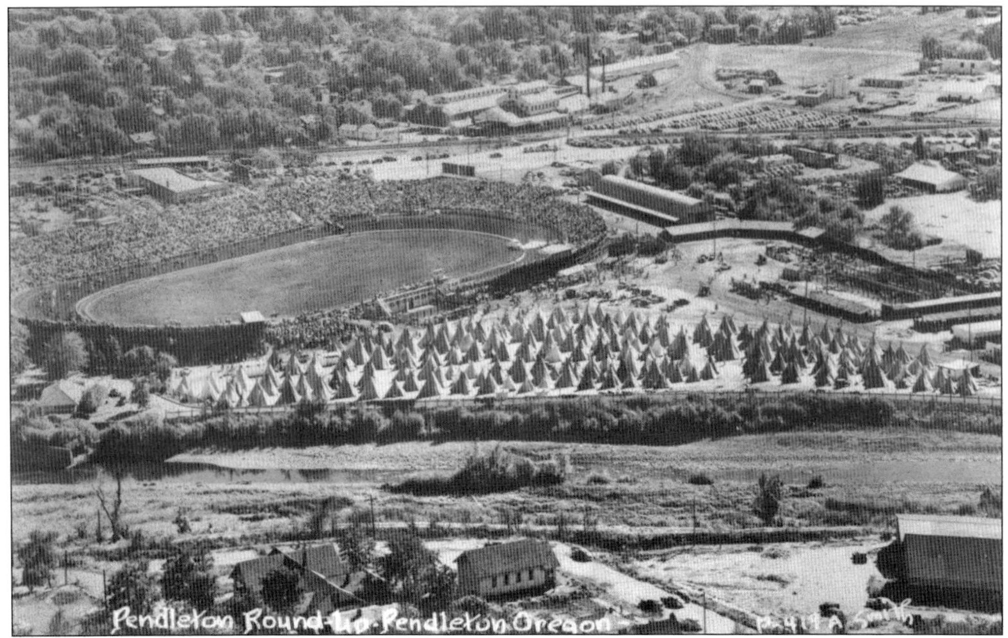

This photograph shows the entire Round-Up arena. The Indian camp is in the foreground, while the main arena is in the center left. The original wooden grandstand burned down in August 1940. This new arena was quickly erected to be ready for that year's event. After that, two more sections were added, for a total seating capacity of 5,000. Because of World War II, the Round-Up was not held in 1942 or 1943. (Elizabeth Gibson.)

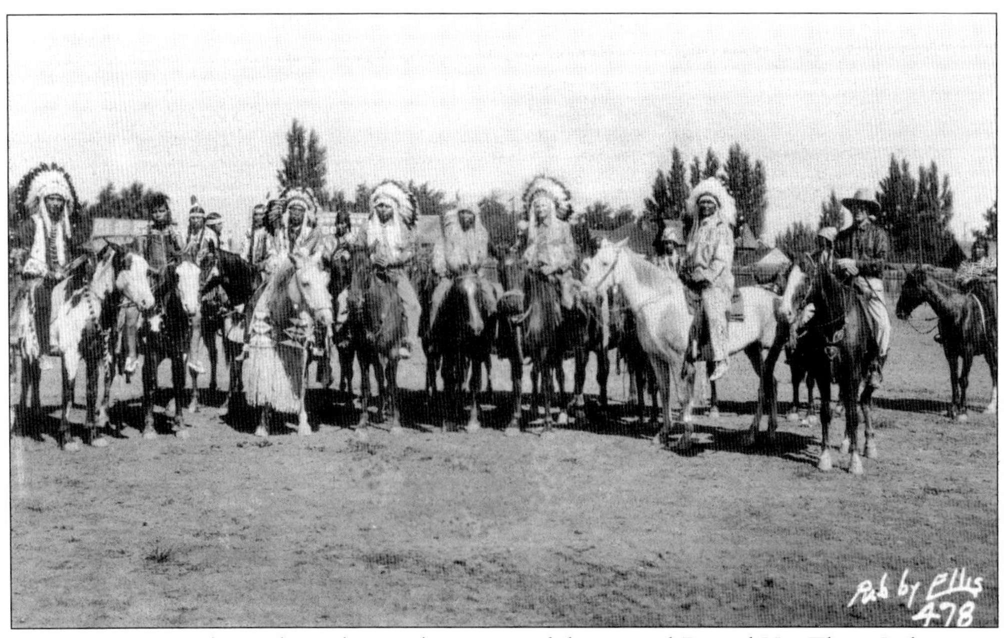

Native Americans have always been a large part of the annual Round-Up. These Indians are dressed in full regalia, probably for a 1950s event. (Tamástslikt Cultural Institute.)

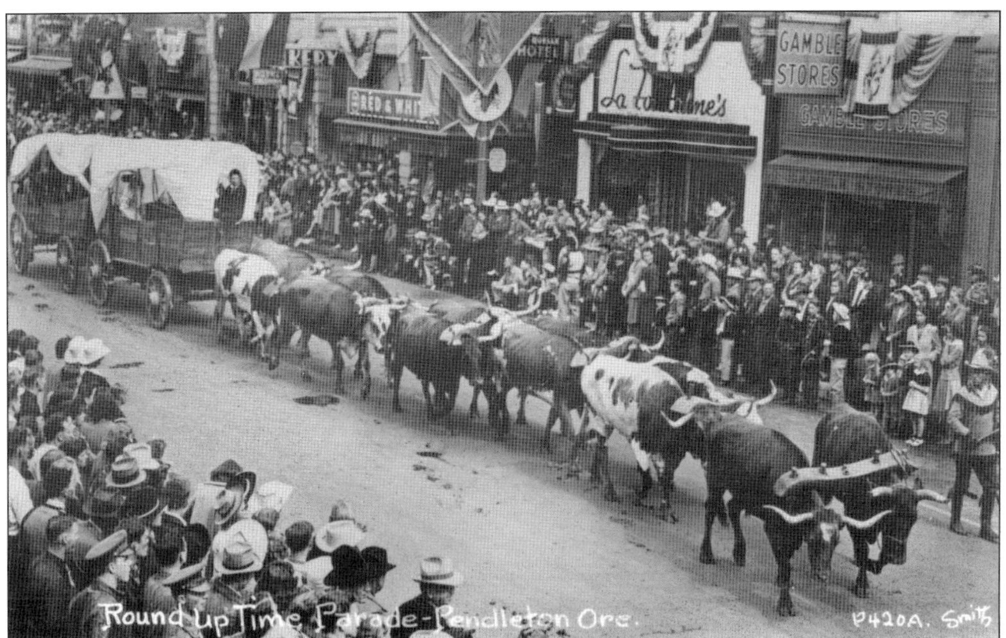

The photograph above of the Westward Ho parade dates from the 1940s. When the arena burned, historic covered wagons were lost. Replicas had to be used in later years. Only a few wagons still remained by the year 2000. (Glen Thiesfeld.)

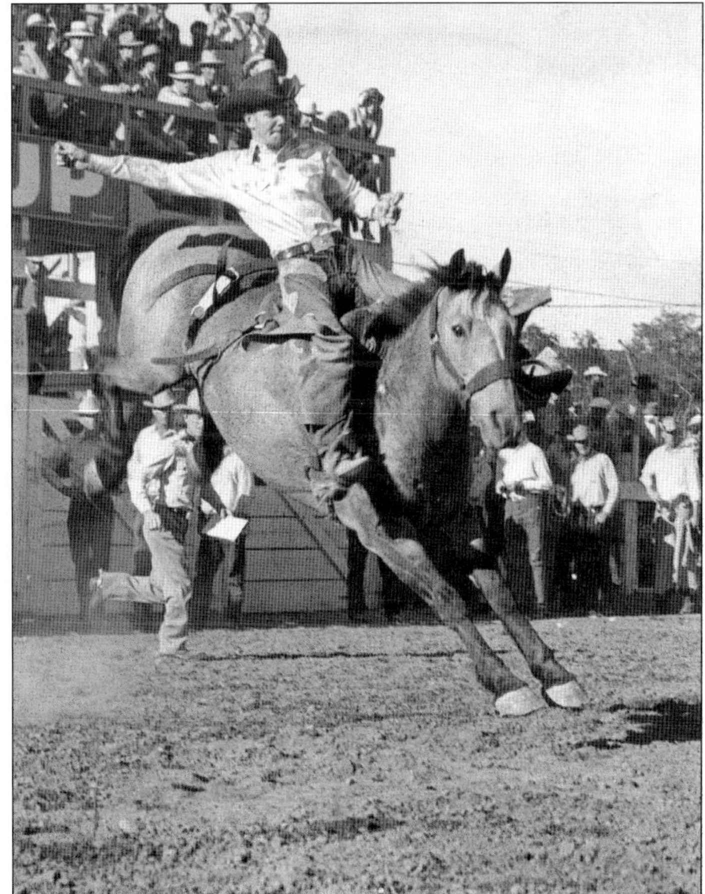

Casey Tibbs is seen here in 1947 riding Reservation at the Round-Up. He was one of only two men to win Round-Up titles in both saddle and bareback bronco riding. He won the bareback bronc riding contest in 1950 and the saddle bronc crown in 1959. In 1949, he was the International Rodeo Association saddle bronc champion. He was the youngest winner at age 29. He died in 1990. (Hamley & Company.)

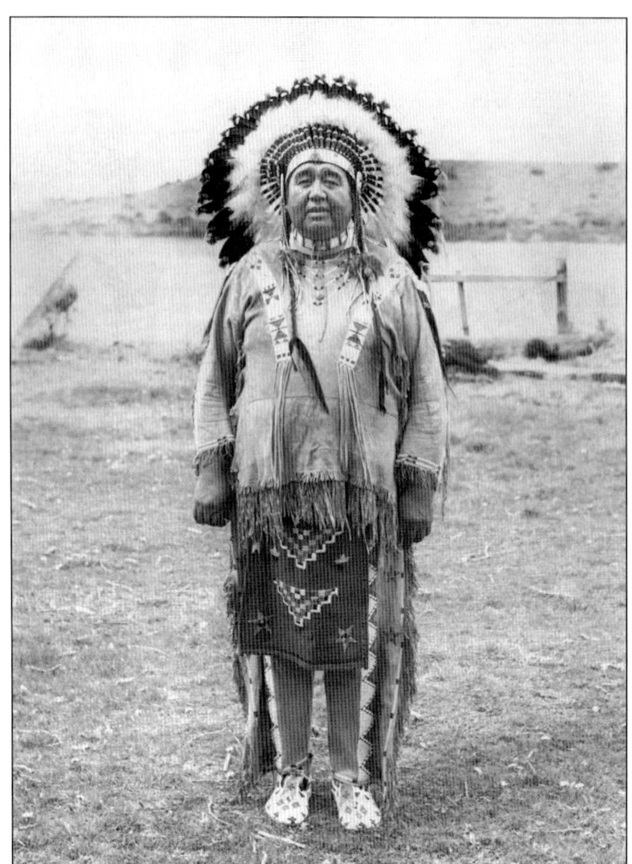

Chief Clarence Burke is one of the most photographed Indians in America. The oldest of three children, he was born at Thornhollow, on the reservation. His father, "Poker Jim" Burke, served as the Round-Up chief for many years. When his father died, Clarence took over the role for the next five decades. His brothers Robert and Richard also competed in Round-Up events. (Fort Walla Walla Museum, Daughters of the Pioneers Collection.)

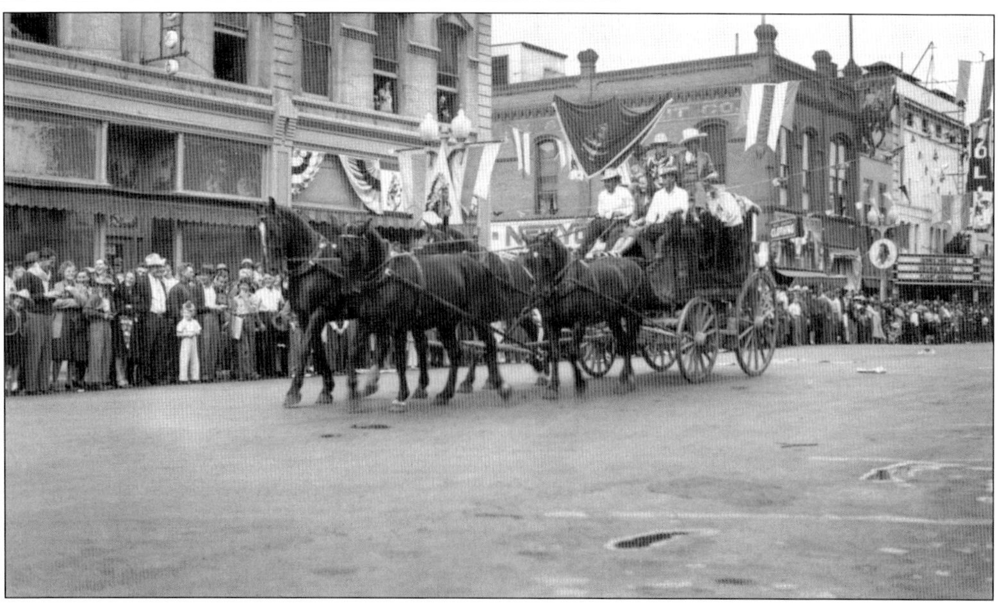

This 1940s Westward Ho parade continues the tradition of only allowing human and horse-drawn vehicles. Participants represented miners, mountain men, cowboys, Indians, and Oregon Trail pioneers. This parade winds its way south on Main Street. (Elizabeth Gibson.)

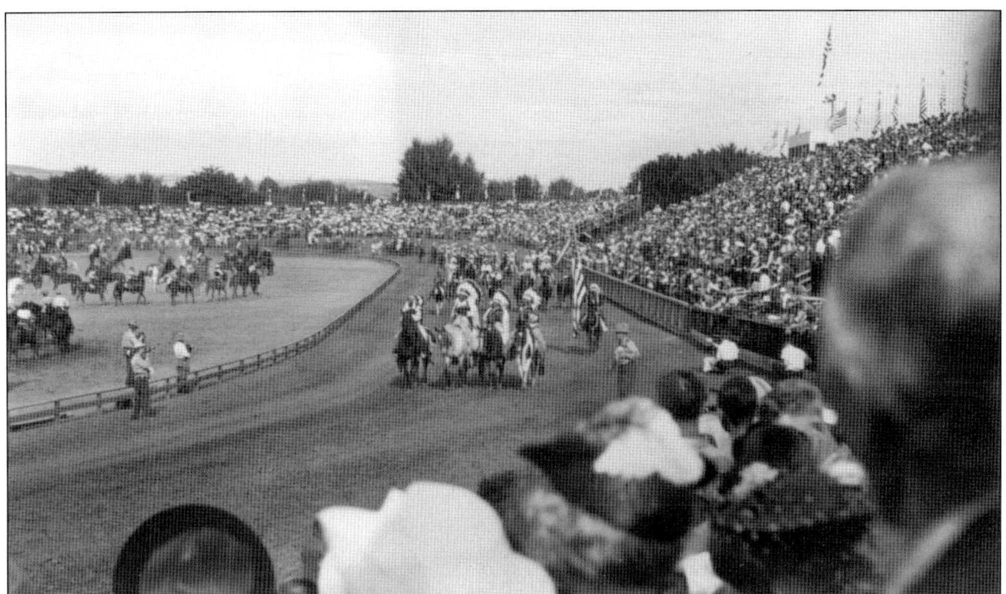

Tribal members enter the arena in parade form in the 1940s. These were the final years of the dirt arena. In 1951, city planners planted grass in the arena so that it could be used throughout the year for high school football games and other events. The Round-Up became the only major rodeo conducted on grass, making it a more challenging field. (Elizabeth Gibson.)

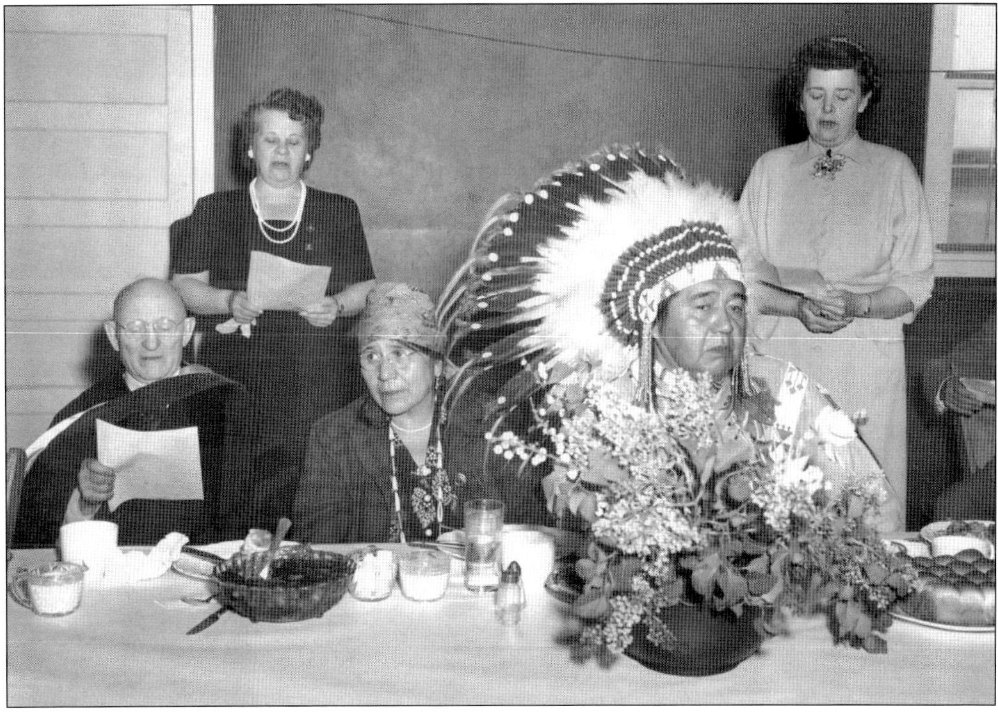

Chief Clarence Burke served as Round-Up chief and attended many Round-Up events. He is seen here at a Round-Up banquet. Burke, Steve Sohappy, and Ron Pond were also responsible for reviving the Indians' Washat faith, a practice that been outlawed by the Indian agent and the churches on the reservation. (Fort Walla Walla Museum.)

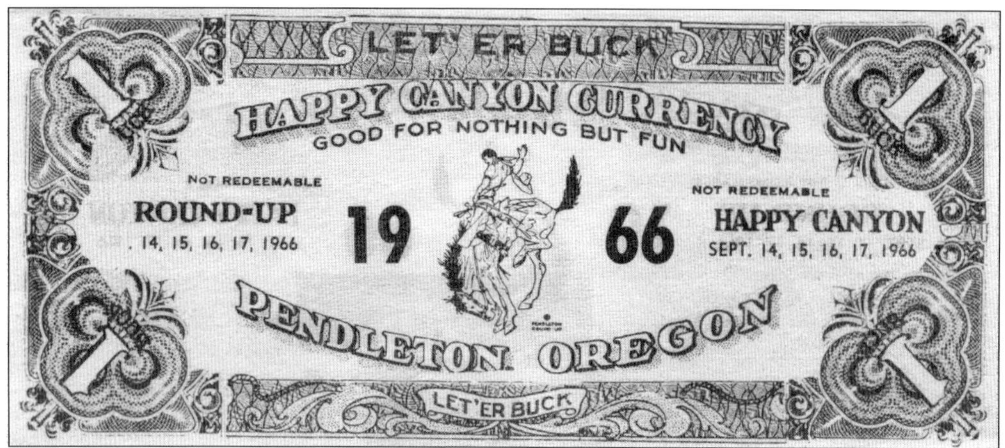

Many souvenirs have been created for the Round-Up over the years. Products from plates to blankets to poker chips have been created to commemorate the event. This is a piece of Pendleton "currency" created to celebrate the event in the 1960s. (Elizabeth Gibson.)

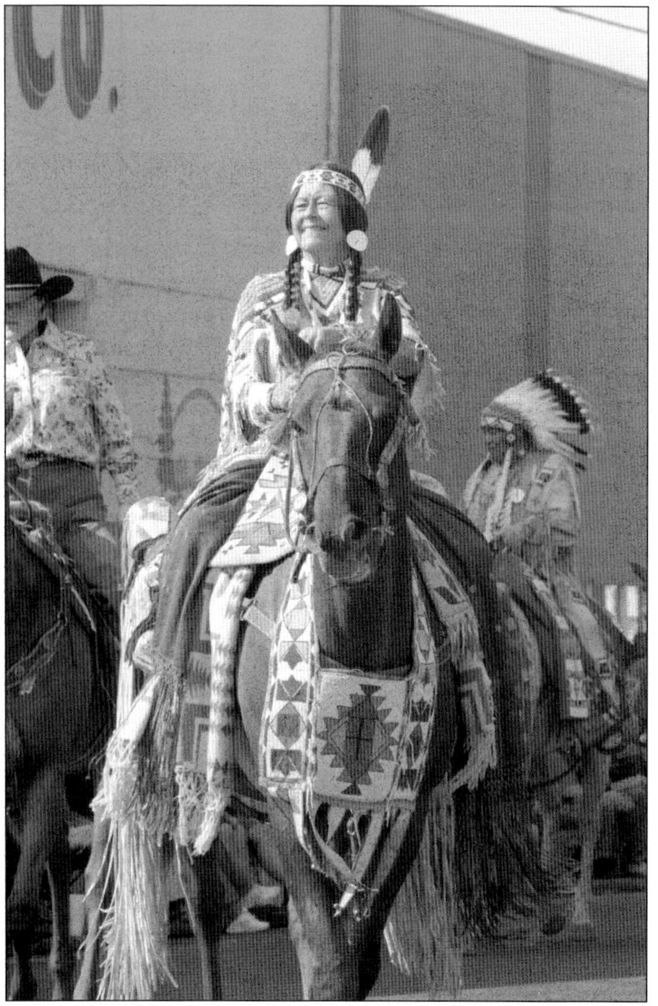

Caroline Motanic Davis is seen here 2012, when she was inducted into the Round-Up and Happy Canyon Hall of Fame. She first won honors in 1955 when she became the first Happy Canyon princess. She participated in the Happy Canyon pageant from 1959 to 2012 and never missed a year. She had five children, all with her first husband, Douglas Minthorn. In her later years, she married Gilbert A. Davis, who preceded her in death in 2008. (Tamástslikt Cultural Institute.)

Six

The City

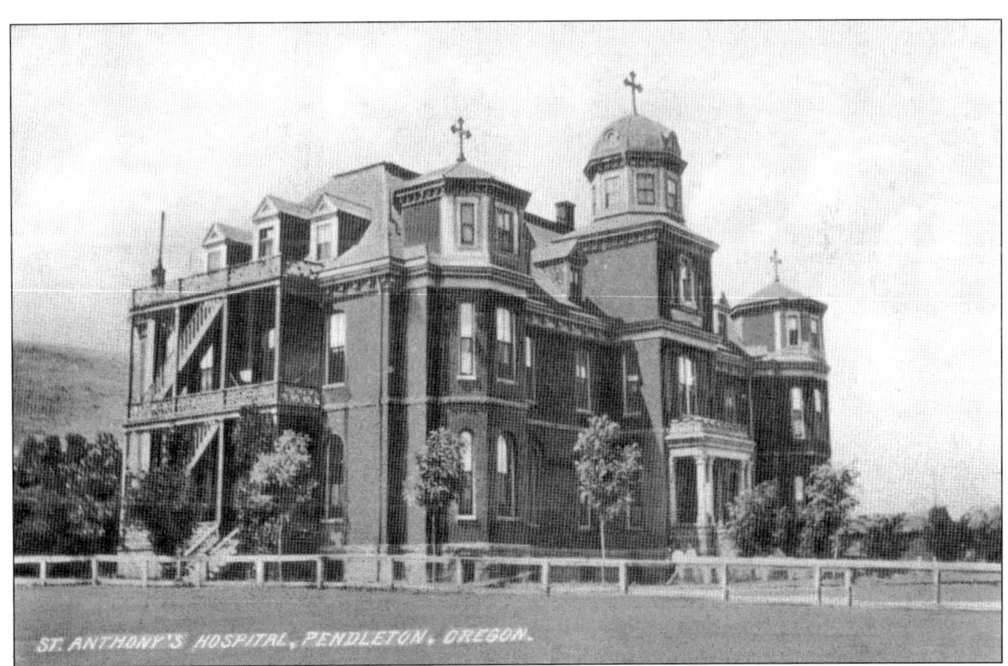

Ground was broken on St. Anthony's Hospital in 1901. Catholic sisters led by Mother Stanislaus collected the money to build it, and it was dedicated in 1902. It ultimately cost $75,000. A nursing school was added in 1909. The hospital has been expanded many times over the years and still stands on Court Avenue. (Elizabeth Gibson.)

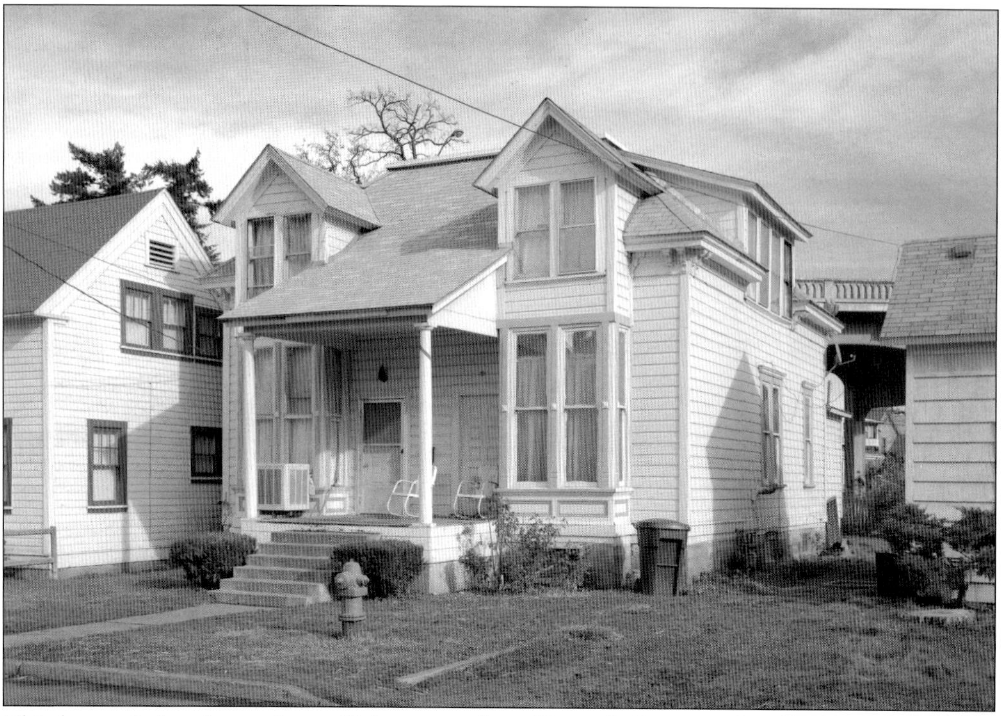

This house, belonging to James Nelson, stood on Eleventh Street in Pendleton. It is a typical home in that area. (Historic American Buildings Survey, Library of Congress.)

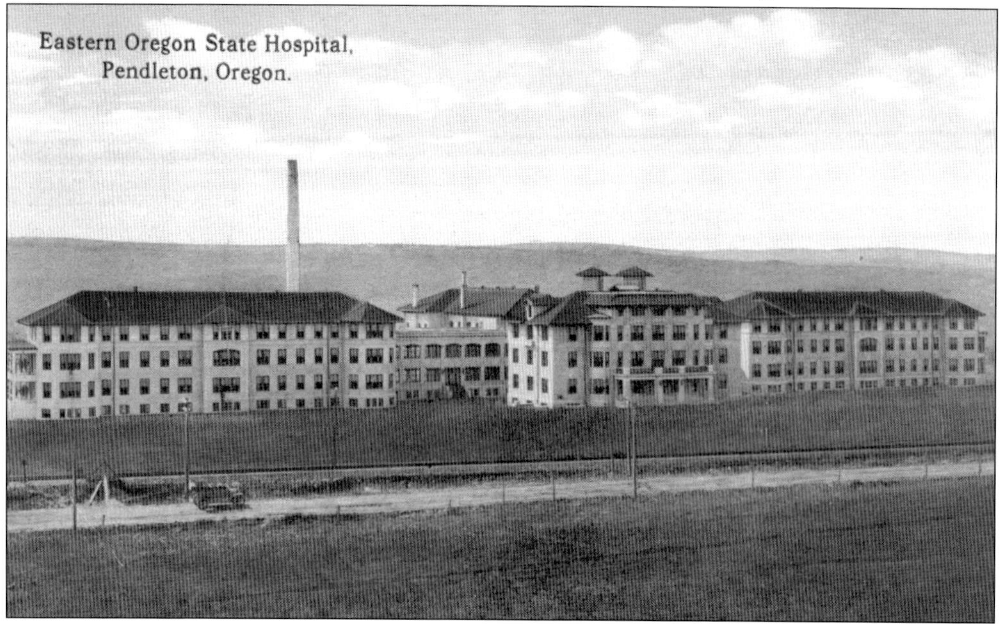

Eastern Oregon State Hospital opened in 1913. The hospital cared for the state's mentally disabled. When it opened, 325 patients were sent from Salem. The residents of the facility operated a dairy and a farm. The local Catholic diocese also provided a chaplain for residents. The facility was eventually closed, which devastated the local economy. In 1985, the old building was reopened as a correctional facility. (Elizabeth Gibson.)

This courthouse was built in 1888 in the French Renaissance style on Fourth Street on land donated by Aura Goodwin, the widow of Moses Goodwin, who had originally donated the land to use for a college. The new building cost about $80,000, including the furnishings. The courthouse contained a supreme court, a district court, a jail, offices, four cupolas, and a central clock tower. (Elizabeth Gibson.)

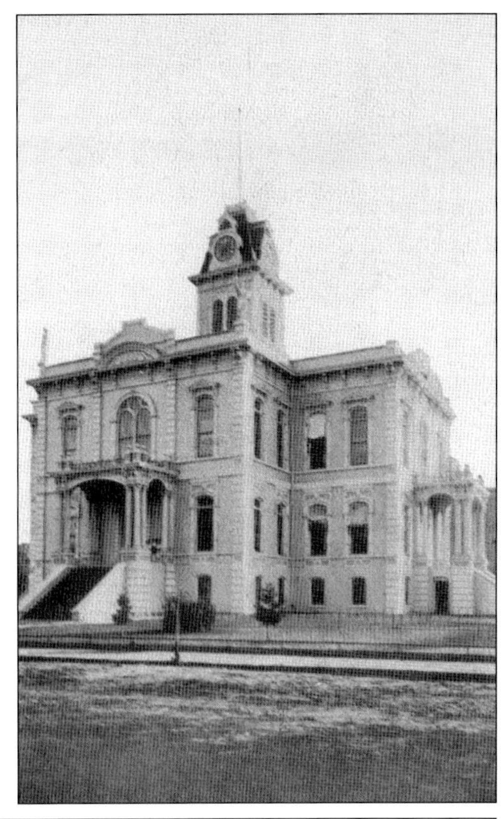

The panorama below dates from the 1890s. Such panoramic maps were commonly made for growing cities around the United States. At this time, the town was confined to the Umatilla River valley; housing had not yet crept up the surrounding hills. The map shows the original names of the streets, which reflected the Southern Democratic leanings of early residents. In 1940, streets were renamed alphabetically and numerically. (Elizabeth Gibson.)

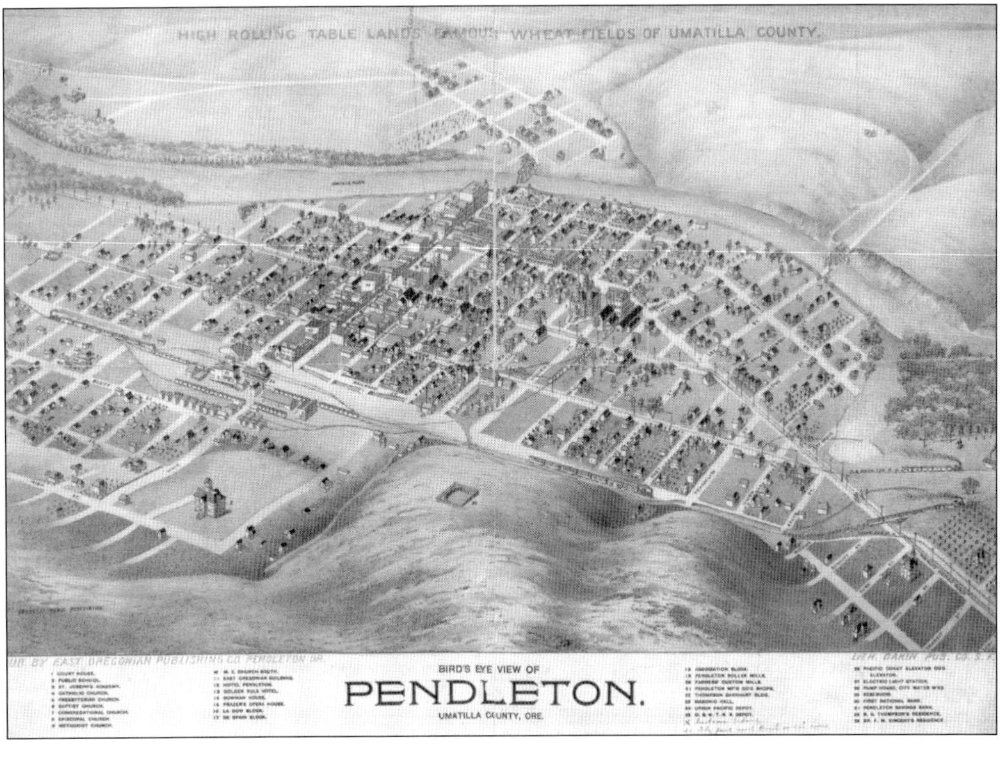

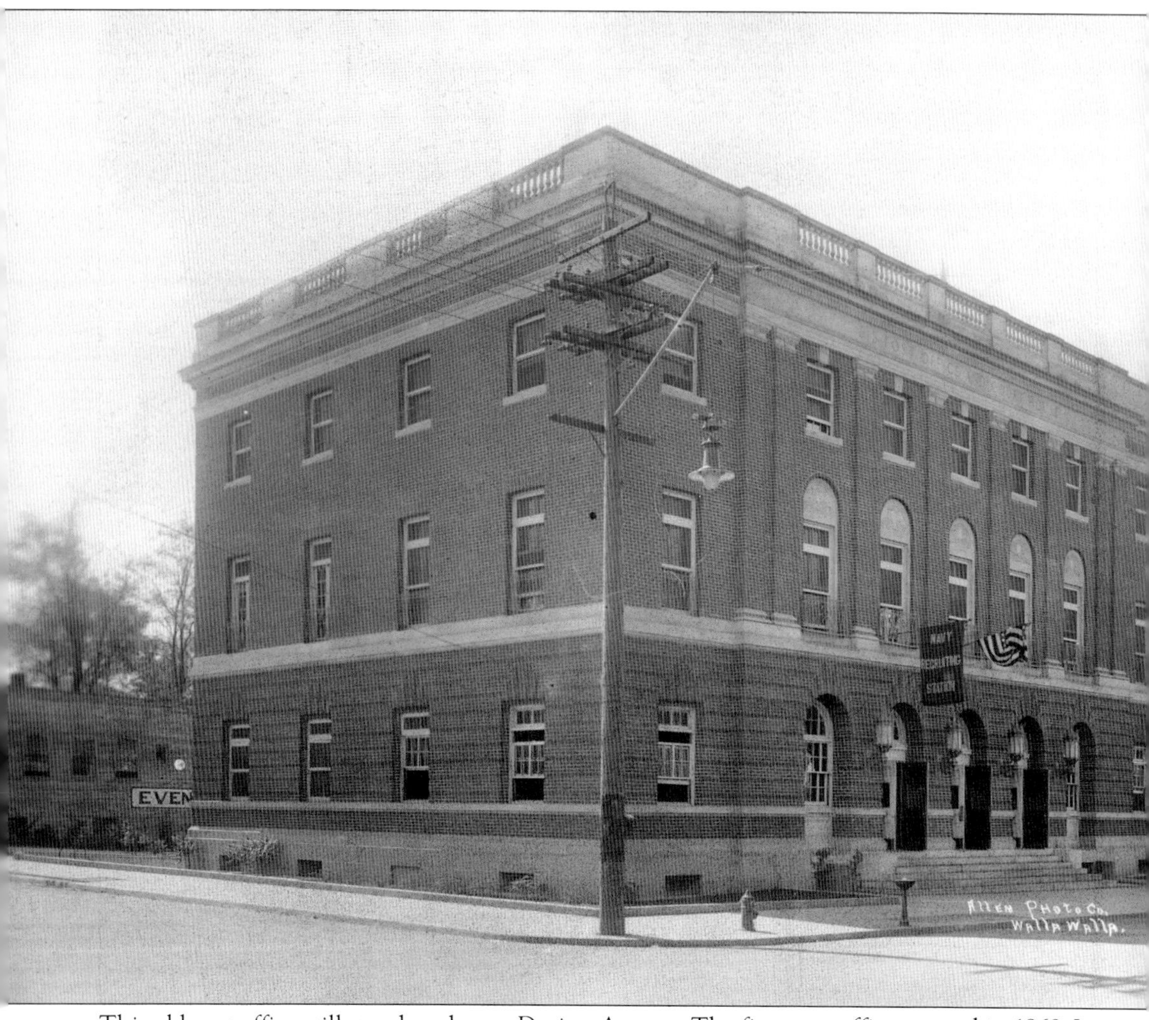

This old post office still stands today on Dorion Avenue. The first post office opened in 1869. It changed locations about eight times before finally coming to rest at this location in 1916. Thomas J. Tweedy was postmaster at the time. The building is an example of Georgian-style architecture, with seven bays and a parapet. The supervising architect was Oscar Wenderoth. The building is listed in the National Register of Historic Places. The building was renamed the John F. Kilkenny United States Post Office and Courthouse in 1984. Kilkenny was a federal judge who practiced law in Pendleton and a past president of the Happy Canyon Board of Directors. (National Archives and Records Administration.)

The first city hall was built in 1908 on Dorion Street. The fire and police departments were housed in the building. These police officers served in 1928. They are, from left to right, (first row) police chief R.B. Montgomery, Maj. L.J. McAtee, and day patrolman J.L. Gammel; (second row) city traffic officer F.F. Hutton, officer Charles Lemons, and night patrolman D.C. Gurdane. (Pendleton Police Department.)

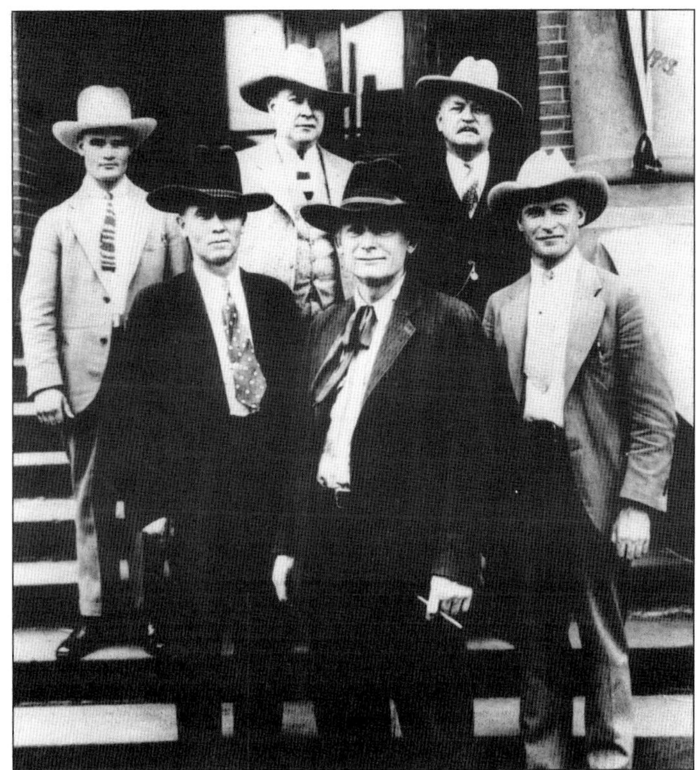

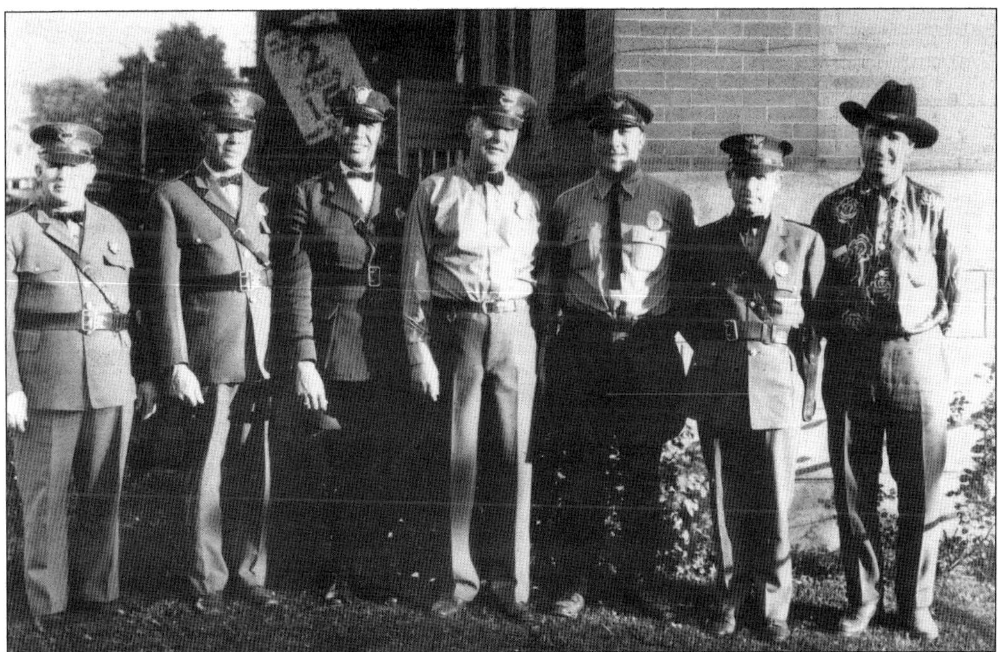

This photograph was taken in front of the city hall building between 1930 and 1932. From left to right are city officer T. Skinner, two unidentified men, police chief Charles Lemons, officer Buck Lieuallen of the Oregon State Police, unidentified, and federal agent Charles Hoskins. (Pendleton Police Department.)

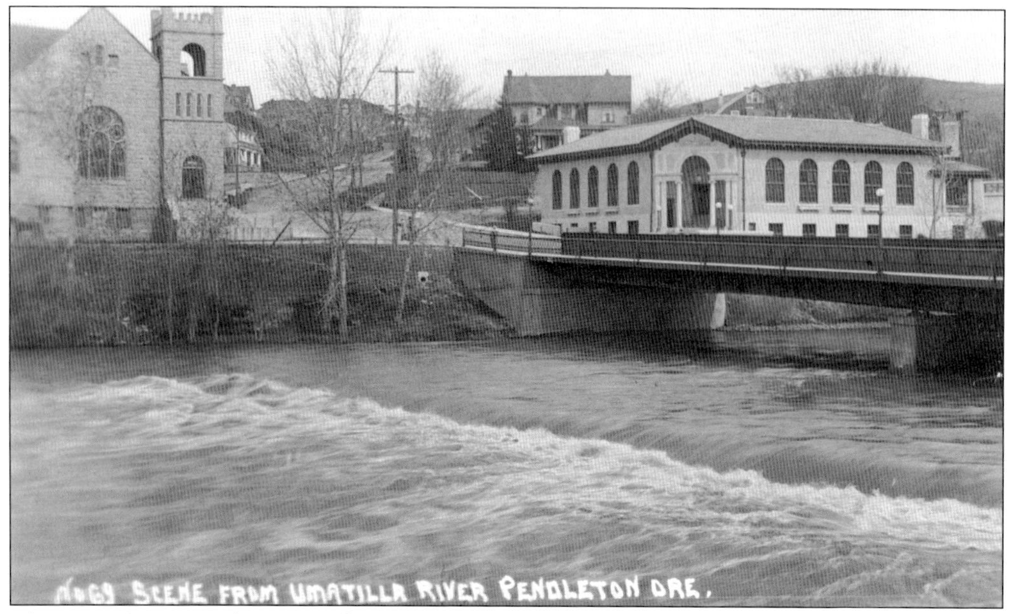

The Main Street Bridge is seen here around 1929. The new Christian church is on the left. To the right is the Carnegie library, which was funded and built by philanthropist Andrew Carnegie in 1915. Both buildings still stand today. The library is now used by the Pendleton Center for the Arts. (Elizabeth Gibson.)

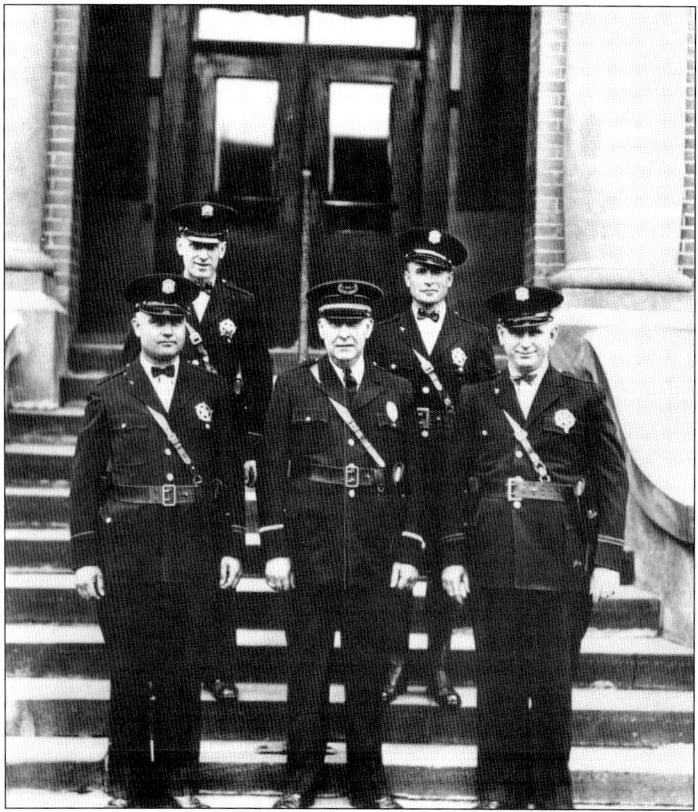

These police officers posing outside the city hall building served in 1934. They are, from left to right, officers Hogan, Charles Lemons, Bogan, Hank Arkell, and F.F. Hutton. Lemons was the police chief at the time. (Pendleton Police Department.)

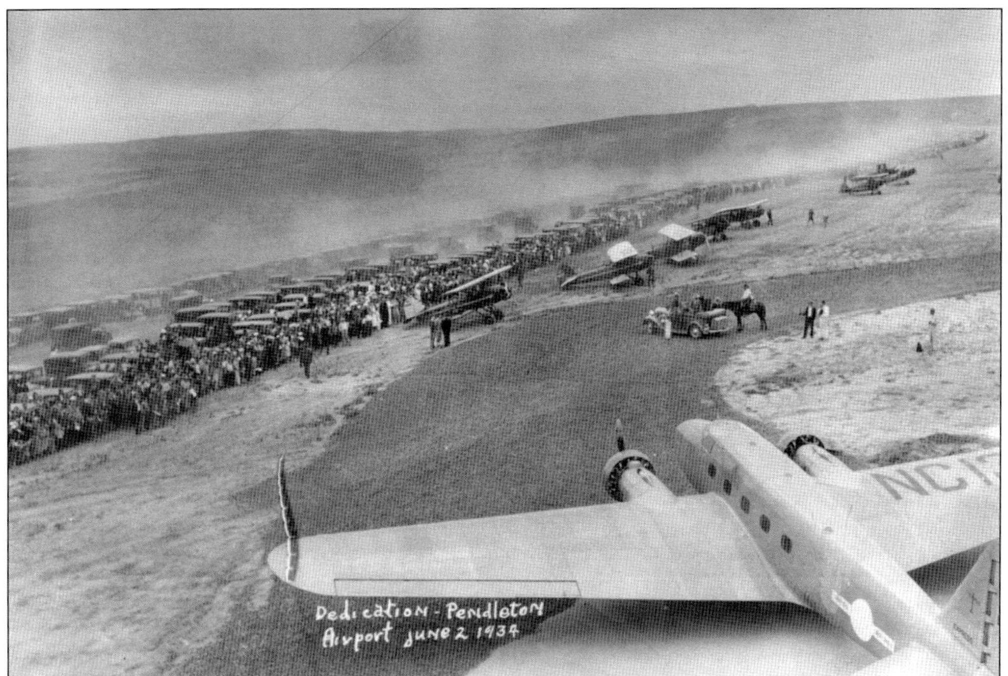

The new city airport was dedicated on June 2, 1934. The facility cost $150,000, including a $65,000 administration building. A daylong program included a large parade that wove its way through town to celebrate the event. Cowboys, Indians, Pony Express riders, and other Western characters participated. The mayor was also on hand, as were several news agencies. Tex Rankin performed airplane stunts, and Eddie B. Winfield performed a parachute jump. (Umatilla County Historical Society, 1998.022.002.)

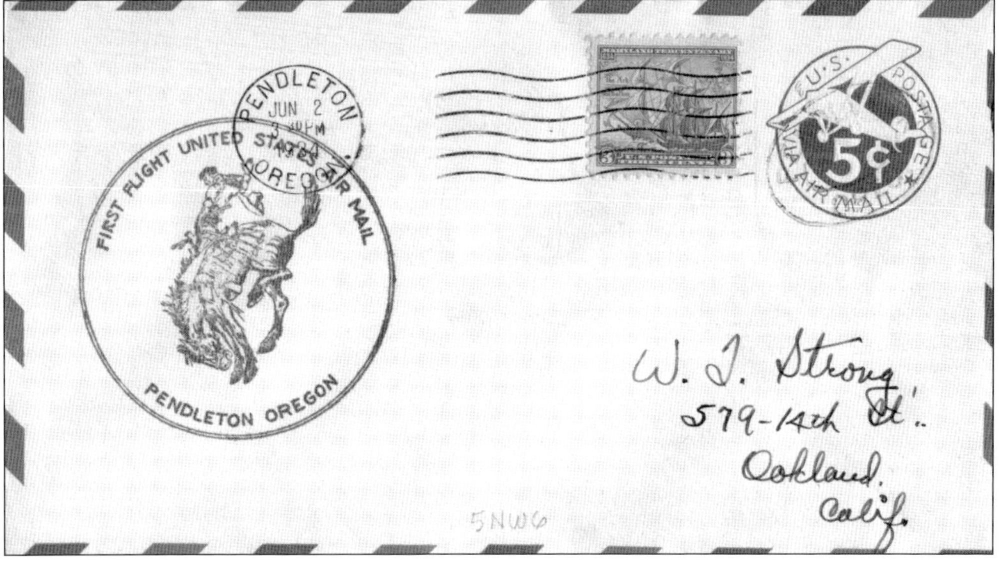

The first airmail also left the airport on June 2, 1934. The postmark contained a special cachet that commemorated the 25th anniversary of the Pendleton Round-Up. A special letter was sent to Pres. Franklin Roosevelt inviting him to the 25th anniversary celebration of the Pendleton Round-Up. The first mail was brought to the plane by an old-time stagecoach. (Elizabeth Gibson.)

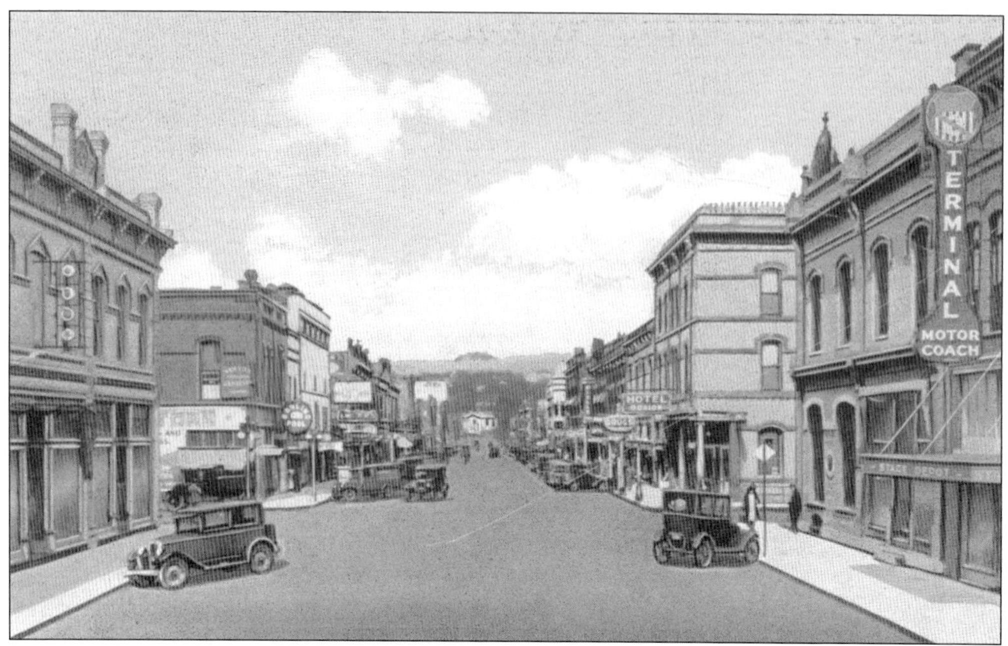

Main Street is seen here around 1936, looking north toward Court Street. The streets had been paved by this time, and power poles visible in earlier photographs had been moved or relocated underground. (Glen Thiesfeld.)

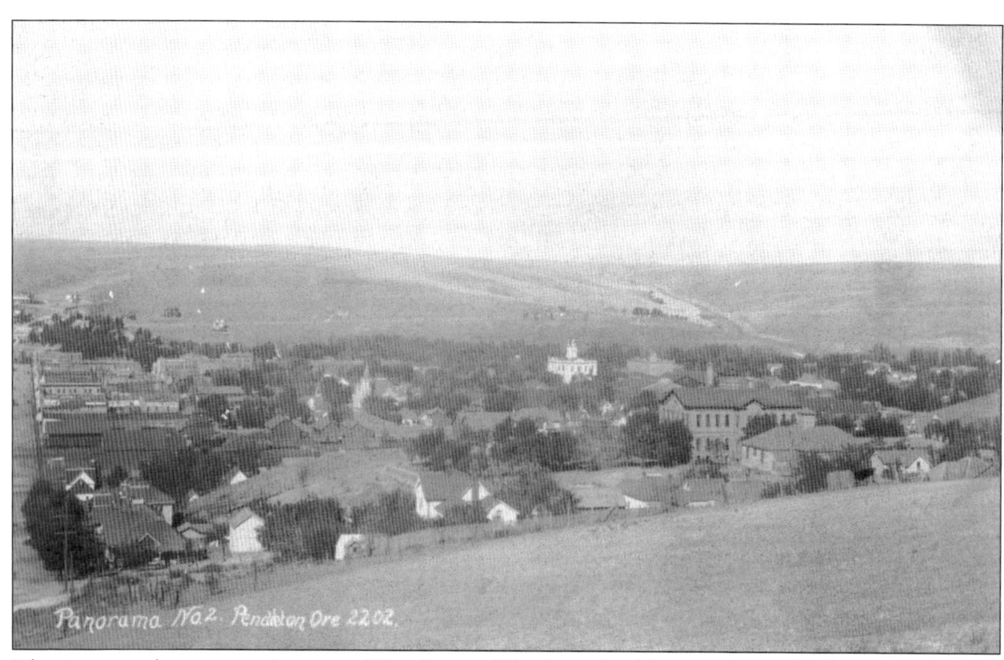

This is an early panoramic view of Pendleton. The large building in the right foreground is the Pendleton Academy. The white building in the background is the county courthouse. The church in the center is the Methodist church. (Elizabeth Gibson.)

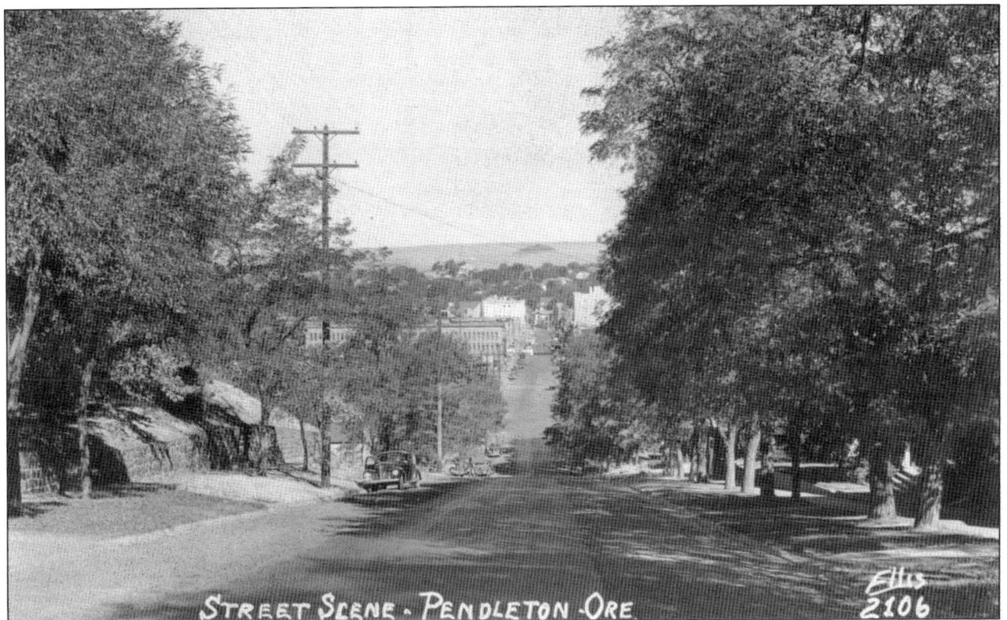

This residential street is the north end of Main Street as it leaves the downtown area. The photograph dates from the 1940s. Many of the streets in this section of town have similar orientations and designs as they climb up the north hill. (Elizabeth Gibson.)

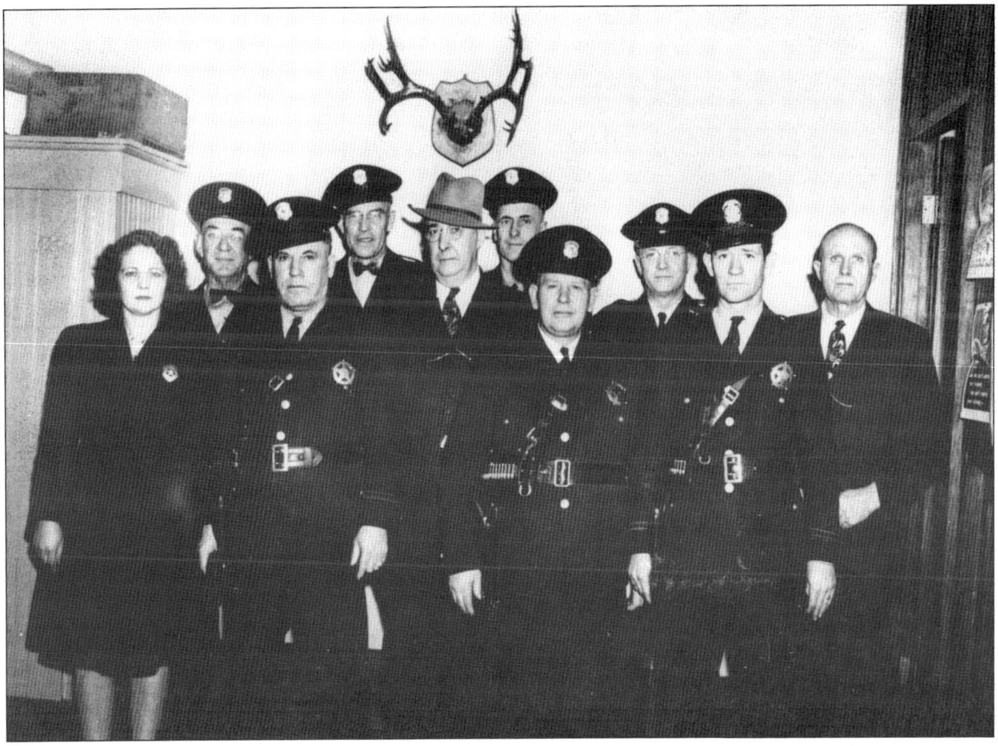

This photograph shows local officers in 1944. They are, from left to right, (first row) Fern Masters (matron), D. Bush, T. Skinner, and unidentified; (second row) E. Brubbs, unidentified, police chief Charles Lemons, Hank Arkell, unidentified, and T. Thomas. (Pendleton Police Department.)

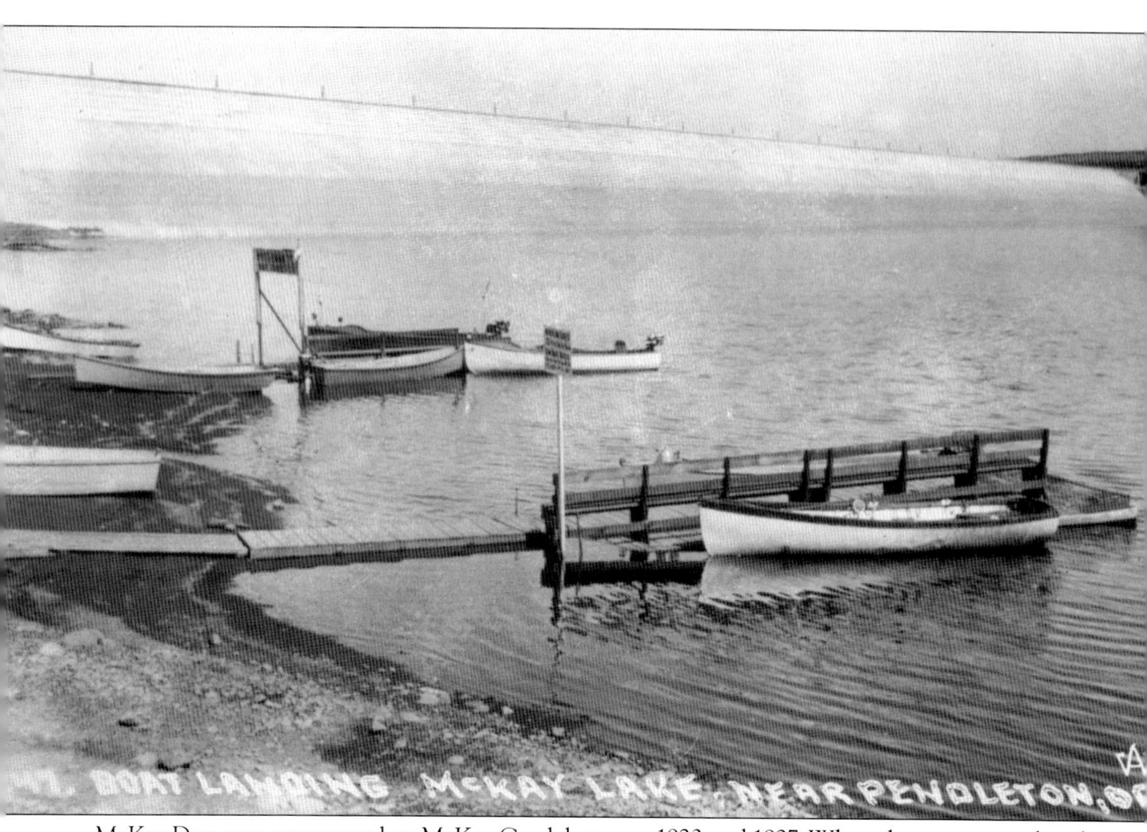

McKay Dam was constructed on McKay Creek between 1923 and 1927. When the gates were closed in 1927, this reservoir of 73,800 acre-feet was created. Originally, the purpose of the reservoir was to supply water to the Stanfield and Westland Irrigation Districts. It was built by the US Bureau of Reclamation. The reservoir and creek are named for Dr. William C. McKay, an early pioneer in the Pendleton area who settled near the mouth of McKay Creek about 1851. The place was originally called Houtama. McKay died in Pendleton in 1893. (Elizabeth Gibson.)

This photograph was taken outside of the city hall building on Court Street in 1946. Sgt. R. Bond shows off the department's new three-wheel motorcycle to police chief Charles Lemons (standing). (Pendleton Police Department.)

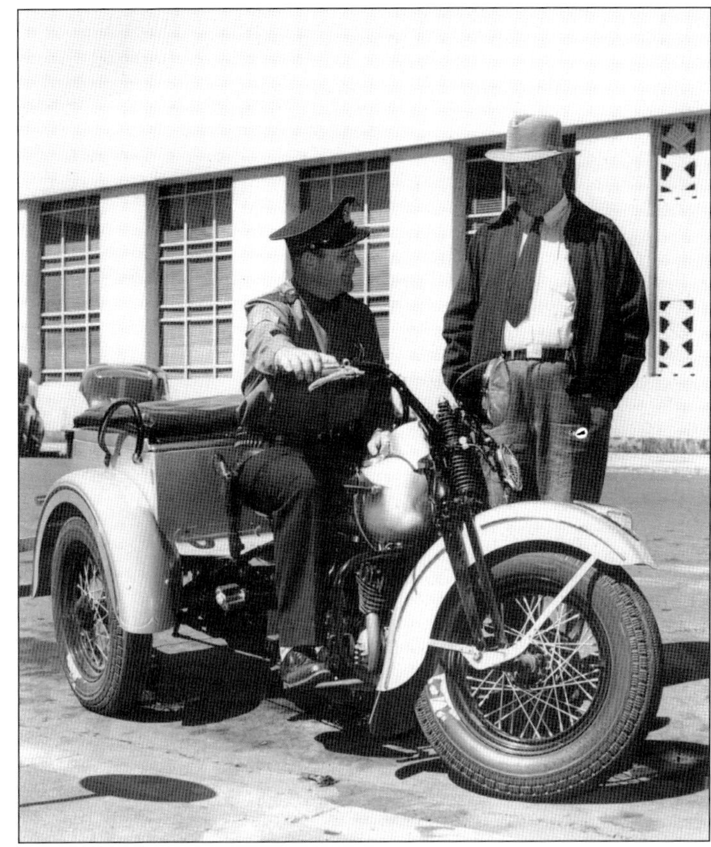

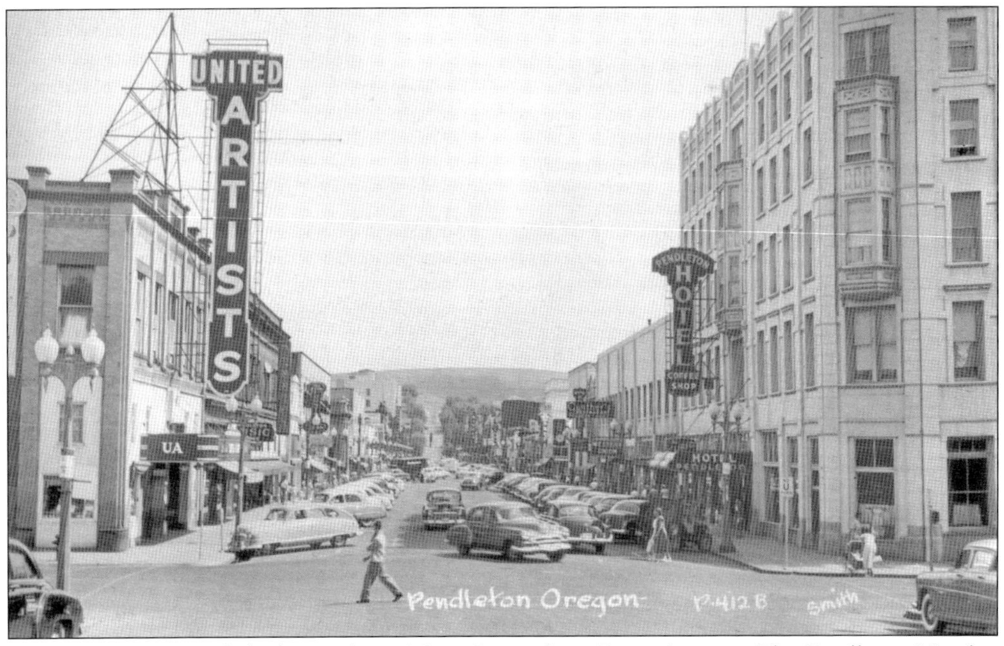

This later photograph looks south on Main Street from Byers Avenue. The Pendleton Hotel is on the right. (Elizabeth Gibson.)

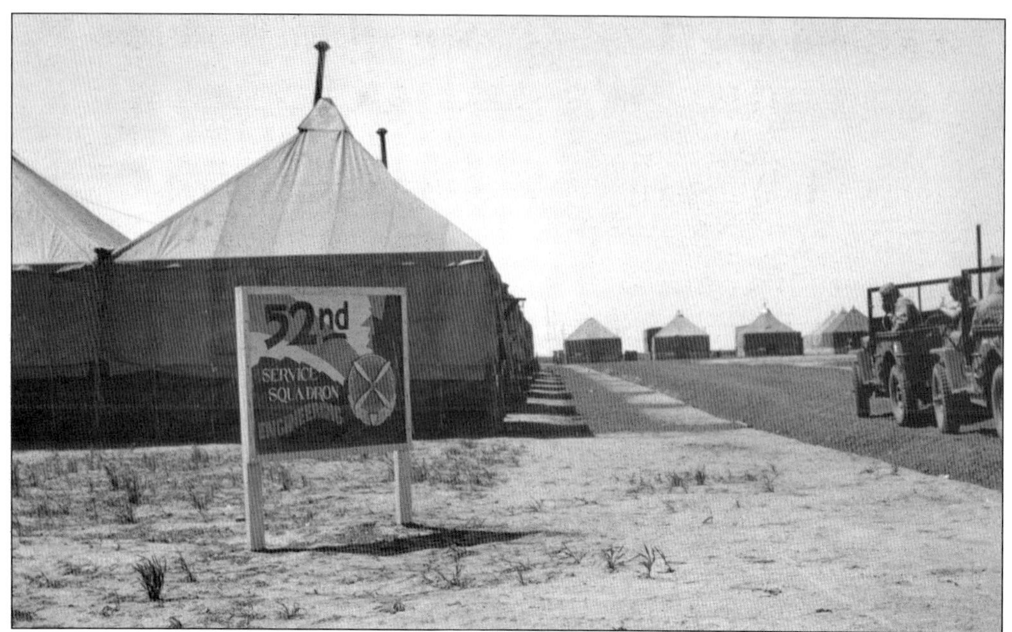

In 1941, a military airbase was established in Pendleton that would become the home of the 52nd Squadron. There was nothing but wheat fields in the area before construction began. W.D. Smith Co., Inc., was the chief contractor, working under the direction of the Army Corps of Engineers. By July, the base was ready for partial occupation, and several hundred men moved in. (Umatilla County Historical Society, 1991.034.015.)

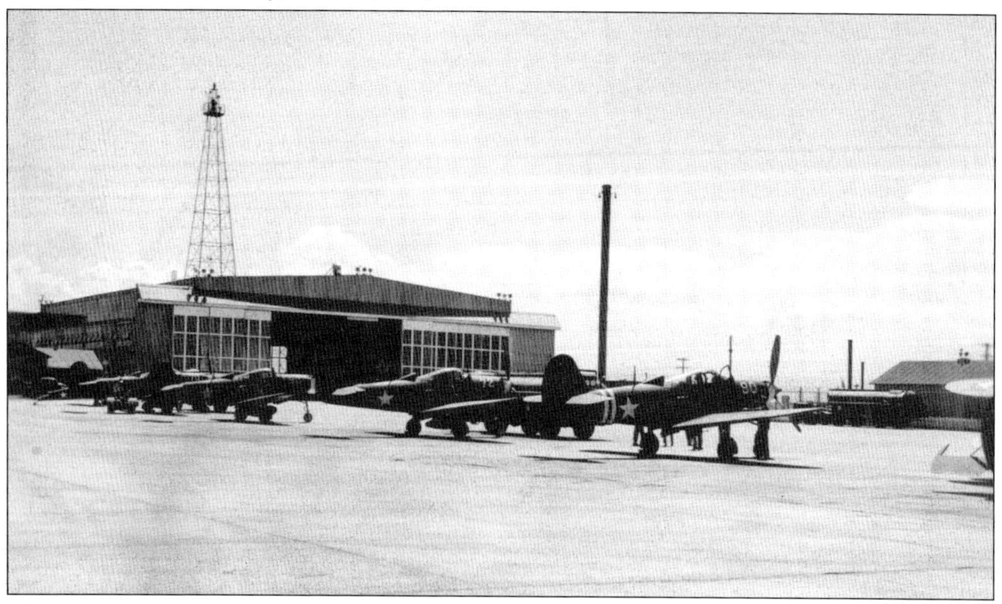

The 17th Bombardment Group, under the command of Lt. Col. Walter R. Peck, and the 89th Reconnaissance Squadron were housed at the airbase. It was rated a class-four airport, which meant runways were longer than 5,000 feet. The 17th Medium Bomb Group was also stationed at Pendleton field following the Japanese attack on Pearl Harbor. From this group, flying ace James B. Doolittle selected his crew for his daring raid on Japan. (Umatilla County Historical Society, 1991.034.026.)

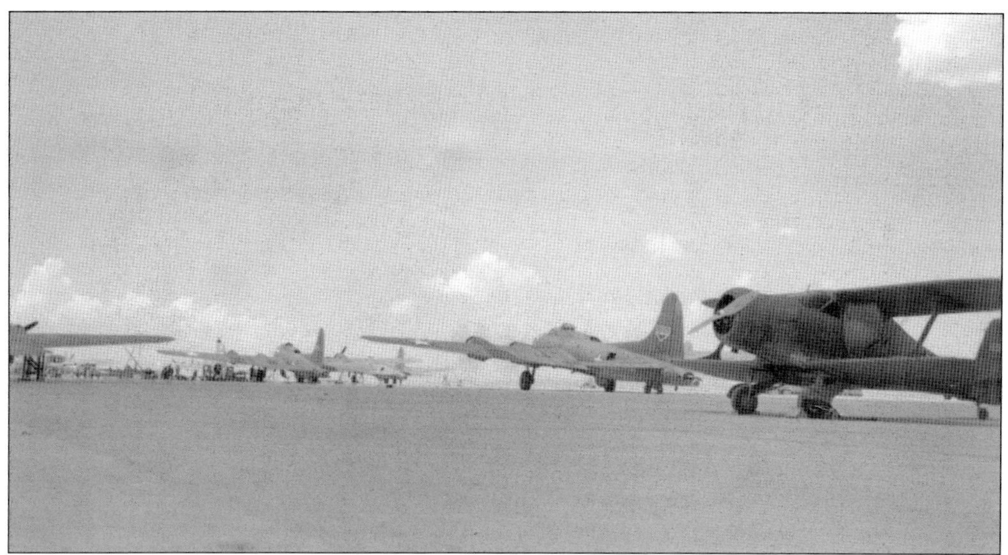

The airbase, which would ultimately consist of 127 buildings, typically used B-25 bombers. During this time period, Lt. Gen. Curtis LeMay, who was later the chief of staff of the Air Force, was awarded the Distinguished Flying Cross. (Umatilla County Historical Society, 1991.034.027.)

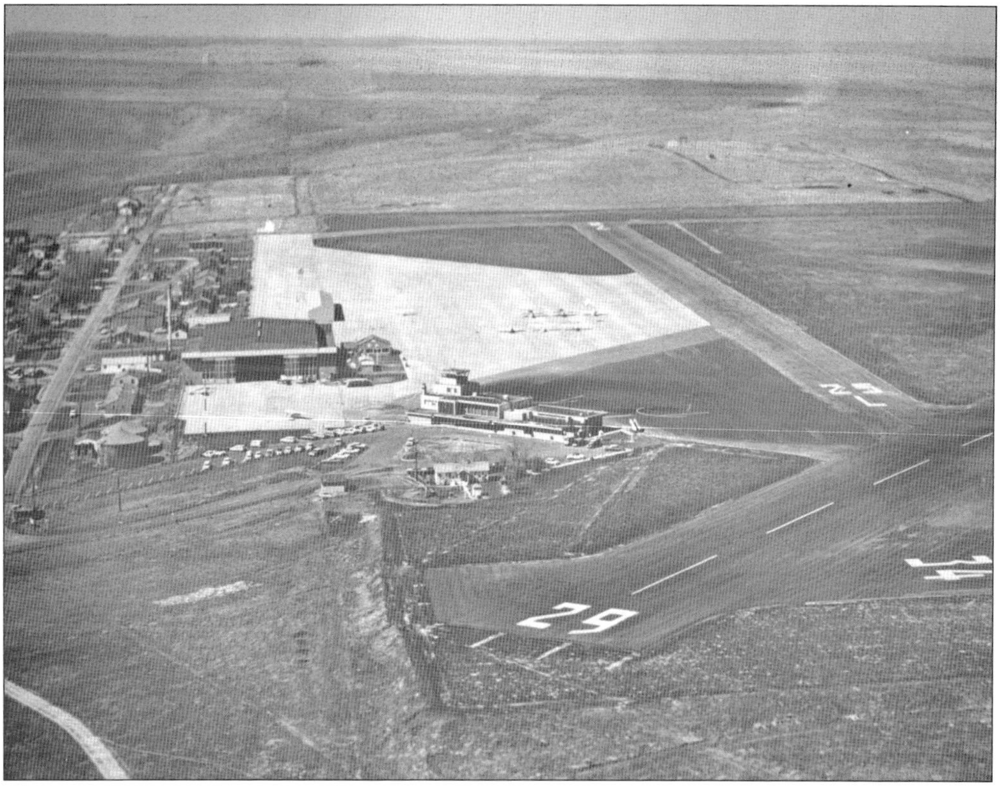

This aerial view of the airbase shows its size. The base would ultimately house 303 officers and 2,218 enlisted men. The base included a post office, a chapel, a recreation building, a warehouse, an officers' club, and bombsight storage. The base commander was Col. Frank M. Wright. (Umatilla County Historical Society, 1992.040.005.)

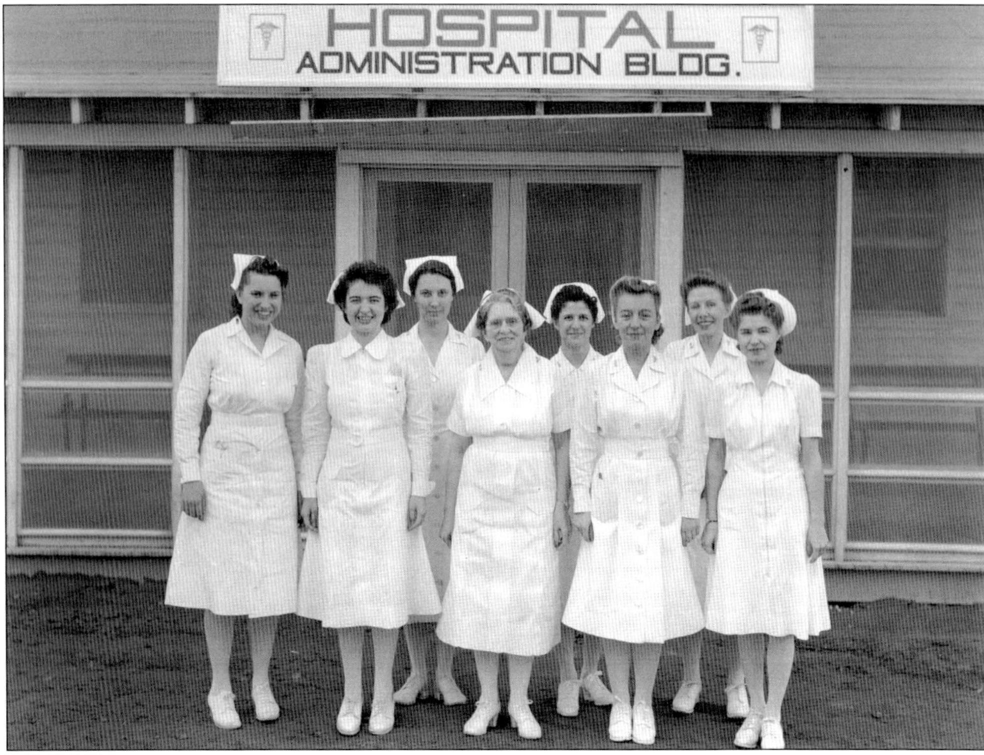

Nurses served the airbase as well. Note the slight differences in the uniforms worn by the women. These were likely the uniforms established by the various teaching hospitals under which they trained. (Umatilla County Historical Society, 2000.100.017.)

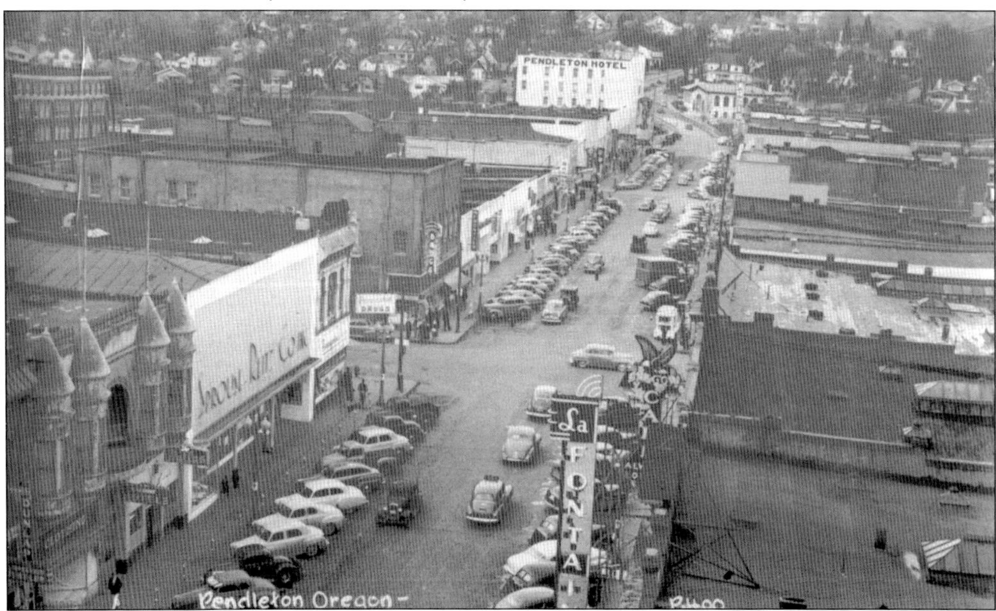

This overhead view of Main Street was taken in the 1940s. A Sprouse Reitz store is in the left foreground. The Pendleton Hotel is still standing in the center background. Today, there is only parallel parking on this street. Also, few of the old marquees still line the street. (Elizabeth Gibson.)

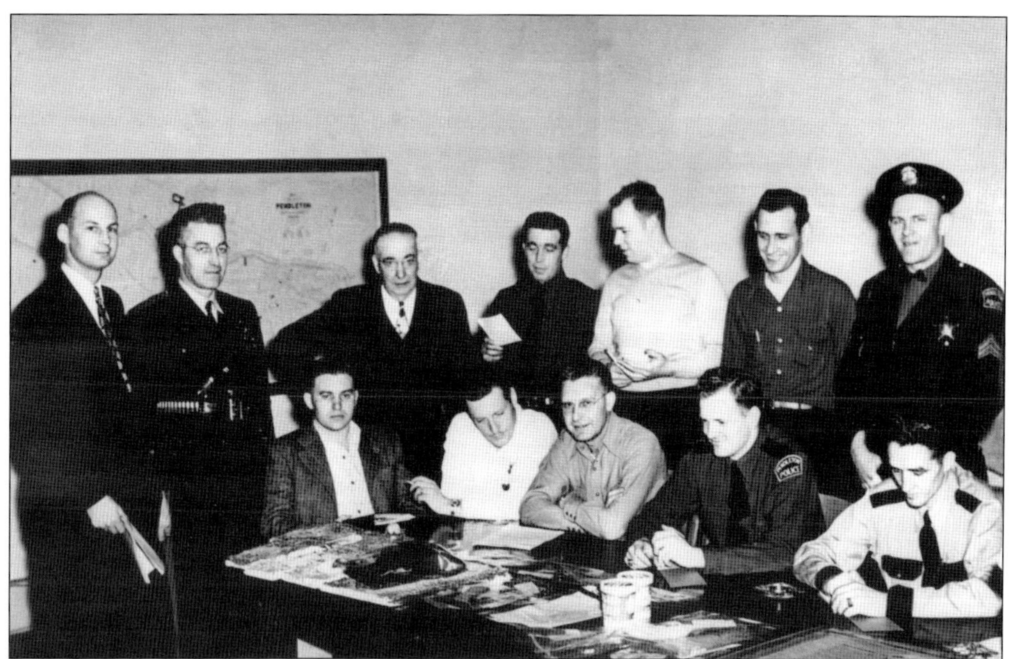

These officers are attending a training class in the use of evidence and plaster casts in 1948. They are, from left to right, (seated) T. Skinner, unidentified, W. Silvey, T. Nielsen, and unidentified; (standing) unidentified, Sgt. R. Smith of the Oregon State Patrol, police chief Charles Lemons, J. Smith, two unidentified men, and Sgt. R. Bond. (Pendleton Police Department.)

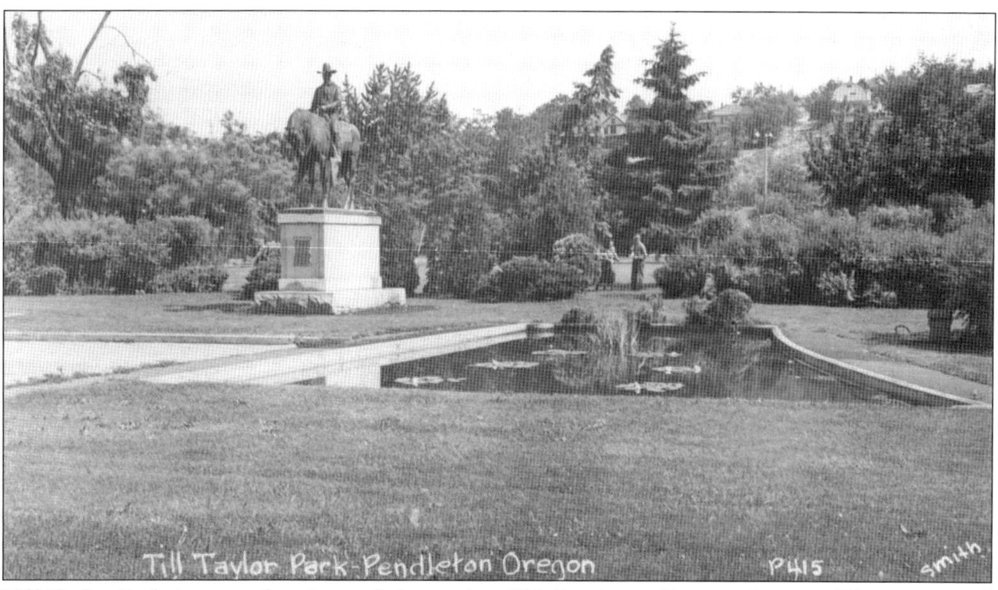

Till Taylor Park is a popular city park located at 700 Southeast Dorion Avenue. The statue and park honor the memory of Tilman Taylor, the Umatilla County sheriff who was killed in the line of duty in 1920. Taylor was also one of the founders of the Pendleton Round-Up. The park and statue were dedicated in his honor in 1929. The sculpture was designed by sculptor Alexander Phimister Proctor. (Elizabeth Gibson.)

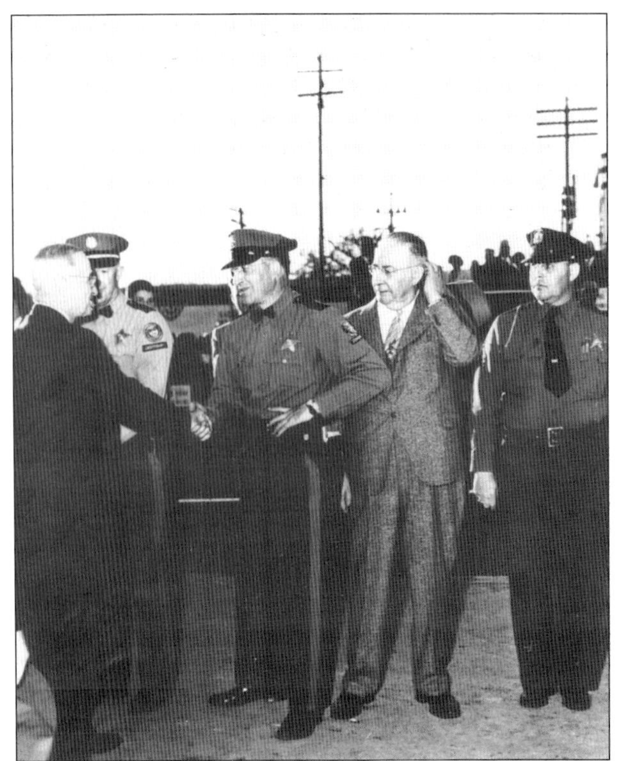

On May 10, 1950, Pres. Harry S. Truman (far left) visited Pendleton. Greeting him were, from left to right, Lieutenant Harrel of the Oregon State Patrol, Sergeant Smith, Pendleton police chief Charles Lemons, and Sgt. A. Campbell. President Truman was on his way to dedicate Grand Coulee Dam in Washington State. He spoke from a platform erected near the Union Pacific train station. (Pendleton Police Department.)

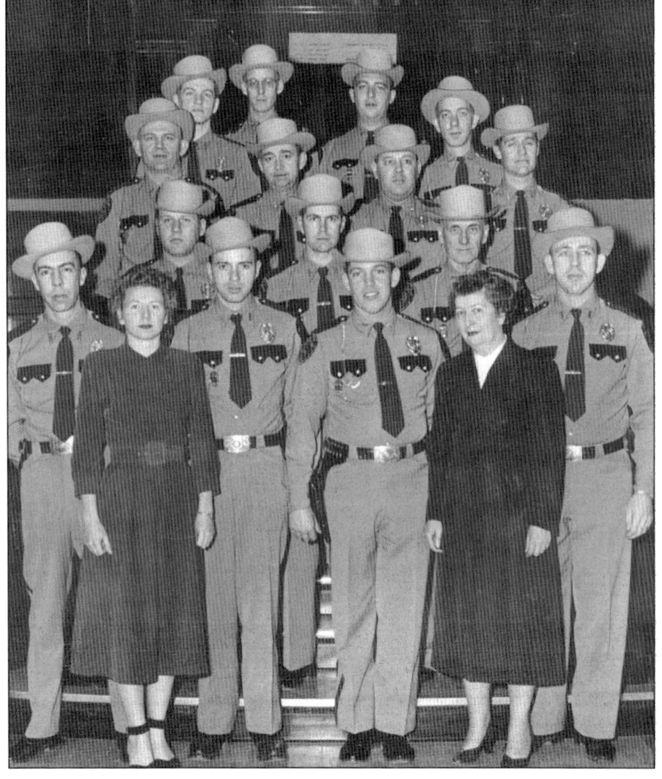

The 1954 Pendleton Police Department included, from left to right, (first row) Mildred Turner and Bonnie Story; (second row) Dick Haskill, Bill Bawks, Cap Jessup, and Ernest Gallaher; (third row) Don Luft, Bob Deeter, and Hank Arkell; (fourth row) Ralph Bone, Lee Hutchinson, Archie Campbell, and Clifford Murray; (fifth row) Dean Wittwer, Mike Doney, Dick Kinne, and Bert Lindsay. (Pendleton Police Department.)

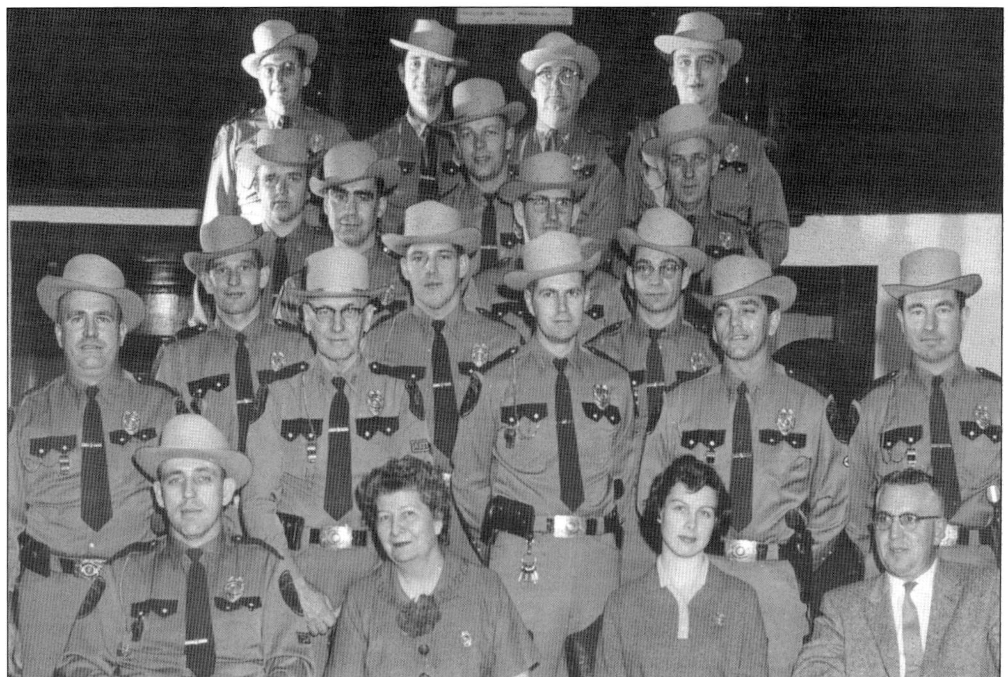

Many of the officers seen here in 1959 served long terms. They are, from left to right, (first row) police chief Ernest Gallaher, Bonnie Story, Doris Smith, and Andy Browning; (second row) John Hascall, Hank Arkell, Bob Deeter, Tony Martinez, and Don Eagle; (third row) Jim Swanson, Cap Jessup, and Dale Keller; (fourth row) John Kain, Lyle Earlley, Bill Boysen, Gib Branstetter, and Chet Nordstrum; (fifth row) Paul Carter, Bill Crooke, Lee Hutchinson, and Dick Kinne. (Pendleton Police Department.)

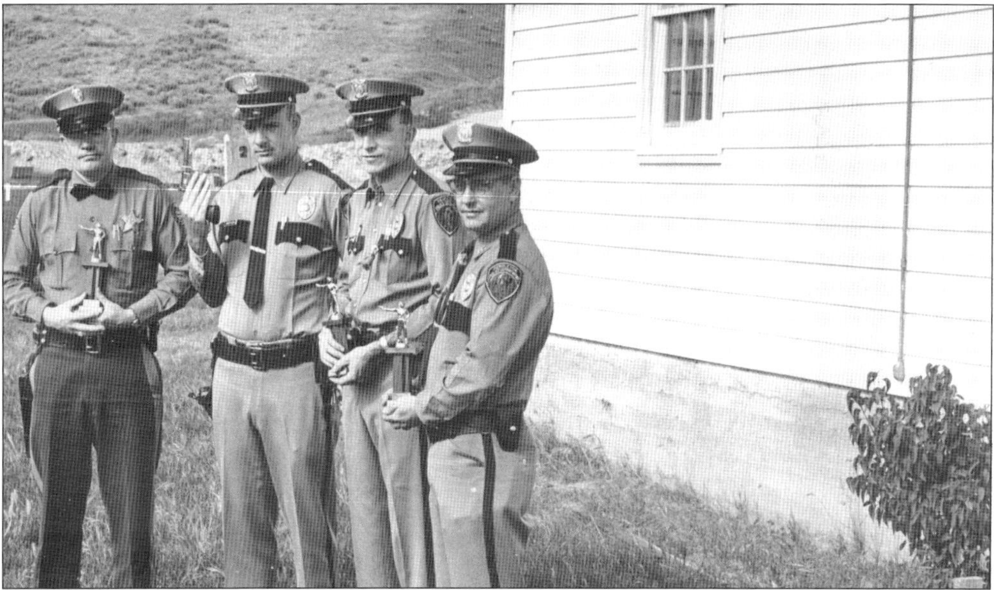

These men served in 1966. They are, from left to right, Officer Elliott, 1st Oregon Association Chief of Police (OACPO) Anderson, 3rd OACPO Christensen, and 2nd OACPO Harris. (Pendleton Police Department.)

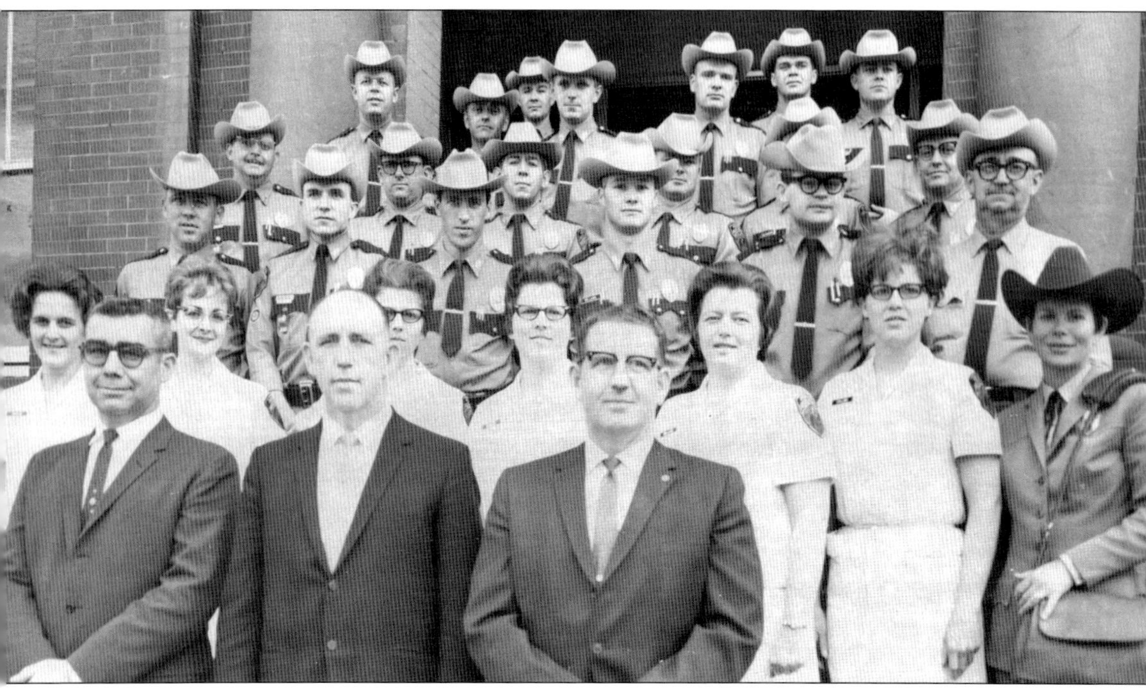

This 1968 department photograph includes, from left to right, (first row) Lyle Earlley, police chief Ernest Gallaher, and Gilbert Branstetter; (second row) Janet Kincaid, Sandra Hauger, Carol Cameron, Elaine Hunter, Billie Wallace, Elsie Collins, and Carol Ayers; (third row) Dale Hulse, John Christensen, Gary Lytton, Ron Williams, Verlon Dawson, and Lee Hutchinson; (fourth row) Paul Carter, Barry Clift, Raymond Hughes, Jim Banks, Argel Collinsworth, and Delbert Harris; (fifth row) Bill Boysen, George Hammons, Wayne Hamilton, Barry Forrest, Allen Anderson, Wayne Moore, and John Collins. (Pendleton Police Department.)

Seven

Businesses

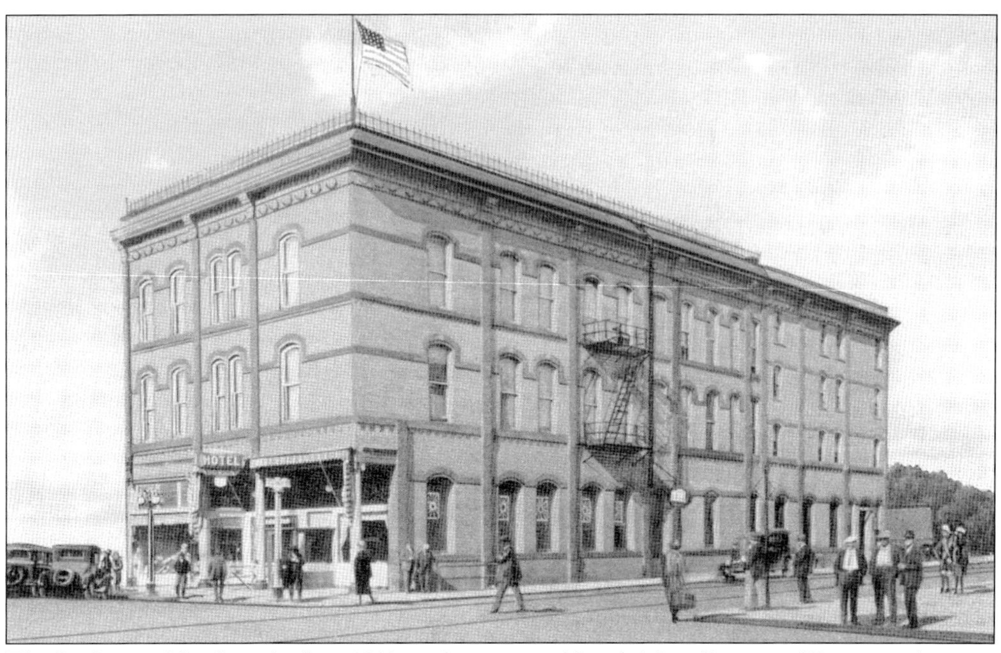

The St. George Hotel was built in 1910 on the corner of South Main Street and Emigrant Avenue. In 1922, Dr. Isaiah Ulysses Temple bought the hotel and renamed it Hotel Dorion. It was known by that name from 1922 to 1927. After that, it was known as the Temple Hotel. Several additions were built onto it over the years. (Elizabeth Gibson.)

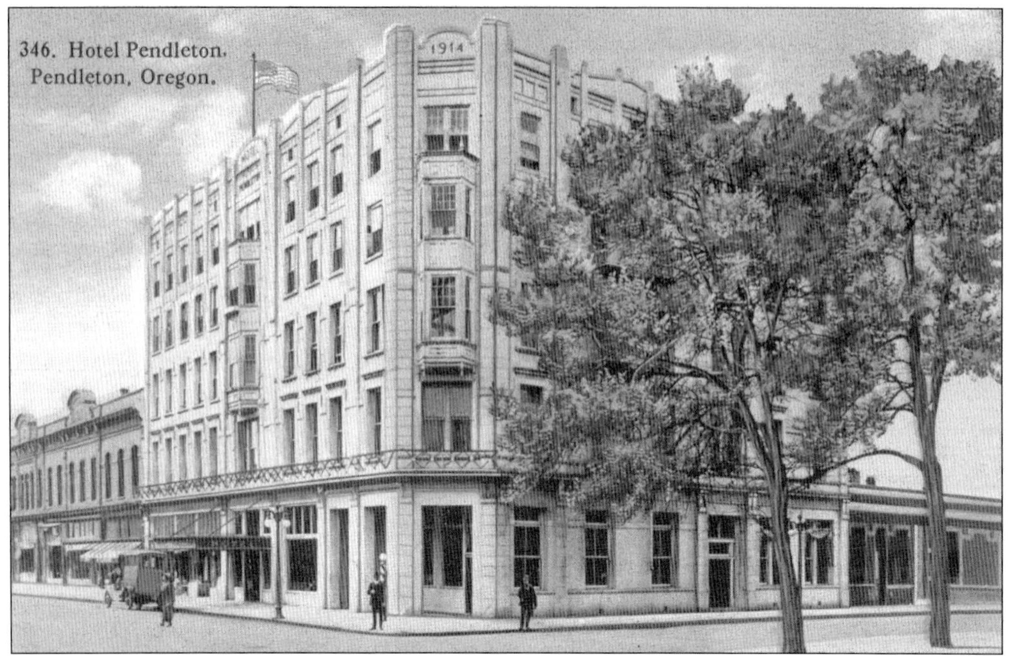

Hotel Pendleton was located on the corner of Main Street and Byers Avenue. Originally a wooden structure, it was rebuilt with brick in 1891. By 1906, it had steam heat and electric lights. The hotel was very popular until the 1920s, when the highway department routed traffic around it. This fact, combined with competing business from motels, forced its eventual closure. (Elizabeth Gibson.)

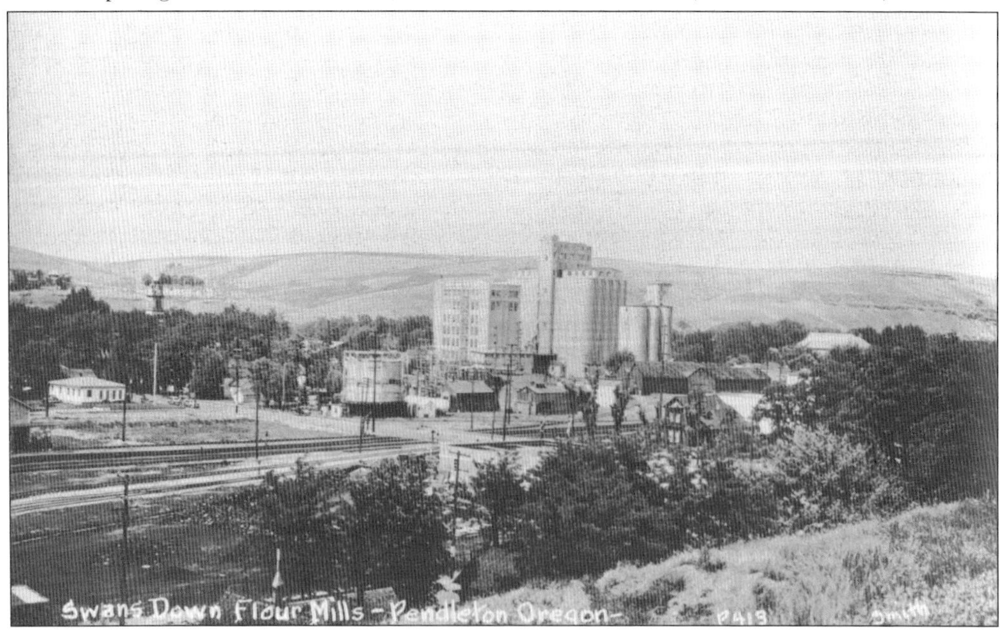

The Byers Flour Mill produced Swan's Down Flour, a specific type of cake flour for General Mills. The flour was considered exceptional, made out of soft winter wheat and sifted multiple times for fineness. The original mill was built in 1875 by W.S. Byers and burned down in 1897. The new brick structure eventually burned down in 1947. Byers Avenue was named for Byers. (Elizabeth Gibson.)

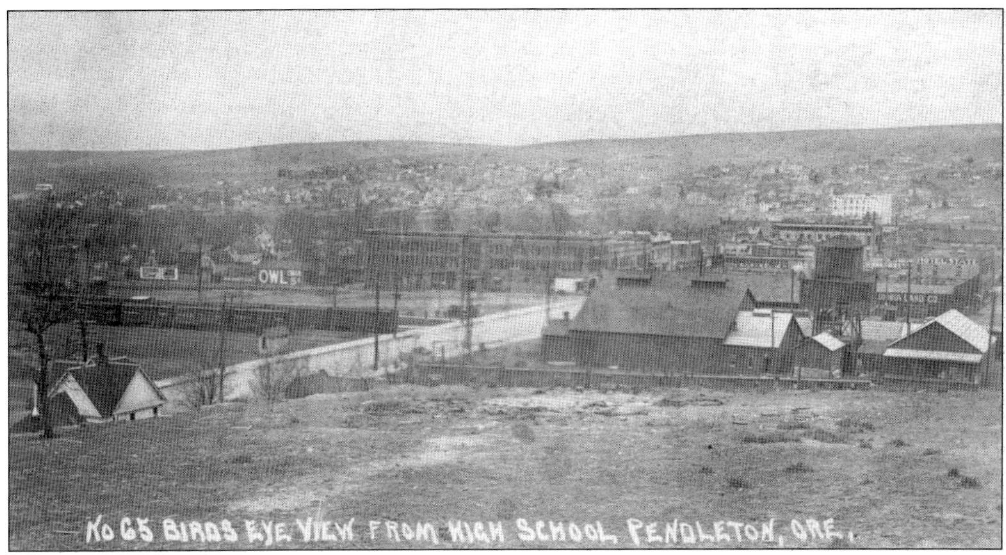

This view looks north from South Hill. The railroad tracks and depot are in the foreground. Also visible is the Bowman Hotel, built by Oliver Purl Bowman in 1906. In 1890, Bowman bought the land and a building called the Transfer House. Shortly afterward, the building burned down. He replaced it in 1906 with the current building, which had 59 rooms but no room No. 13. (Elizabeth Gibson.)

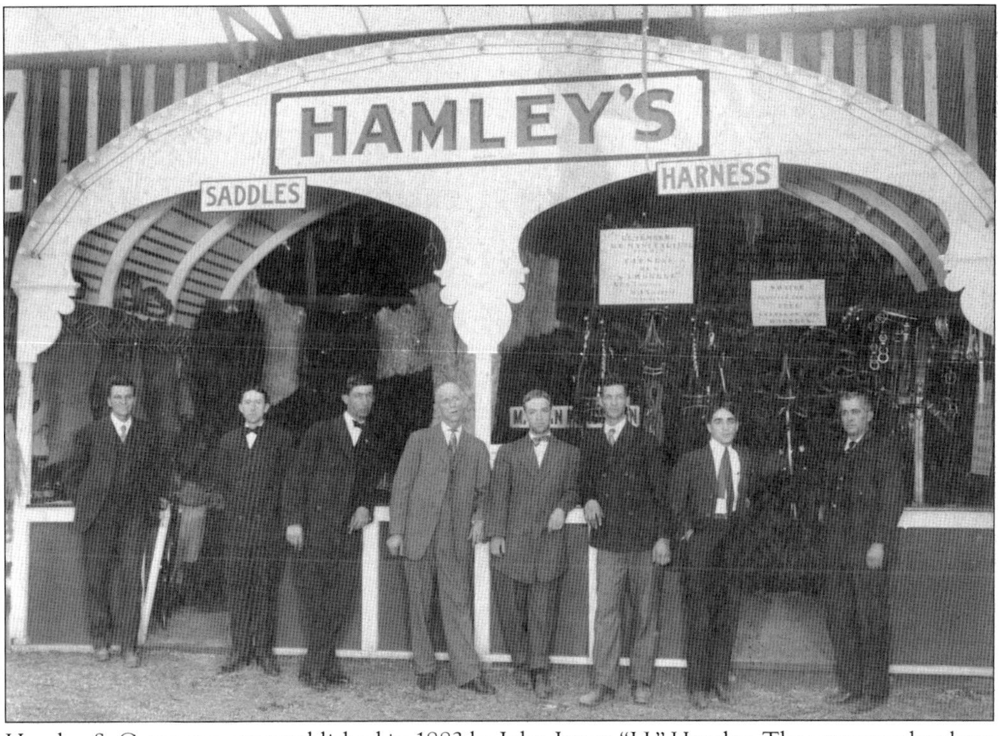

Hamley & Company was established in 1883 by John James "J.J." Hamley. The company has long been known as a harness and saddle maker, originating in 1905 in Cornwall, England. In 1908, the company set up this booth at the local county fair. The older gentleman in the center is J.J. Hamley. His son Lester is next to him on the right. (Hamley & Company.)

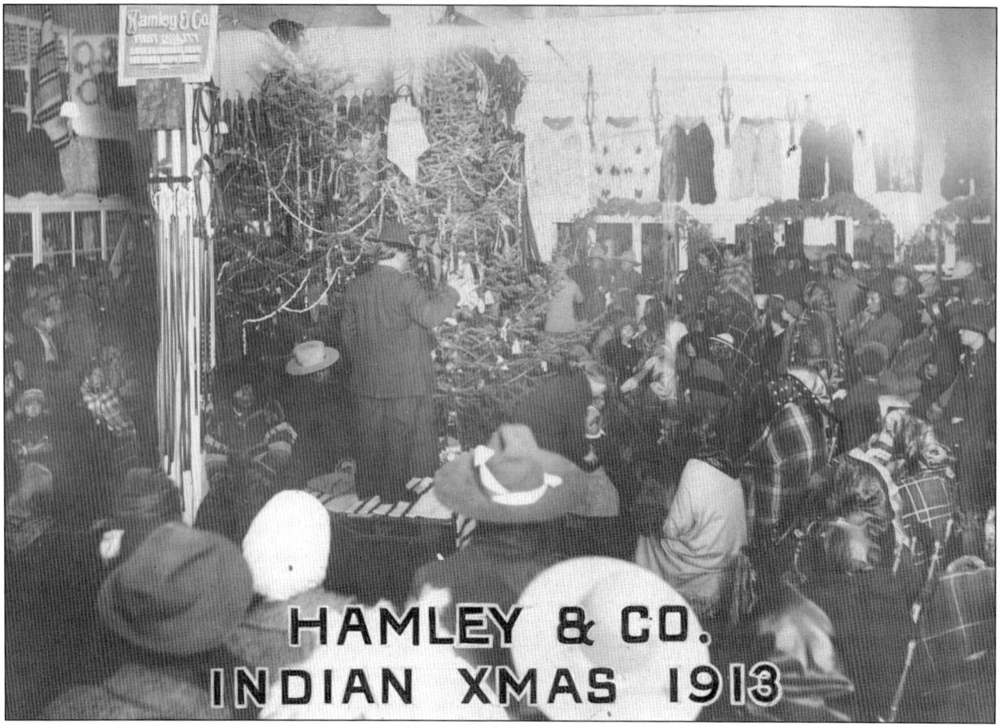

Hamley & Company always maintained good relations with the local Indians living at the nearby Umatilla Indian Reservation. For years, the company held an annual Christmas celebration. This photograph shows the 1913 celebration. The company gave gifts to Umatilla, Cayuse, and Walla Walla tribes. (Hamley & Company.)

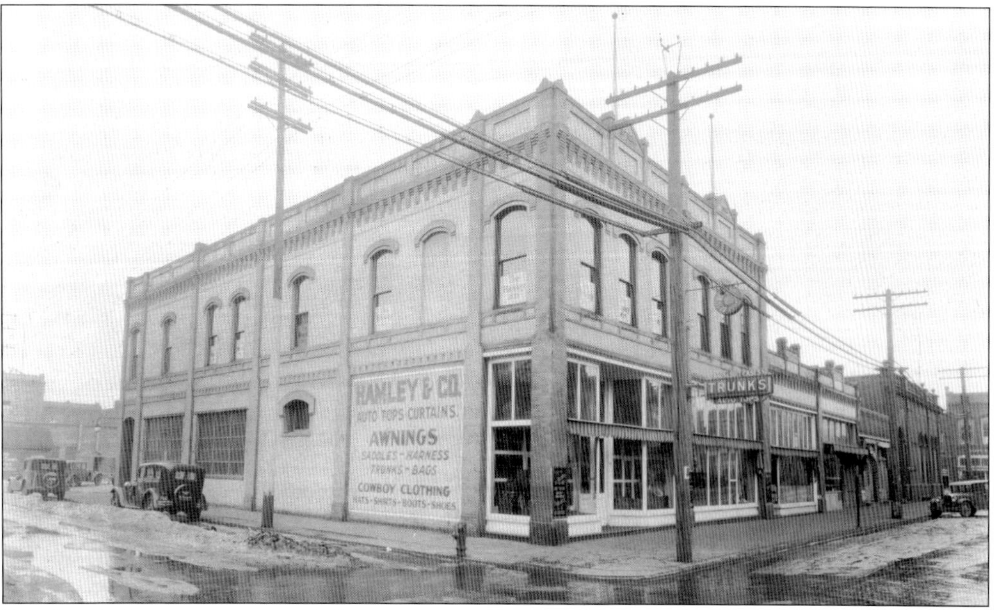

Hamley & Company occupied the same space on Court Street since 1905. The building, seen here in 1921, has undergone a number of remodels and expansions. The business operated there until it was sold in 1980. (Hamley & Company.)

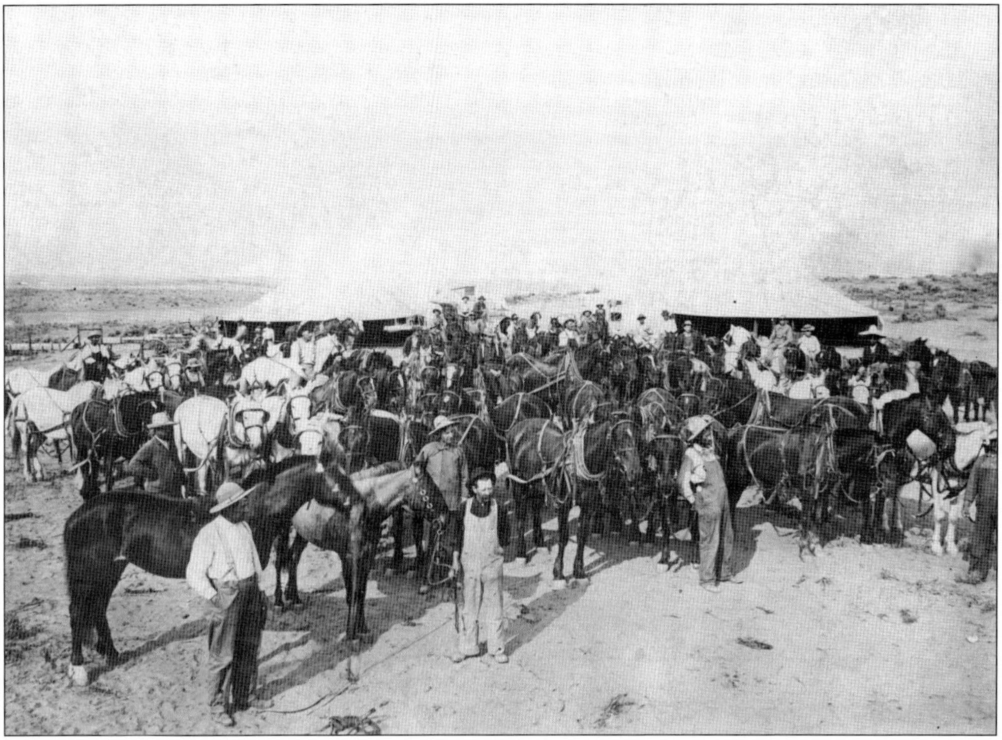

In 1947, construction began on the McNary Dam, downstream from Pendleton on the Columbia River. These men contributed to the building of the dam, and their horses were outfitted with Hamley saddles. (Hamley & Company.)

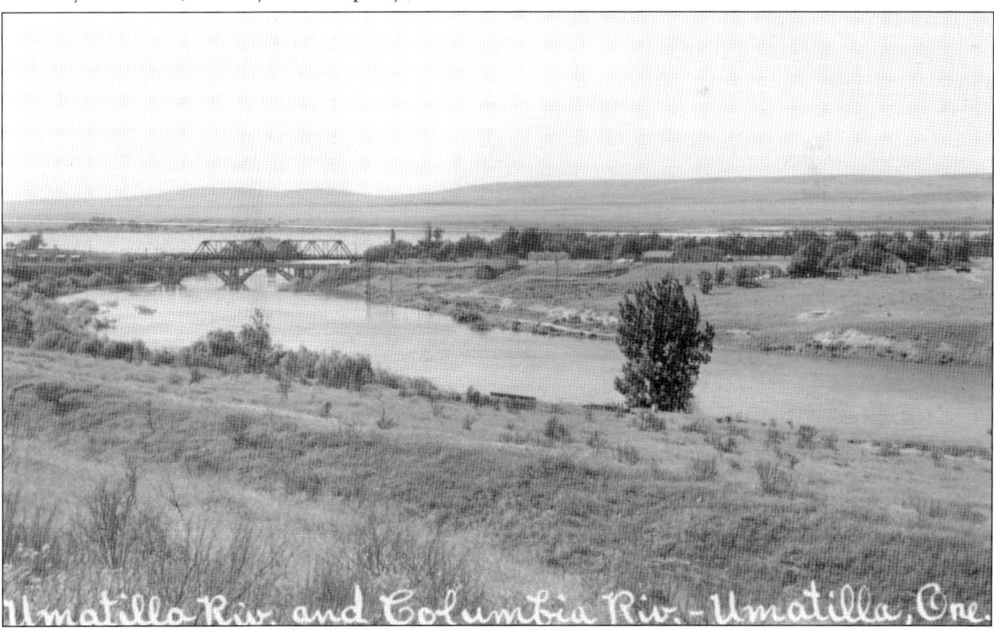

This photograph shows the mouth of the Umatilla River where it joins the Columbia River, just below the McNary Dam. The Umatilla River flows through the middle of downtown Pendleton. (Elizabeth Gibson.)

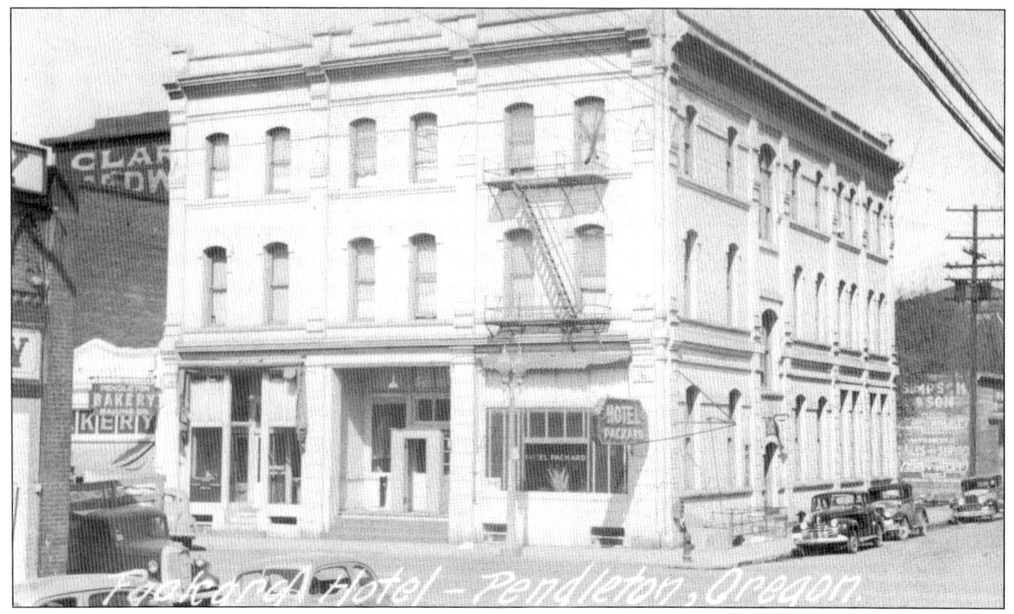

The Packard Hotel was originally called the Golden Rule Hotel. It was later owned by Arthur Packard. Upon his death, his wife, Dora, took over operation of the hotel. Her brother Fred Zurfluh worked as the hotel clerk from 1919 to 1954. He then worked as the manager until 1970, when the hotel finally closed. (Elizabeth Gibson.)

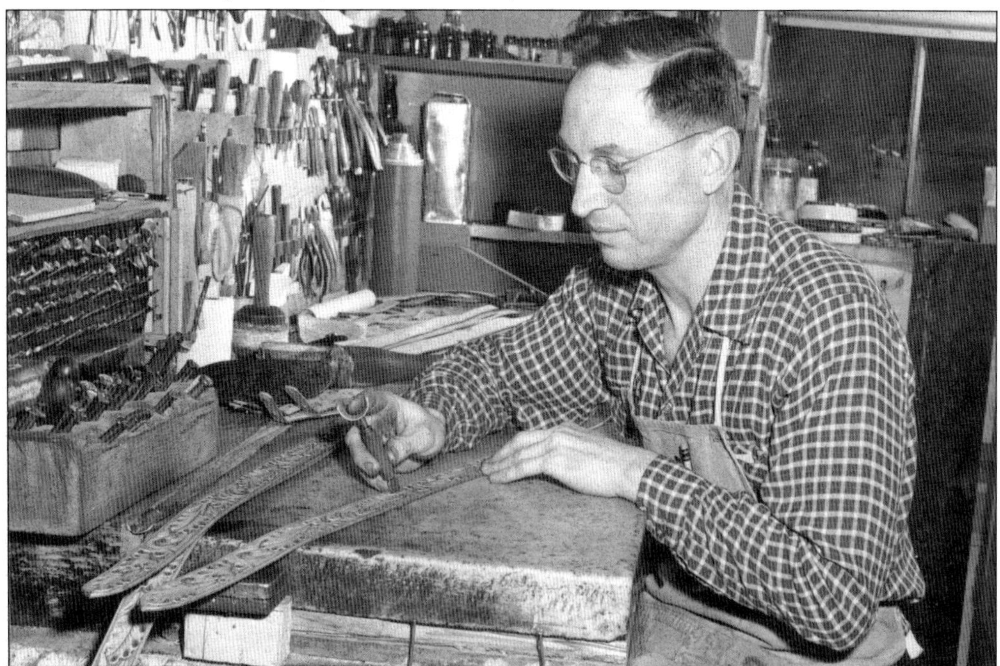

Seen here is Bill Knight, a saddle maker for Hamley in the 1950s. Knight was well respected for his designs and saddle-making techniques. Many future employees emulated his techniques. Knight later went into the insurance business to provide a living for his growing family, but he loved his time at Hamley & Company the best. When he died in 2013, his family returned his vintage tools to the company, where they will be cherished. (Jim Knight.)

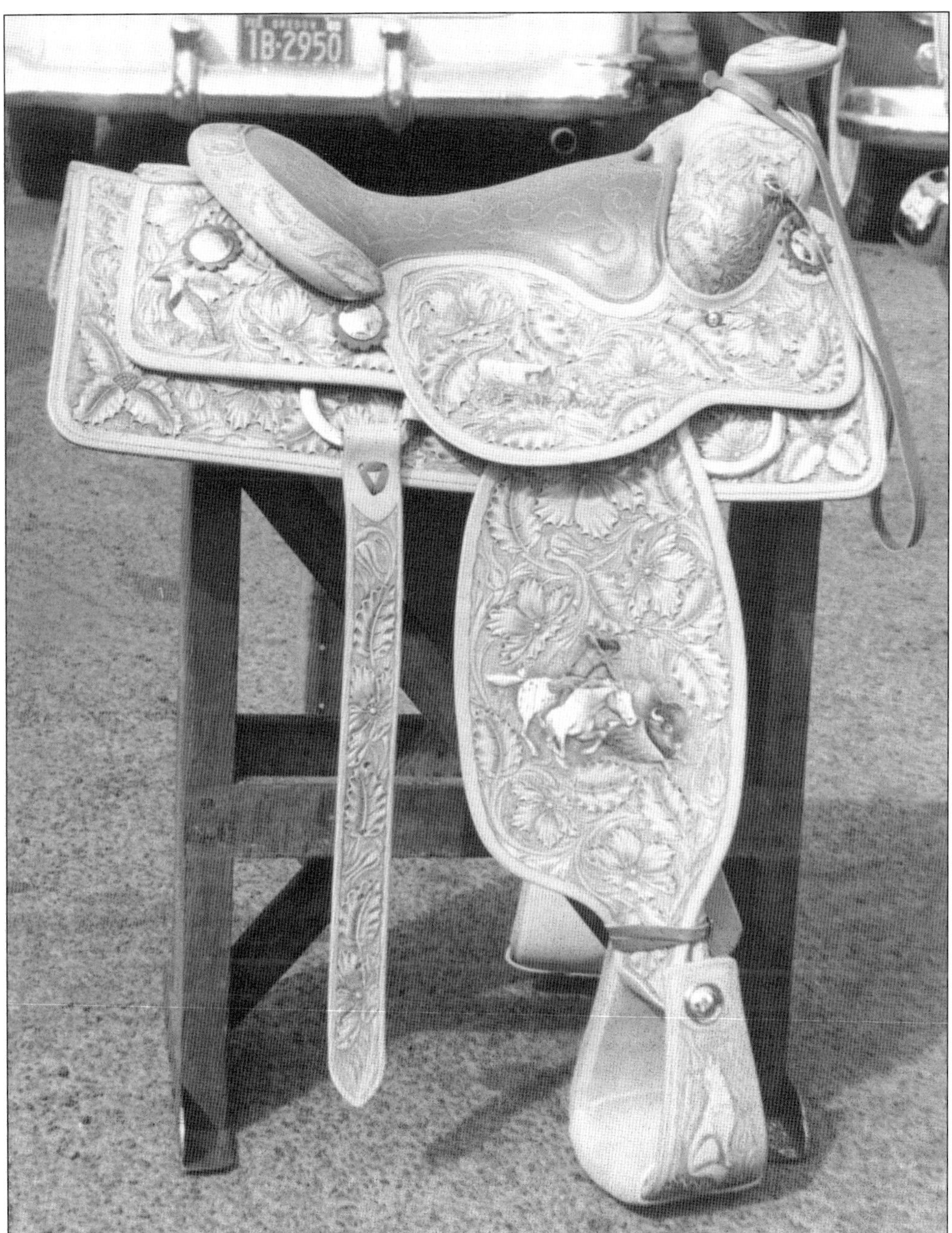

Besides having a healthy retail business, Hamley & Company also provides the trophy saddle for the Pendleton Round-Up. This has been a company tradition since the beginning of the Round-Up in 1910, when J.J. Hamley helped organize the first event. This saddle was given away in 1959 to the steer-roping champion. This one was special because it commemorated the state's centennial and included many state emblems like the state bird (meadowlark) and the state flower (Oregon grape). (Jim Knight.)

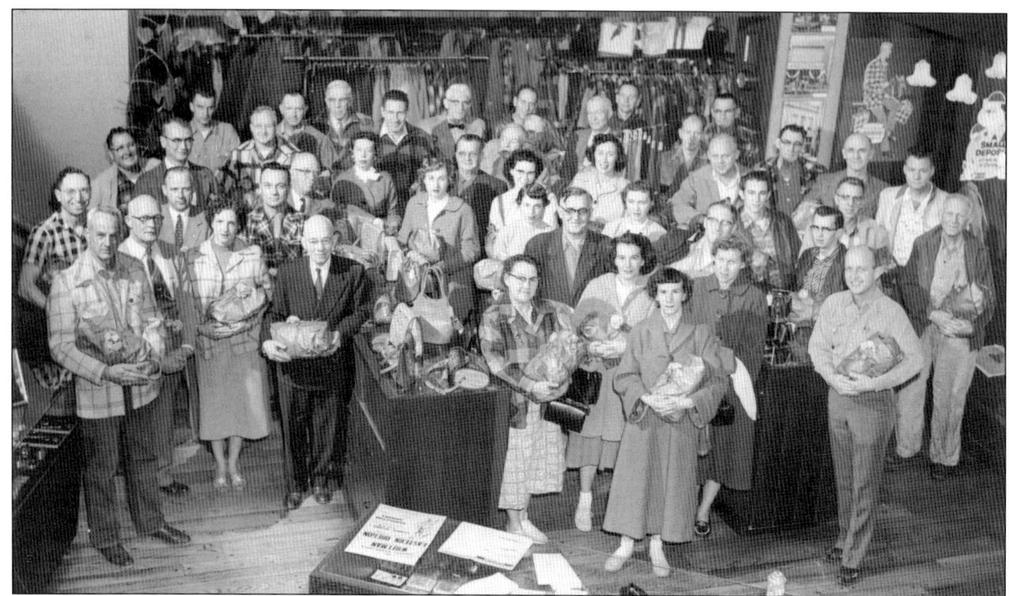

Hamley & Company employees tended to work for the company for a very long time. For their loyalty, the company gave each employee a goose for Thanksgiving every year. This photograph from 1956 shows each employee holding his or her annual gift. Dave Hamley, the president of the company during that era, holds a goose in the center-left foreground. (Jim Knight.)

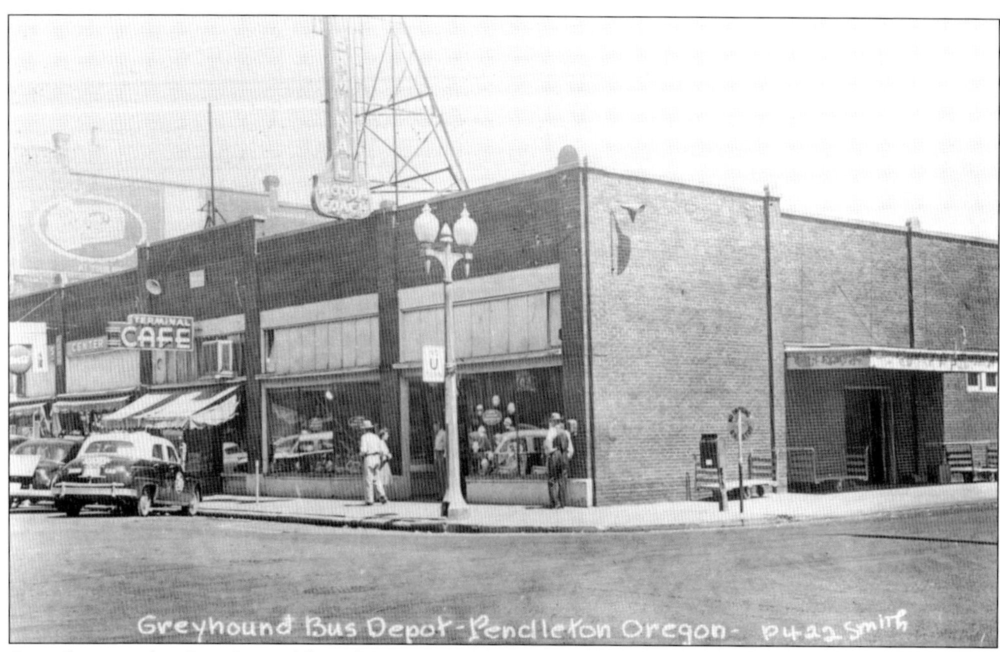

Seen here is the Greyhound bus depot, at 801 Southeast Court Street. It has stood at the same location for many years. This photograph dates from around 1950. (Elizabeth Gibson.)

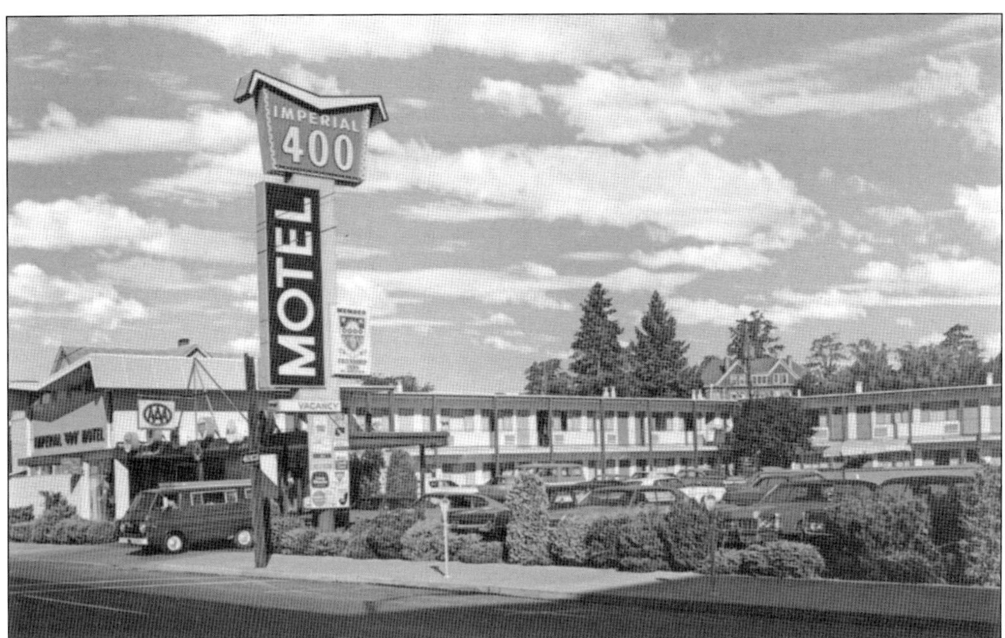

The Imperial 400 Motel (above), at 201 Southwest Court Street, stood on land once owned by the Bowman family. F.M. "Mac" and Norma McClure were the owners and managers. This motel is now part of the America's Best Value chain. It has 51 rooms and a heated pool and underwent major renovations in 2005 and 2006. (Elizabeth Gibson.)

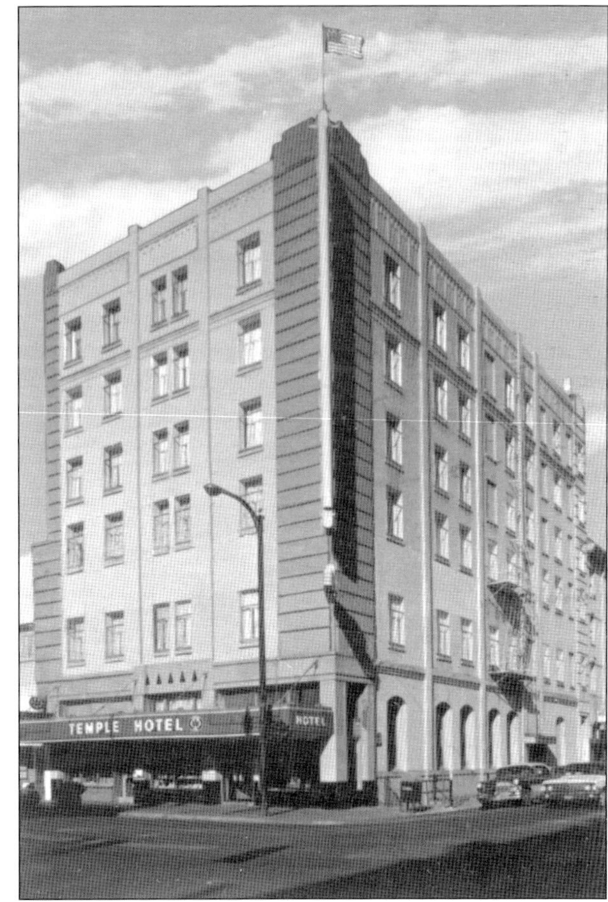

The Temple Hotel, seen here, was formerly the Dorion Hotel. At the time this photograph was taken, it had 100 rooms, a coffee shop, a dining room, a cocktail lounge, a heated rooftop swimming pool, free parking, and free television. It eventually closed due to its location away from traffic patterns. It is currently used as apartments, with retail shops occupying the ground floor. (Elizabeth Gibson.)

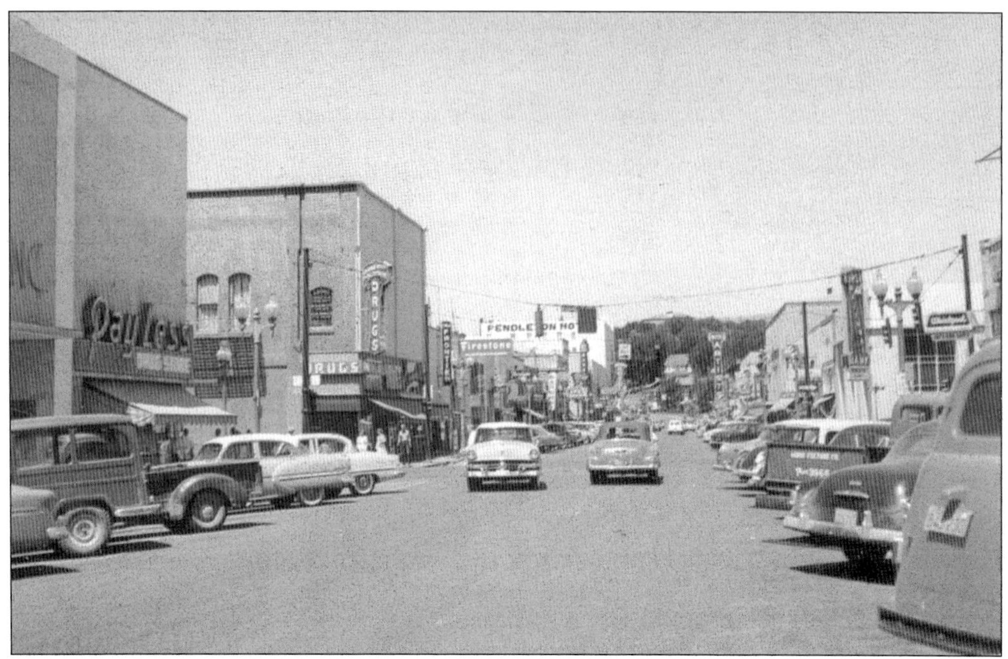

This street scene of Main Street was taken just a few years after the 1940s-era photograph on page 98. The vehicles are still parked at an angle, not parallel parked. Many of the businesses are still the same, although some of the facades have changed. (Elizabeth Gibson.)

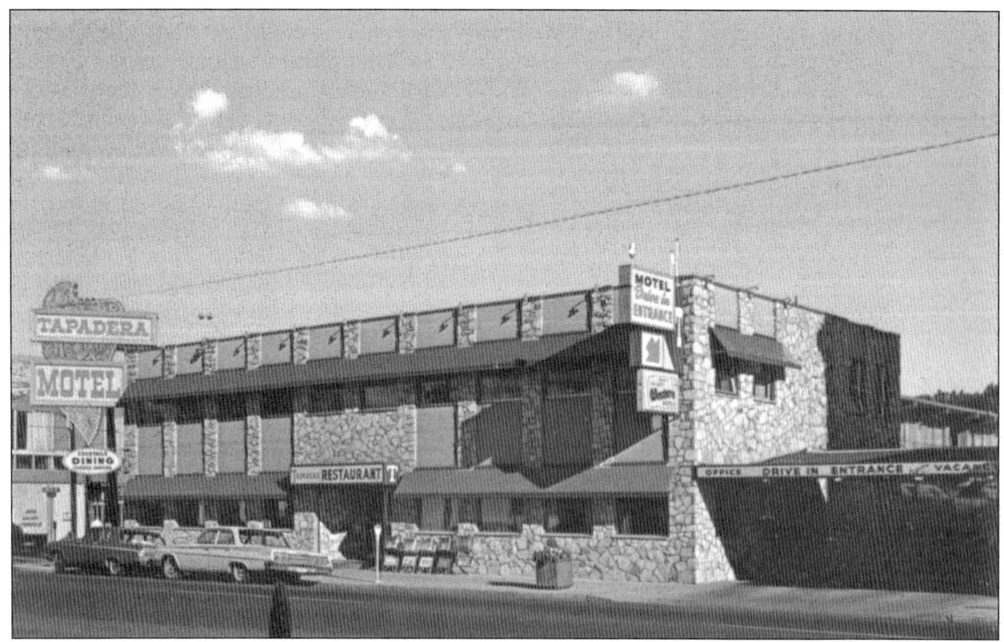

The popularity of the Pendleton Round-Up necessitated more overnight accommodations, and many hotels were built in the 1960s. The Tapadera Motel was on the east side of town, on Court Street. It is now part of the Knight's Inn chain and the Wyndham family of hotels. (Elizabeth Gibson.)

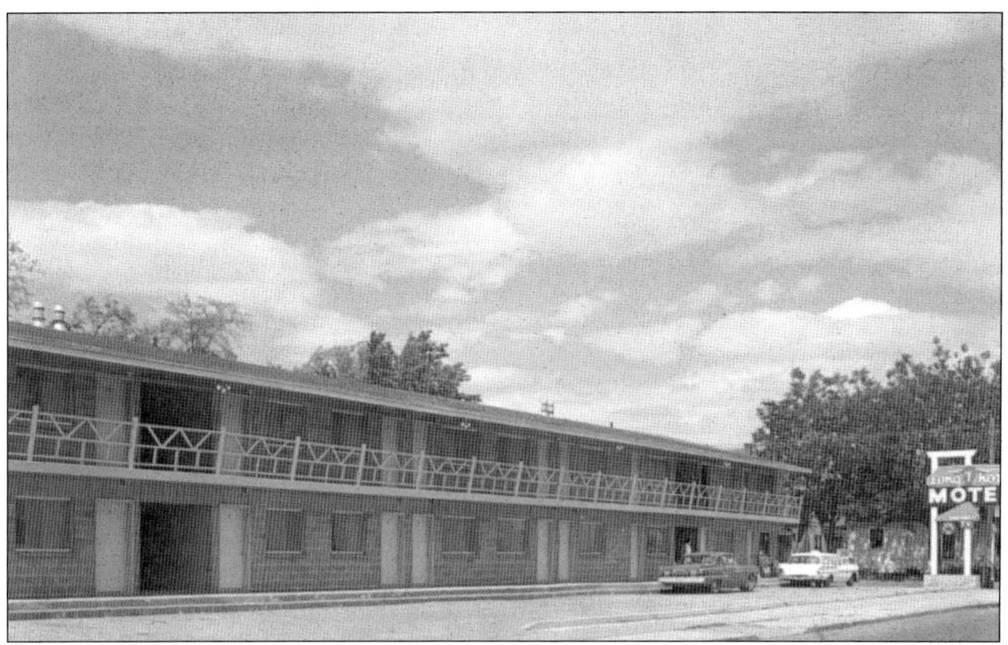

Another popular motel was the Longhorn Motel, located at 411 Southwest Dorion Avenue. It had 37 units with free radio and television and central heating. Its location, on the northeast corner of Dorion Avenue and Southwest Fourth Street, is now the home of a TraveLodge. (Elizabeth Gibson.)

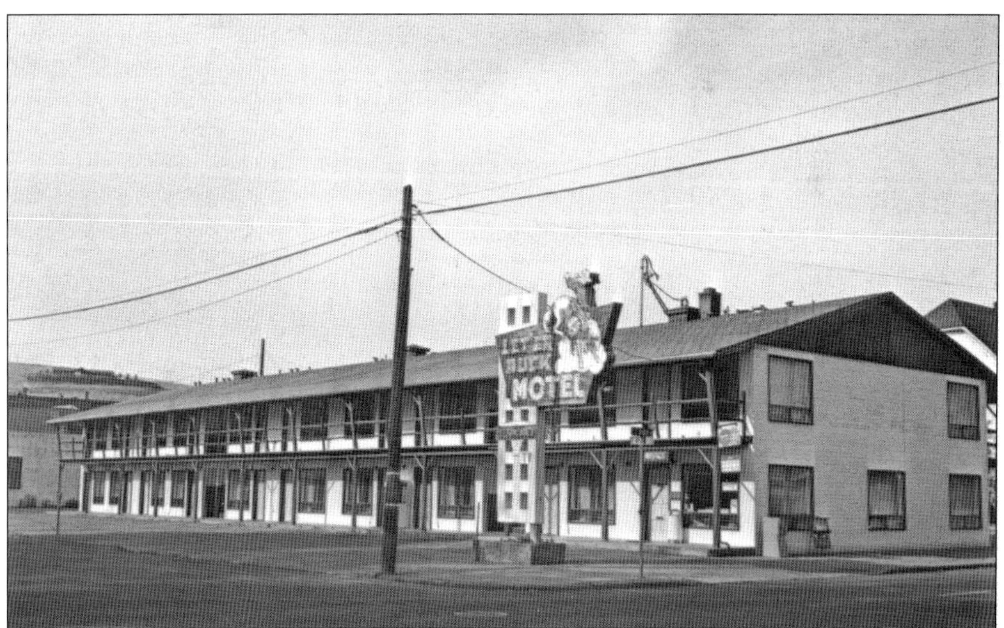

The Let 'Er Buck Hotel was located at 205 Southeast Dorion Avenue, two blocks east of Main Street. This property is now home to the Relax Inn, a 36-room hotel on the corner of Southeast Second Street and Southeast Dorion Avenue. (Elizabeth Gibson.)

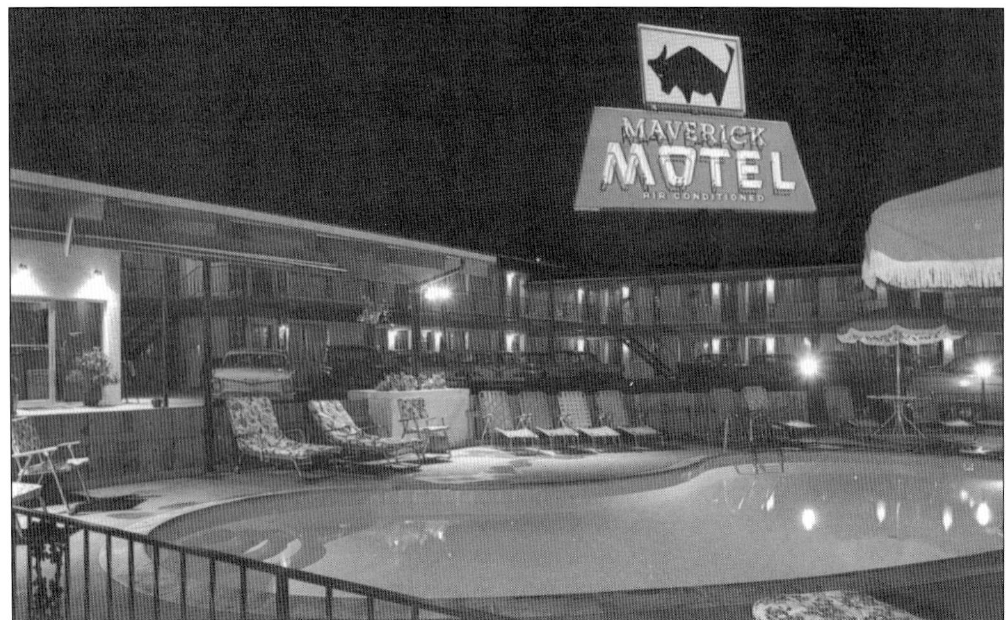

The Maverick Motel was at 310 Southeast Dorion Avenue, three blocks east of Main Street. It had 40 rooms and electric baseboard heat. The property is now a Rodeway Inn, part of the Choice Hotel chain, and offers 43 rooms and a heated outdoor swimming pool. (Elizabeth Gibson.)

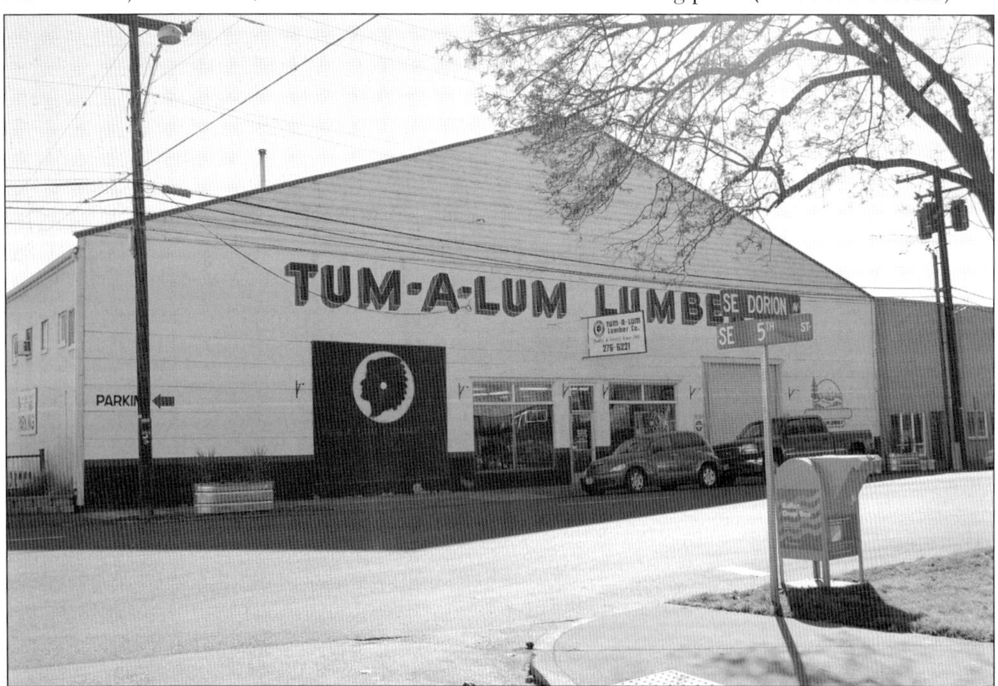

Tum-a-Lum Lumber Company was established by J.M. Crawford in 1906 to supply the lumber and hardware needs of the area. Crawford chose the name, a Umatilla Indian phrase meaning "spreading waters," because of the way water ran off the nearby Blue Mountains. The company now has branches in Hood River and The Dalles as well as in Susanville, California. This building is located on Southeast Dorion Street. (Elizabeth Gibson.)

Eight

Modern Times

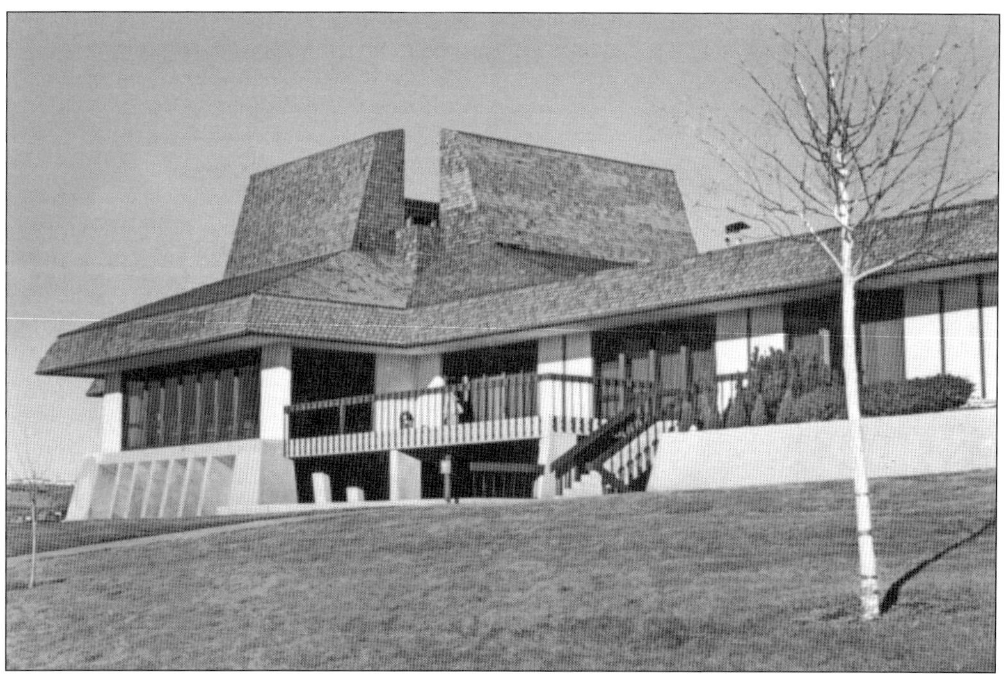

Blue Mountain Community College was established in 1962 and initially offered vocational classes in a junior high school. In 1965, the school moved to permanent facilities on the north hill overlooking the city. The school has continually expanded and now provides traditional and distance learning for Baker, Grant, Morrow, Umatilla, and Wallowa Counties in northeastern Oregon. (Elizabeth Gibson.)

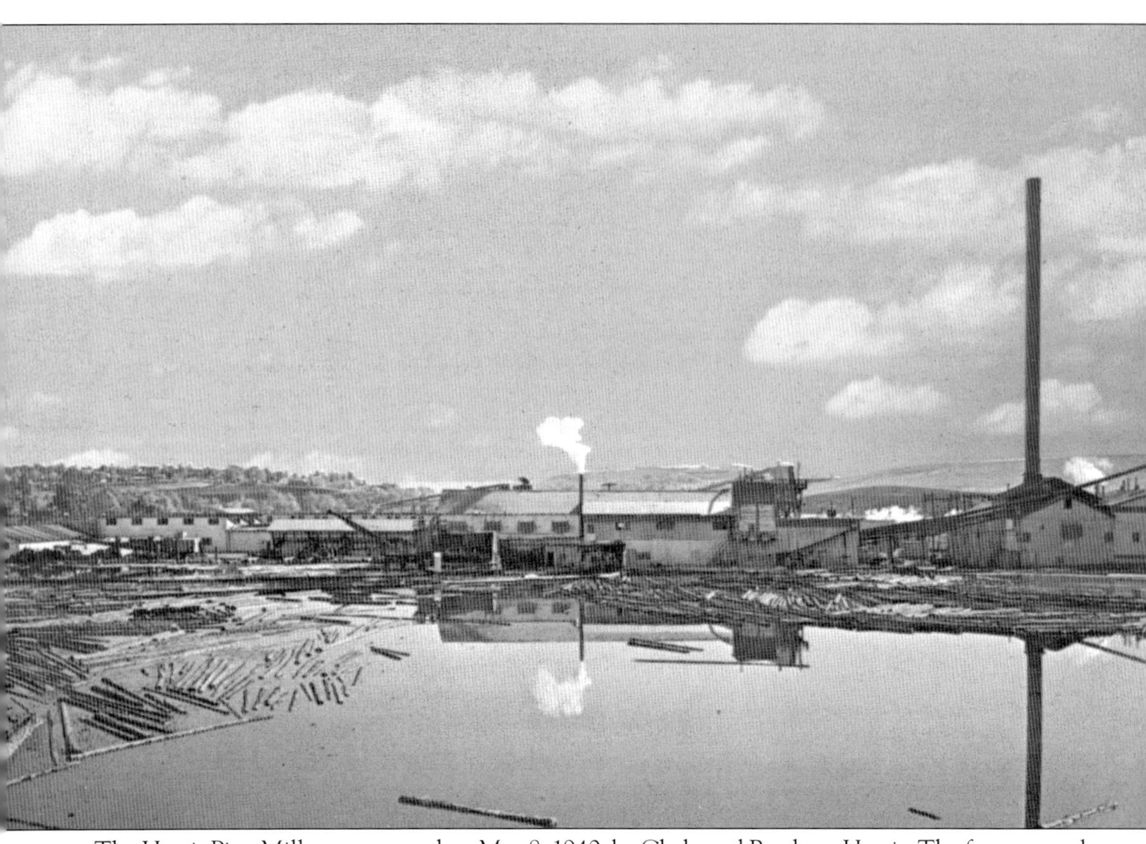

The Harris Pine Mills were opened on May 8, 1940, by Clyde and Burdette Harris. The factory used timber owned by the family in the Umatilla National Forest. The mills could produce 75,000 feet of lumber in an eight-hour shift, and the log pond could hold three million feet of logs. The mill was known for its furniture and could not produce it fast enough. The mill opened 16 fabrication plants to build furniture. The company also made packing crates for the Pacific Northwest fruit industry. Clyde and Mary Harris, who were devout Seventh-Day Adventists, donated the mill to the church in 1951. The church operated the plant until it closed in 1986. The closure was a devastating blow to the Pendleton economy, as it was one of the largest employers at the time. (Elizabeth Gibson.)

Till Taylor Park is seen here in the 1960s. This view of the city pool looks north toward Dorion Avenue. Emigrant Avenue lies to the south. The park is bordered by Southeast Eighth Street to the east and Southeast Seventh Street to the west. Across the street from the park in this photograph are a gas station and Phil Winters Motors. The pool is still part of the park today. (June Tassie.)

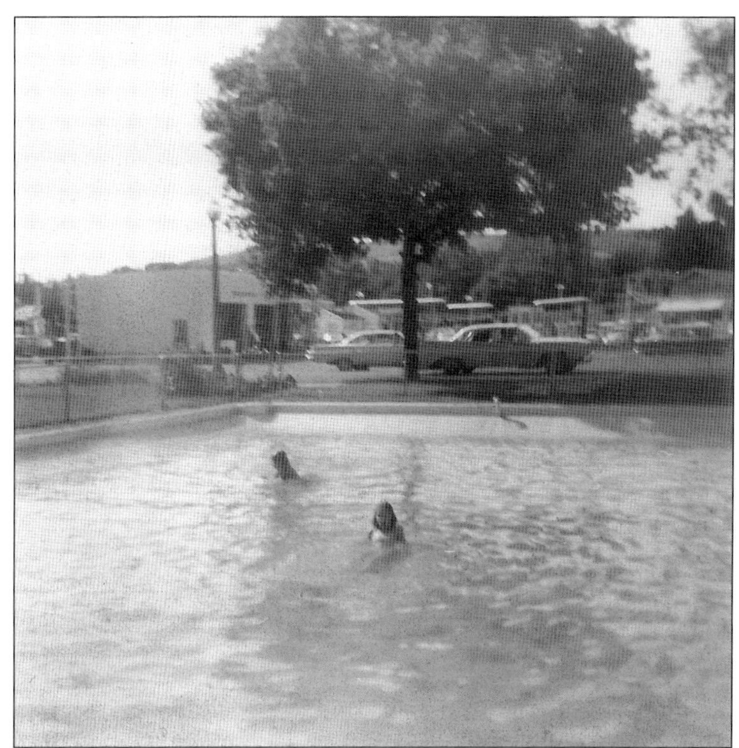

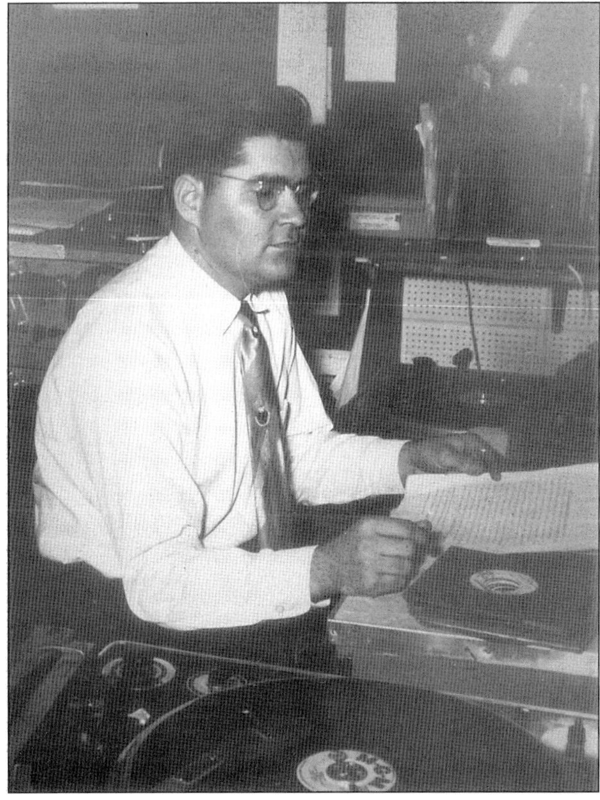

Troy Gene Young lived in Pendleton in the 1960s and 1970s. "Tex," as he became known, was the half owner of a radio station on South Hill. Once named KKID, it was later changed to KTIX. The channel played country and western music. Tex arranged local performances by famous singers such as Marty Robbins and Charley Pride. During the Pendleton Round-Ups of the 1960s, he announced the play-by-play. (June Tassie.)

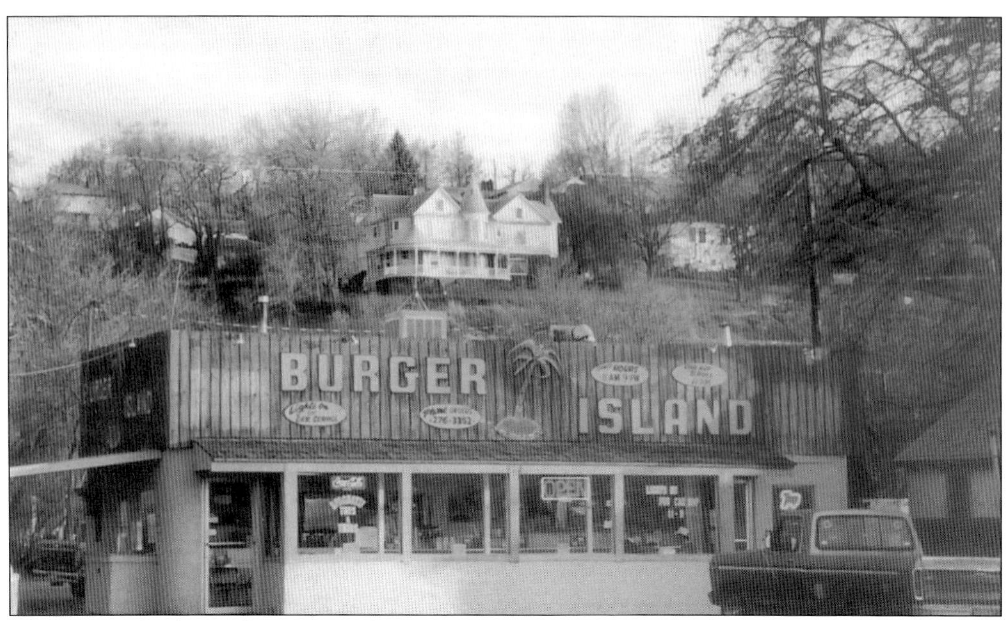

Burger Island is located at 912 Southeast Emigrant Avenue. The restaurant is a favorite hangout in Pendleton. (June Tassie.)

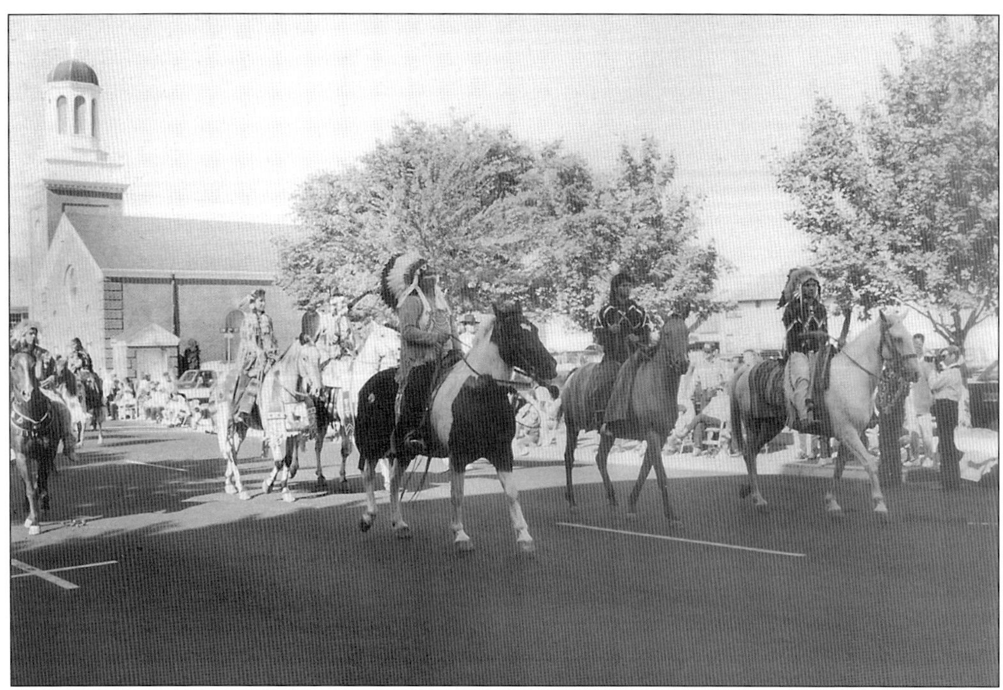

The Westward Ho parade is a long-standing tradition at the Pendleton Round-Up. This photograph from the 1990s shows riders on horseback as they head east down Dorion Avenue. The First Presbyterian Church, on Southwest Dorion, is in the background. This congregation has been part of Pendleton since 1885, and its most recent building was established in 1936. (June Tassie.)

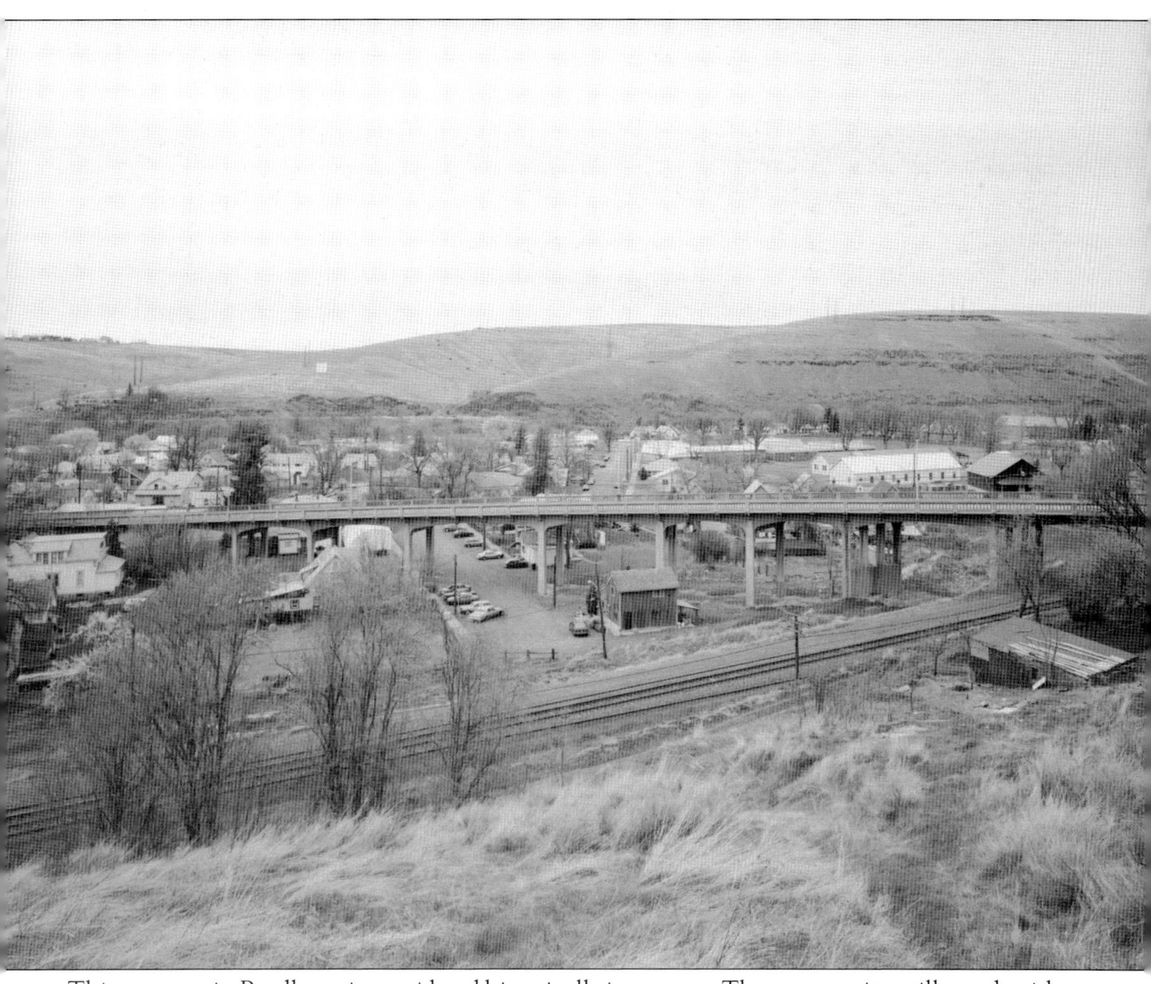

This overpass in Pendleton is considered historically important. The overcrossing still stands with very little change since it was built in 1936–1937. It is important as an example of the work of engineer Conde B. McCullough, the state bridge engineer and the assistant state highway engineer for Oregon from 1919 until 1946. It is one of the best surviving examples of a McCullough-designed slab, beam, and girder bridge. There were more than 900 of them in the state at one time. The bridge features 16 arches of varying lengths. The overall length of the overcrossing is 824 feet. It is 37.5 feet wide, with the roadway making up 26 feet of the width. (Library of Congress, Prints and Photographs Division, Historic American Buildings Survey, reproduction number HAER ORE, 30-PEND, 1-2.)

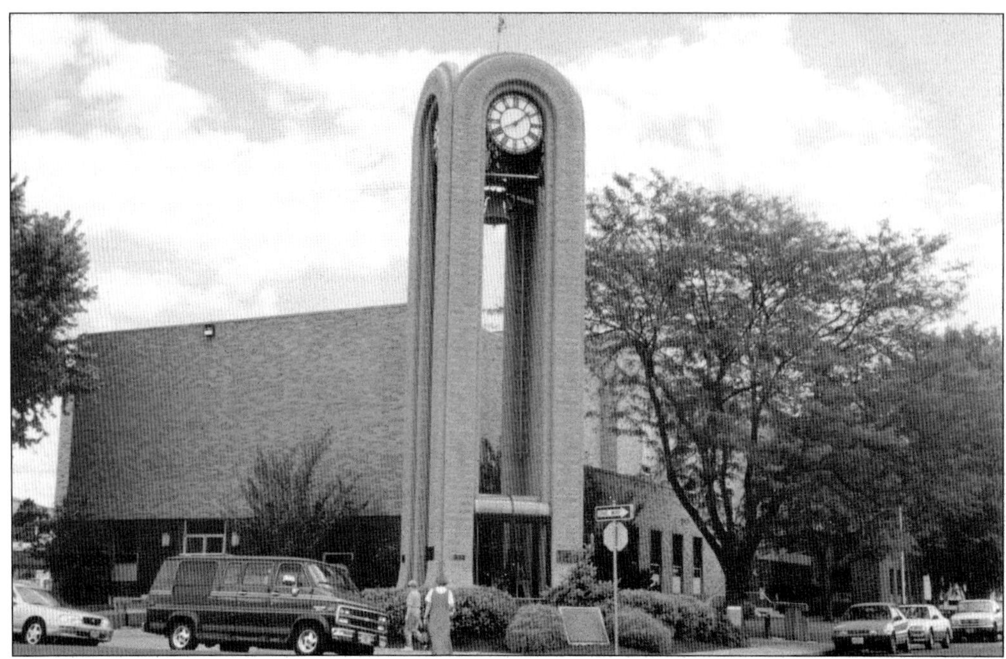

The courthouse was built in 1954 on the site of old courthouse. It was designed by Roald, Schmeer & Harrington of Portland, which also designed the courthouses of Harney and Hood River Counties. The original Seth Thomas clock was saved from the old stone courthouse. In 1989, a tower was built to house the 100-year-old clock. The tower was paid for, in part, by the sale of individually inscribed bricks. (Elizabeth Gibson.)

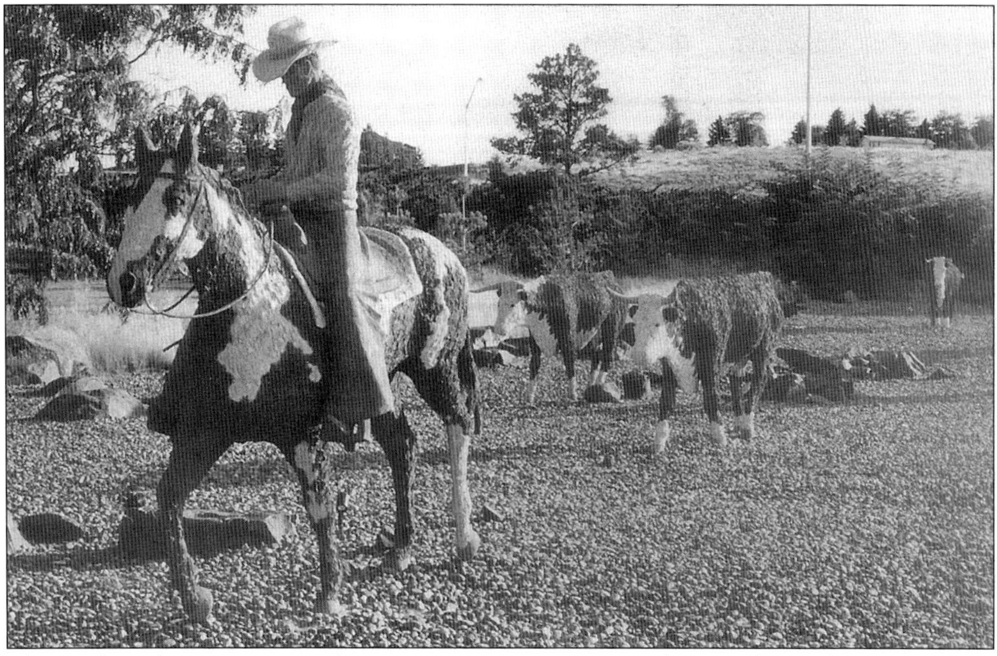

This cattle sculpture on exit 208/209 on Interstate 84 was created in 1999 by Michael Booth. The structure consists of eight cows, two horses, two cowboys, and one dog, all made of concrete. The structure cost approximately $150,000. (June Tassie.)

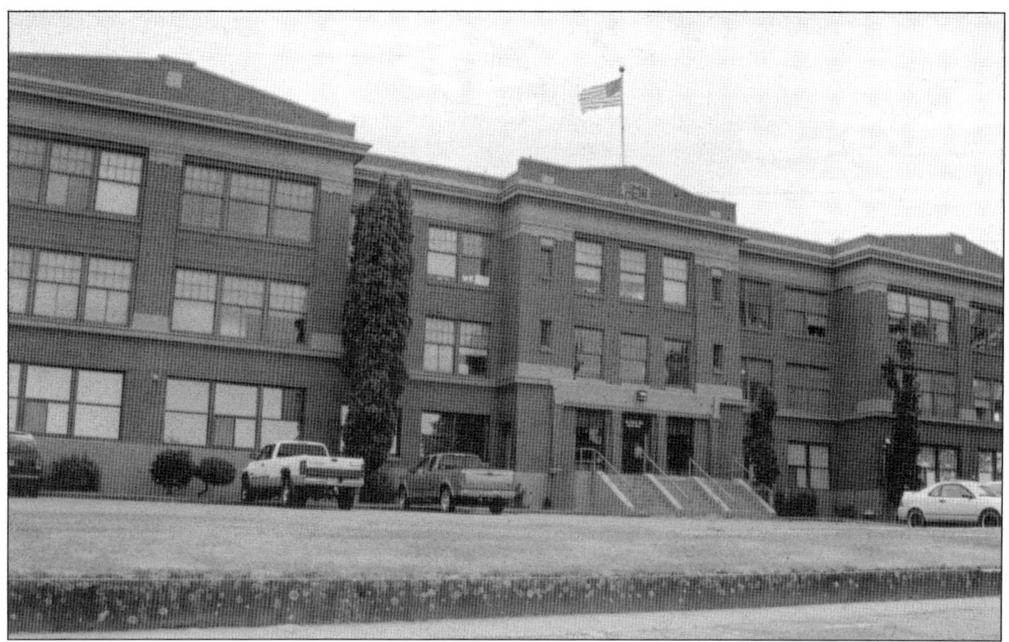

Now known as the John Murray Building, this is on the site of the first public high school, on Hailey Street. When the high school moved to another site, this building was used as a junior high school until 1982. This building was remodeled in the 1980s to accommodate government offices. The county health department occupied part of the space for a few years. The US Department of Agriculture also uses the building. (Elizabeth Gibson.)

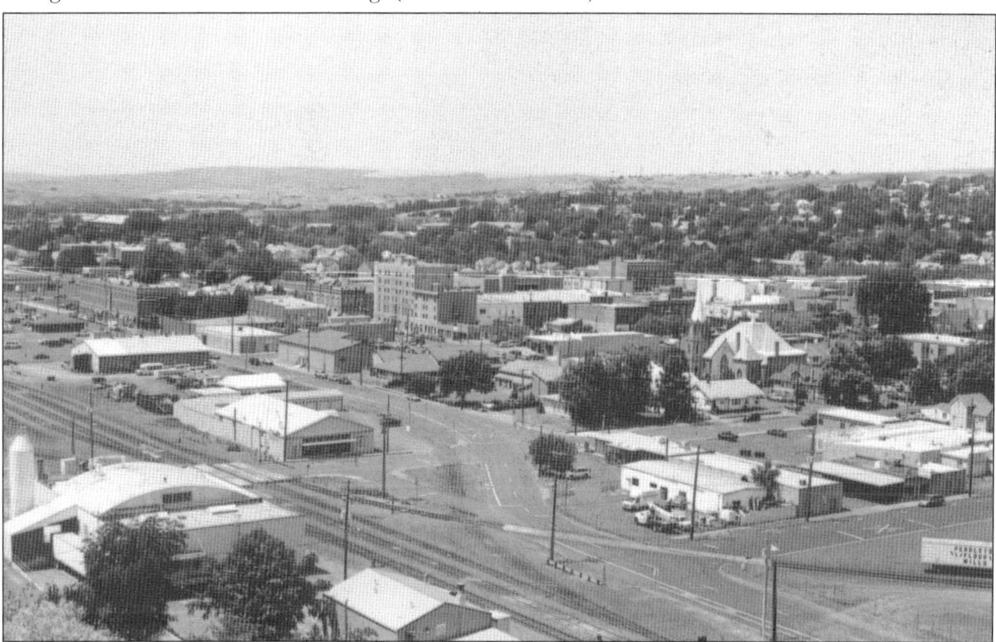

This panoramic view was taken looking west from Goodwin Avenue. The Heritage Station Museum and the old Bowman Hotel building are on the left. The tall building in the center is the old Temple Hotel. The church on the right is the Methodist church on Southeast Second Street and Emigrant Avenue. (Elizabeth Gibson.)

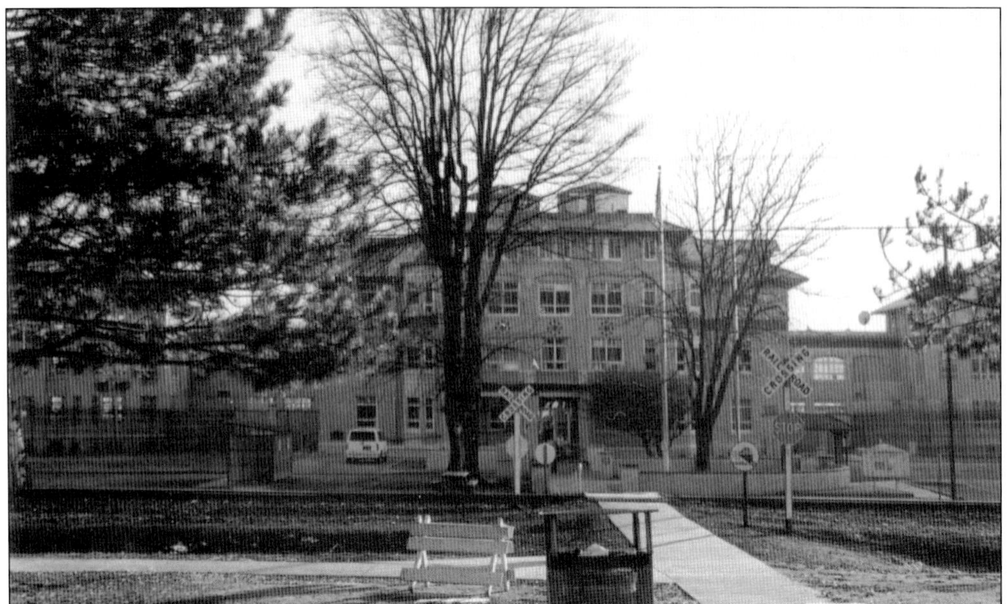

The Eastern Oregon Correctional Facility took over the campus of the former Eastern Oregon State Hospital, which was one of 14 facilities in the state. It was converted into the prison in 1983, and it contained 1,600 beds. Most of the buildings on the property were built in 1912 and 1913. The first prisoners were transferred to this facility in 1985. By 2009, it was the fourth-largest employer in Pendleton. (Elizabeth Gibson.)

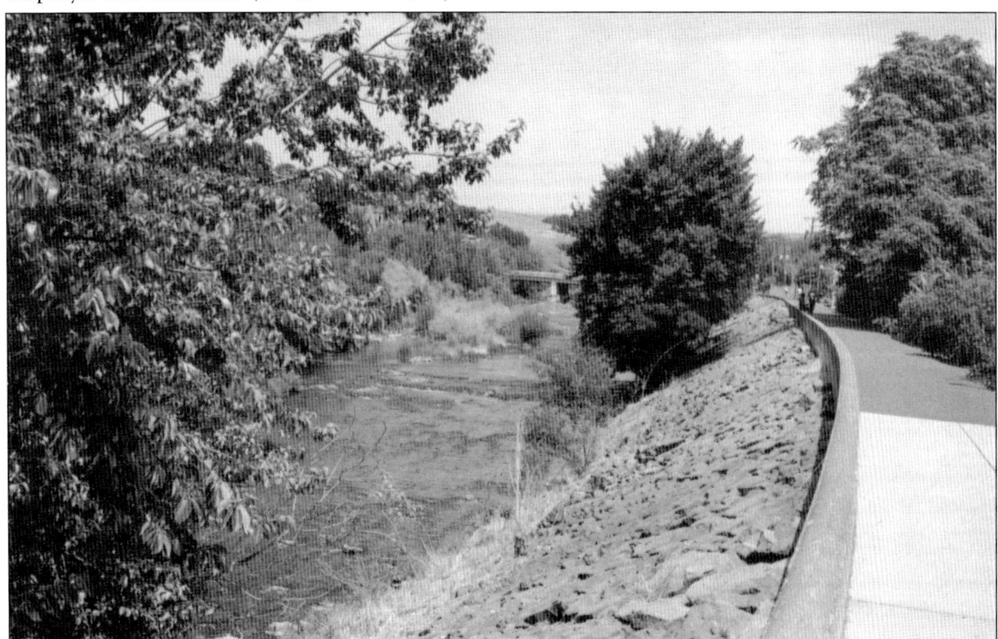

The Pendleton River Parkway runs for three miles along the Umatilla River. This peaceful paved path is perfect for walkers, joggers, cyclists, and skateboarders. This walkway offers river access, nature viewing, and exercise. There are several access points throughout the city to take advantage of this city gem. An adopt-a-parkway program encourages volunteers to keep the parkway looking nice and clean. (Elizabeth Gibson.)

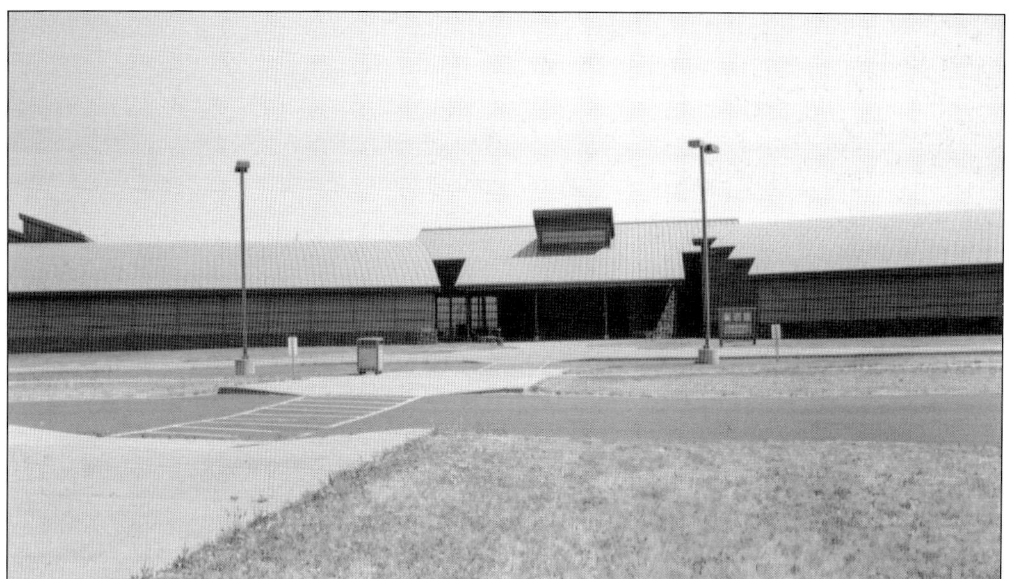

The Tamástslikt Cultural Institute, just outside of Pendleton, celebrates the history and culture of the Walla Walla, Cayuse, and Umatilla tribes. About 2,800 members of the tribes live on or near the reservation, now known as the Confederated Tribes of the Umatilla Indian Reservation. Besides a world-class museum, the institute also houses a gift shop, a café, meeting rooms, a research area, and offices. The institute opened in July 1998. (Elizabeth Gibson.)

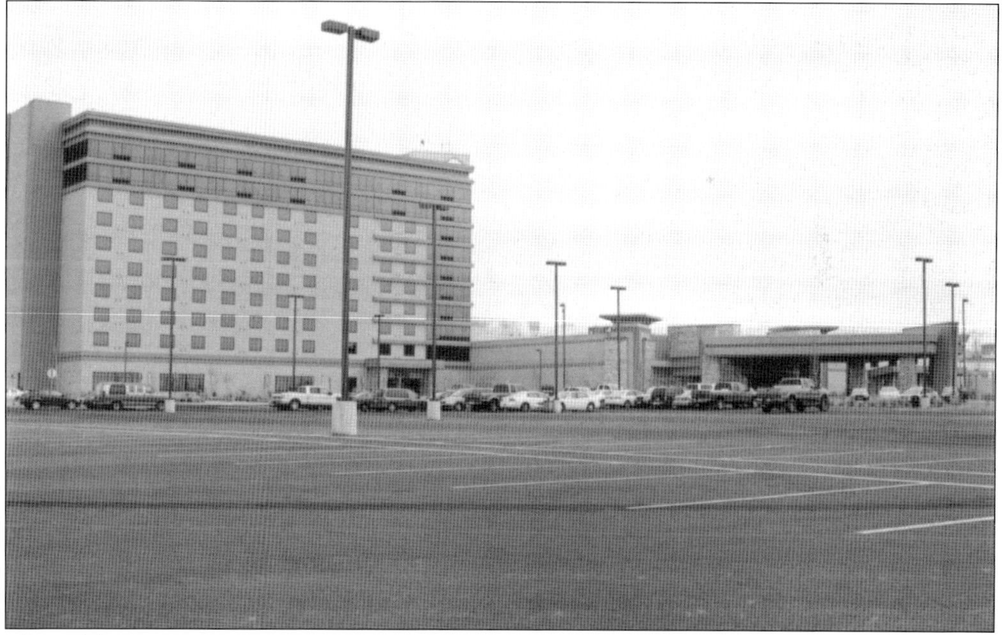

The Wildhorse Casino, operated by the Confederated Tributes of the Umatilla Indian Reservation, opened in March 1995. Besides gambling, the casino offers a gift shop, a movie complex, a sports bar, a restaurant, conference rooms, and live entertainment. The resort also includes the Wildhorse Hotel, the Wildhorse RV park, and a golf course. Together, revenues from the Wildhorse enterprises represent approximately 20 percent of the income of the tribal members. About 700 people work at the resort. (Elizabeth Gibson.)

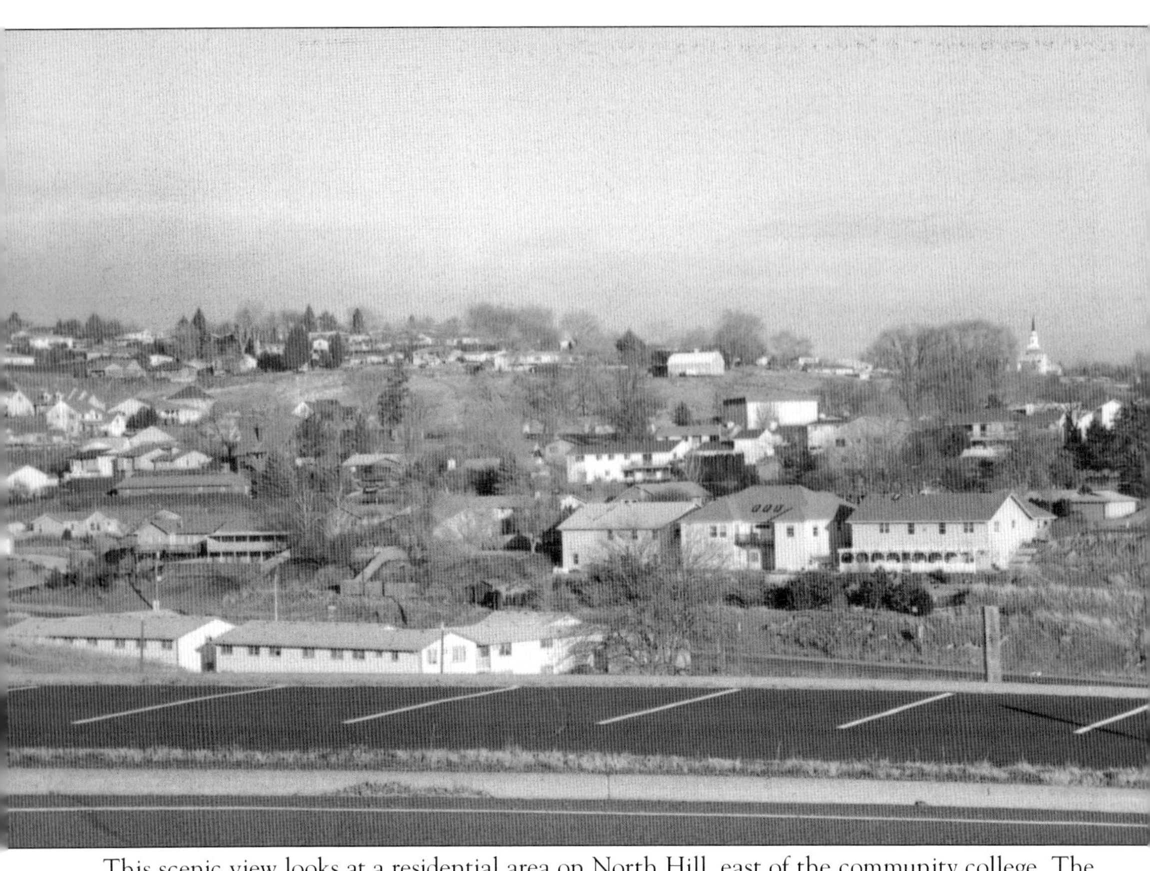

This scenic view looks at a residential area on North Hill, east of the community college. The tall church tower in the right background is the Mormon church. (Elizabeth Gibson.)

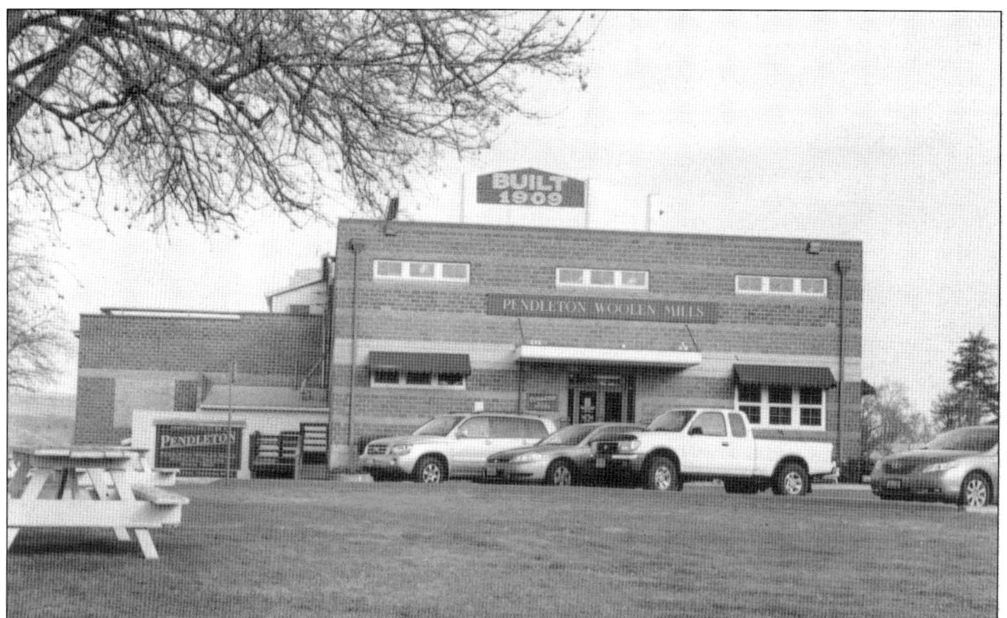

Pendleton Woolen Mills has always welcomed visitors. The visitor center, seen here, has volunteers who conduct tours of the mills. Visitors can also purchase various products from the mills and other Oregon-related souvenirs. (Elizabeth Gibson.)

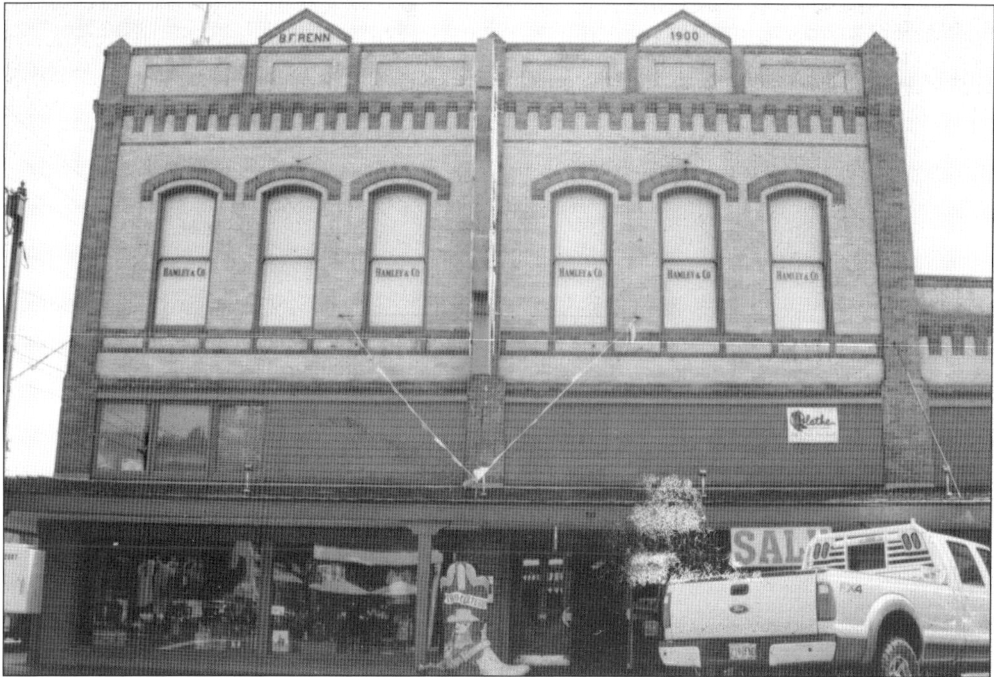

The current home of Hamley & Company, the B.F. Renn Building on Court Street, is seen here as it appears today. The building was constructed in the Italianate style. The second story looks much as it did when it was built. The upper story has a large meeting hall with a beautifully restored bar. The front of the first floor has changed somewhat to accommodate modern shopping. (Elizabeth Gibson.)

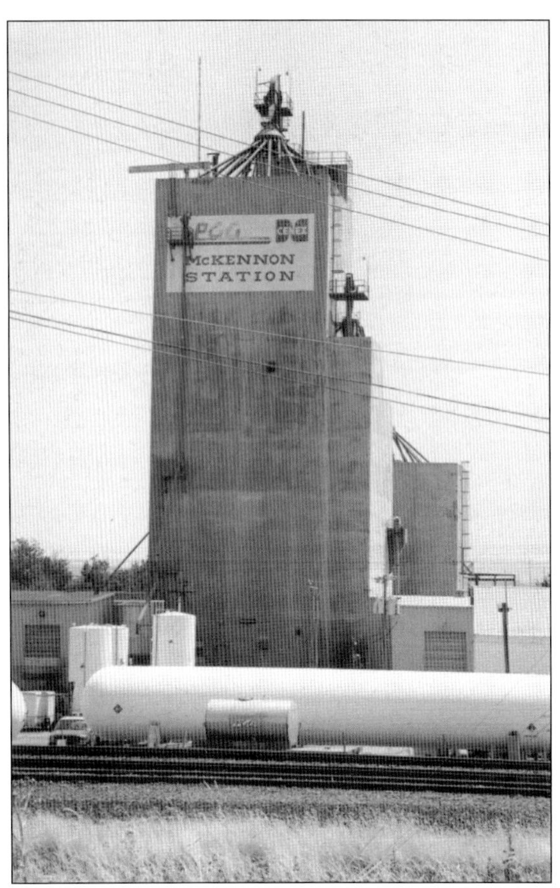

Pendleton Grain Growers is one of the area's oldest businesses. It began in 1930 as the brainchild of several local businessmen during the Great Depression. They came up with the idea to store grain in bulk and then use the Columbia River to transport their products to market. Today, the business has about 2,400 stockholders and over 200 employees. The co-op has 28 storage facilities in three eastern Oregon counties, as well as six retail stores. (Elizabeth Gibson.)

At one time, Continental Mills (below), in Pendleton, produced Krusteaz muffin and pancake baking mixes. The Krusteaz brand was started in 1932 by a Seattle-based company that expanded throughout the Pacific Northwest. In the past, the mill has participated in relief efforts for Oregon food banks. Recently, the plant was sold to Chicago-based Newly Weds Foods. The company makes batters, breading, and similar products. (Elizabeth Gibson.)

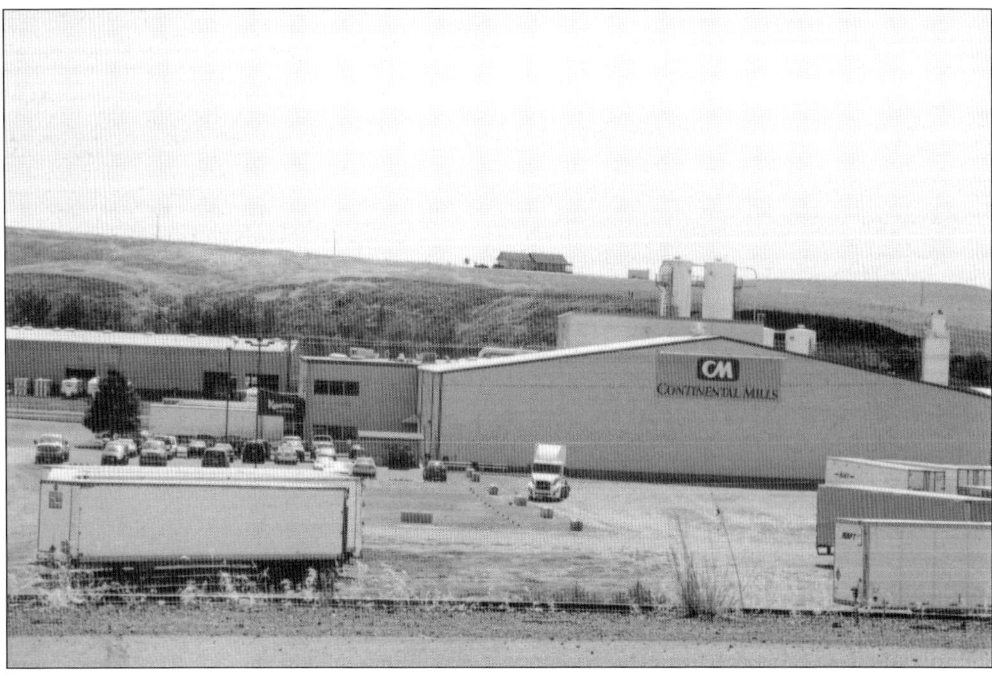

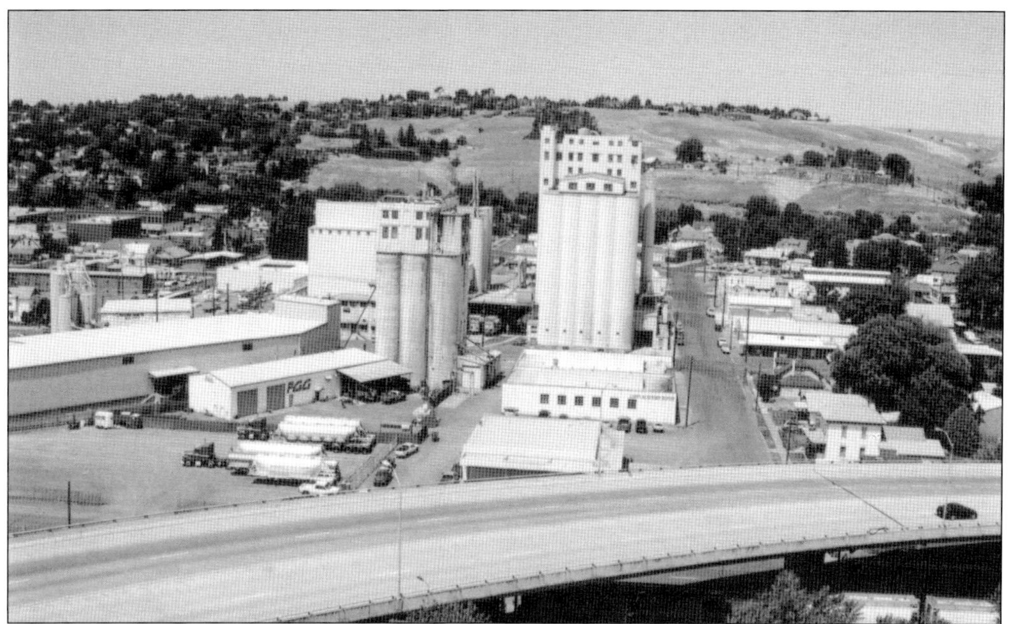

Pendleton Flour Mills has operated in Pendleton for over 100 years. It has been known for its Power brand, which is a high-gluten product. Its Mondako flour is also popular with pizza makers and noodle manufacturers. Besides the mill in Pendleton, the company also has six other mills, in the southeast, Hawaii, and Idaho. (Elizabeth Gibson.)

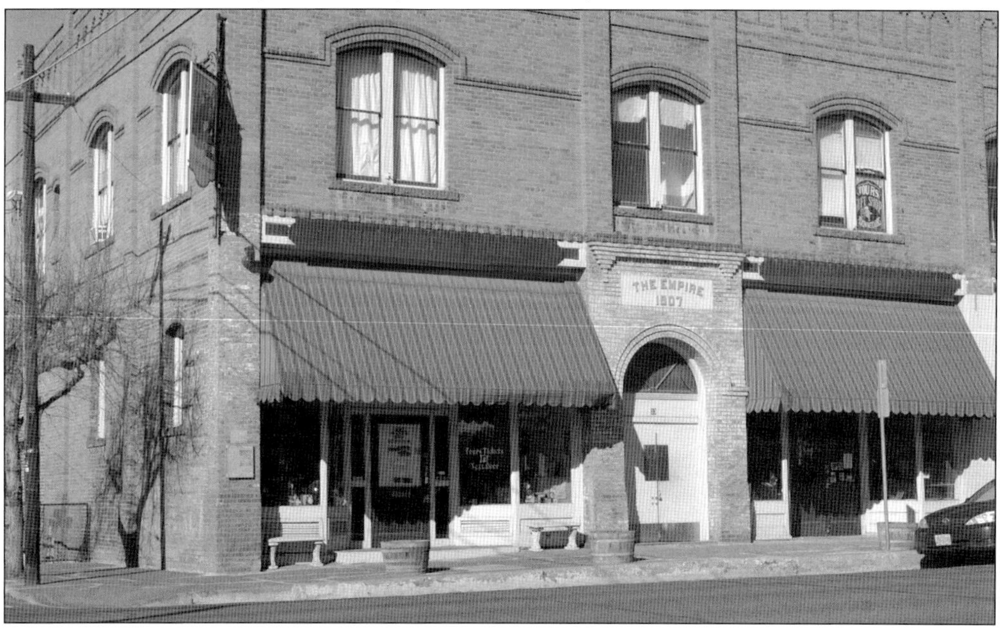

A hidden part of Pendleton's past involves the underground tunnels and businesses that were built by Chinese immigrants in the 1800s and early 1900s. The Chinese were not welcomed by the local population and tried to stay out of sight when they were not working. Today, this office on Emigrant Street guides visitors through this underground area to get a taste of the old underground Chinatown. The guides also show visitors old converted bordellos that once existed in the same area. (Elizabeth Gibson.)

Consistent with our mission to preserve history on a local level, this book was printed in South Carolina on American-made paper and manufactured entirely in the United States. Products carrying the accredited Forest Stewardship Council (FSC) label are printed on 100 percent FSC-certified paper.

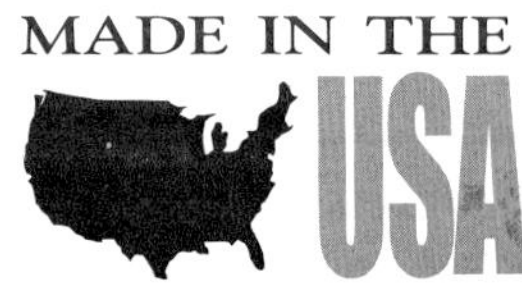